Governance of natural resources

Governance of natural resources: Uncovering the social purpose of materials in nature

Edited by Jin Sato

United Nations University Press

TOKYO · NEW YORK · PARIS

United Nations University Press
United Nations University, 53–70, Jingumae 5-chome,
Shibuya-ku, Tokyo 150–8925, Japan
Tel: +81-3-5467-1212   Fax: +81-3-3406-7345
E-mail: sales@unu.edu   General enquiries: press@unu.edu
http://www.unu.edu

United Nations University Office at the United Nations, New York
2 United Nations Plaza, Room DC2–2062, New York, NY 10017, USA
Tel: +1-212-963-6387   Fax: +1-212-371-9454
E-mail: unuony@unu.edu

United Nations University Press is the publishing division of the United Nations University.

Cover design by Andrew Corbett

Printed in the United States of America for the Americas and Asia
Printed in the United Kingdom for Europe, Africa and the Middle East

ISBN 978-92-808-1228-2
e-ISBN 978-92-808-7197-5

Library of Congress Cataloging-in-Publication Data

Governance of natural resources : uncovering the social purpose of materials in nature / edited by Jin Sato.
    pages   cm
 Includes bibliographical references and index.
  ISBN 978-9280812282 (pbk.) – ISBN 978-9280871975 (e-book)
  1. Natural resources – Government policy. 2. Natural resources – Social aspects.
3. Environmental policy – Social aspects. 4. Sustainable development – Social
aspects. 5. Human ecology. I. Sato, Jin, 1968– editor of compilation. II. Sato, Jin,
1968– State inaction in resource governance.
HC85.G68   2013
333.7—dc23
                                                                        2013011204

Endorsements

"This book addresses an essential topic in the study of the relations between people and nature: natural resource governance. In contrast to much other work on the topic, it does not take natural resource as given but shows how nature is turned into "natural resources" as part of the very social processes constituting governance. Concepts of nature and definitions of natural resources are just as political as questions about the means (e.g. market-based instruments versus regulation) and levels of governance (e.g. centralized versus decentralized forms). Thus the book achieves to establish crucial connections to research on the social constitution of resources in environmental history and science and technology studies.

The book advances the critical concept of natural resources as "bundles of possibilities". It navigates intelligently between the two schools of environmental determinism and the social construction of nature to demonstrate how natural resources and governance constitute each other recursively. The state, in particular, has often been established historically in close conjunction with the ambition to either exploit or manage natural resources. Yet, as the book rightly argues, natural resource governance goes much beyond the state, and often involves various branches of the state in an uneasy relationship with each other. Disjunctures within the state, between the state and other institutions of governance, and between existing governance arrangements and natural processes make natural resource governance inherently dynamic.

The book employs this exciting conceptual framework to cover an impressive range of conditions in which natural resource governance takes place worldwide, presenting analyses of the transport sector, forests, protected areas, river management, minerals and fisheries from Africa, Asia and Latin America."

Thomas Sikor, Professor of Environment and Development, University of East Anglia, UK

"Jin Sato has assembled an excellent collection of case studies and put together an important core argument around the interplay between resources and political economy. Using examples from several continents, this book goes beyond the many texts that take the term 'governance' for granted. Rather, it both makes and supersedes the important – but well-established – point that resources are not just material facts; rather, materials become resources through human uses and social, economic and political interactions around them. It goes further by showing that resources are, in turn, themselves constitutive of power and politics. This is an important contribution to the broad scholarly fields of natural resource governance and political ecology, and it also has significant messages at the level of policy and practice."

Philip Hirsch, Professor of Human Geography and Director of the Mekong Research Group (AMRC) at the University of Sydney

"The industrial age caused humans to forget that all life, and all industry as well, rests on a foundation supplied by natural resources that are not simply discrete portable objects but are functioning parts of whole ecosystems. Humans are slowly, humbly and painfully rediscovering the fact that we cannot outdo nature in providing ourselves with the ecosystem services that are fundamental to all life, including our own. Our simpleminded insistence on segmenting the natural world into different kinds of resources as an organizing tool (and then assigning similarly segmented units of bureaucracy to deal with each piece) actually blinds us to the interactive way that whole ecosystems actually operate. Finally, the arrogance and greed of economic and political elites who assume that their views about 'resources' and their highest 'uses' are correct has produced conflict with communities who recognize their own dependence on natural systems as well as tremendous resistance among elites to decentralizing decision-making power over the environment. This book tells the story of conflict at this cusp between these old (actually 'modernist') views and new recognition of environmental complexity, legal pluralism and democratic decentralization. It demonstrates that this struggle over perceptions, decision-making power and resource wealth takes place everywhere, from ancestral domains in the Philippines to mines in Zambia to dams in Japan. Most importantly, it provides valuable accounts of restorative efforts meant to correct the errors of our oversimplified industrial-era vision, efforts from which we can draw hope and inspiration."

Margaret McKean, Professor of Political Science and Research Professor of Environmental Policy, Duke University

Contents

List of figures and tables

Contributors

Jin Sato is an associate professor at the Institute for Advanced Studies on Asia at the University of Tokyo. Prior to that, he was an associate professor at the Department of International Studies of the Graduate School of Frontier Sciences at the University of Tokyo. He held visiting appointments in the Agrarian Studies Program of Yale University (1998–1999) and the Project on Democracy and Development at Princeton University (2010–2011). He focuses on natural resource governance, foreign aid and disaster response, with a geographical emphasis on Southeast Asia and Japan. His most recent co-edited book is *The Rise of Asian Donors: Japan's Impact on the Evolution of Emerging Donors* (Routledge, 2012). He has published in journals such as *World Development, Sustainability Science, Development and Change, Development in Practice* and the *Journal of Southeast Asian Studies*.

Doreen Allasiw is an environmental officer in the Department of Agriculture Regional Field Office in the Cordillera Administrative Region, Republic of the Philippines.

William Ascher is Donald C. McKenna Professor of Government and Economics at Claremont McKenna College, USA.

Andrew Cock is a visiting fellow in the Institute for Advanced Studies on Asia at the University of Tokyo, Japan.

Masahide Horita is a professor in the Graduate School of Frontier Sciences at the University of Tokyo, Japan.

Michiko Ishisone is an analyst in the Transferring Pricing Group at Deloitte Tohmatsu Tax Co., Japan.

Tomohiro Oh is a post-doctoral fellow of the Global Center of Excellence at Nagoya University, Japan.

Eri Saikawa is an assistant professor in the Department of Environmental Studies, Emory University, USA

Naofumi Suzuki is an associate professor in the Graduate School of Social Sciences at Hitotsubashi University, Japan.

Naruhiko Takesada is an associate professor in the Faculty of Humanity and Environment at Hosei University, Japan.

Foreword

Jesse Ribot

The step from nature to commodity requires a moment of vision in which the social uses of nature are apprehended. This is a first step in the commodification of what we call natural resources. These essential inputs to capitalism are mixed with labour and mobilized as tradeable commodities. Nature as a commodity, however, is a kind of fiction. Polanyi (1944) understood that land (e.g. nature), labour and money can never be real commodities since they are not produced by and for the market. None is a market creation. Hence none possesses the market magic of self-regulation – none provides a signal to the market that would give these three entities appropriate meaning and value to beget their sound management and protection. Their meaning and value must be imagined, like the vision that starts the path from nature to commodity. These "fictive commodities" require special treatment so that society can envision them in ways that sustain them as productive inputs.

Nature sits precariously with labour and money (and with knowledge, added by Burawoy, 2011) as fictions beyond the immediate concern of market forces – threatened by the very inability of the market to sense their origins and limits.[1] In reaction to these destructive tendencies, Polanyi (1944) described countermovements that demand protection for these productive inputs – inputs that the market cannot produce or reproduce. Polanyi's "double movement", the destructive force of the market countered by the protective impulses of society, emerges from the pain of destruction mixed with the enlightened self-interest of capital.

Governance of Natural Resources: Uncovering the Social Purpose of Materials in Nature recognizes that their envisioning, construction, transformation into resources and commodification are social processes with deep economic, political and ecological implications. They are part of the production and reproduction of the state, civil society and the world of commerce. Attempts to influence the meanings, uses and management of nature, and its governance, are inherently political. The ways we view and engage resources shape the boundaries of state and society – what remains in a state of nature, what is to be brought into use and trade, who has rights, who does not, who is in and who is out, who is friend and who is foe. Resources and their emergence from nature are governed. Government is defined by its relation to these essential inputs to markets and its position on the reproduction of nature, labour, money and knowledge. It is legitimated by what it controls and by the claims that it is able to enforce or mediate. Natural resources in this sense become the material basis of government. As Sikor and Lund (2009) indicate, authorities seek resource claims to enforce in order to come into being as authorities; simultaneously, resource claimants seek authorities to enforce their claims so as to continue to exercise their enjoyment of things. Access and authority are mutually constituted.

It is very important to locate governance within political economy and nature in politics – both of which this book achieves. Polanyi's (1944) double movement – market destructions countered by protections on nature, labour and financial systems – is useful for thinking along these lines. The double movement is not simply about *destructive* markets countered by protective movements. Governments create and dissolve boundaries between state and society. They are part of the making of nature into resources, resources into commodities, movements into protections; they also facilitate the destruction that can undermine the entire workings of enterprise and of state. Social stability and, dare I use the term, ecological "sustainability" are not natural by-products of stateness and resource as fixed categories, but products of the social dialectics that constitute both. Protections are social and political-economic creatures. But do protections manifest only as social movements that counter markets and governments that regulate them? What steers this dynamic interaction? Where does emancipation or marginalization of the governed in governing enter the process of defining and mobilizing states and resources?

Unfettered markets can destroy fictive commodities: but they can also be productive and emancipatory. Disembedding timber markets from the oligopsony control of urban traders can provide income and associated freedoms to forest-edge farmers – simultaneously undermining an oppressive ruling elite. Of course, exposure to such free trade can result in new abuses of land and labour. Countermovements and the social or environmental protections that abuses inspire can be productive and liberating, but can also be socially and economically damaging. Affirmative action aimed at fair access to labour opportunities can reify race identities – requiring the definition and bounding of categories such as Black, Latino or indigenous – creating new forms of inclusion and exclusion.[2] As political ecologists well know, environmental protections can unleash painfully abusive exclusions of resource-dependent people. Balancing these markets and protections is the social struggle to create a healthy and equitable society – to govern those who govern by and for those governed. Fraser (2011) sees a third movement that cuts across Polanyi's (1944) double movement: people subject to markets or protections (social or environmental) mobilize to demand the right to judge and influence the making of both. This third movement is emancipation. It is a demand that state intervention in the creation of markets and in the establishment of social, environmental and financial protections be subject to public scrutiny in which the public judges and decides on a level field of engagement. In this process boundaries between state and society are hammered out again and again. The demand for participatory parity is emancipatory politics.

Against this backdrop, this book outlines multiple ways by which individuals and collectives operating at multiples scales can engage in the making of nature and mediate its transformation into resources. Natural resources are more than just a fictive commodity. They also form a key part of the material basis of production and of authority. Hence they play a double role in the relation between state and society. They are the basis of authority and wealth – as is their protection. These are the very basis of the legitimacy and power of states that govern. The destruction or unjust management of natural resources, then, brings into question the basis of authority and therefore the stability of future wealth – environmental decline is social decline. This volume correctly treats "resources as catalysts that constantly form the constituents surrounding them" (Sato, Introduction).[3]

Resource governance in this volume is about how "people negotiate and interact with each other over the utilization of nature" (see Introduction of this volume by Sato). It is about the relations among people vis-à-vis things. The book expands this property-related concept beyond bundles of rights (Meek, 1938: 1), beyond bundles of powers (Ghani, 1995: 2), to what the authors call "bundles of possibilities" (Sato, Introduction). Hence resource governance becomes the basis of a political possible. The properties of this notion are in the creative negotiated spaces mutually constituted by society and state over the definition and use of natural resources. As Arendt ([1960] 2000: 460) reminds us, the "twofold gift of freedom and action" enables people to "establish a reality of their own". It is creativity through freedom in action that produces the miracle of political change – a miracle more frequent and intentional than that of nature, whose evolution is authored by probability. It is this human creativity that is the basis of the possible and of an emancipatory politics.

Notes

1. To nature, labour and finance, Burawoy (2011) added knowledge – another essential input to all capitalism that is destroyed when our universities and schools are turned into commerce. The very vision that enables us to imagine new boundaries between nature and resource is a product of a creativity born beyond the bounds of market logic – although Schumpeter ([1942] 1994) might disagree.
2. Indeed, by reifying group identity, recognition obscures internal cultural differences and subordinates the "struggles within the group for the authority – and the power – to represent it" (Fraser, 2000: 112; also see Povinelli, 2002: 6–13).
3. Note that this position does not attribute agency to resources (or any other material objects or animals) – as Bruno Latour (2005) would have us do – but shows the ways in which resources form a basis of power and agency of those who govern.

REFERENCES

Arendt, Hannah ([1960] 2000) "What Is Freedom?", in Peter Baehr (ed.) *The Portable Hannah Arendt*, New York: Penguin Books, pp. 438–461.

Burawoy, Michael (2011) Keynote address at Russian East European and Eastasian Center annual conference, "New Postsocialist Ontologies and Politics", University of Illinois, available at www.reeec.illinois.edu/events/conferences/SOYUZ.html.

Fraser, Nancy (2000) "Rethinking Recognition", *New Left Review* 3, May/June, pp. 107–120.

—— (2011) "Marketization, Social Protection, Emancipation: Toward a Neo-Polanyian Conception of Capitalist Crisis", in Craig Calhoun and Georgi Derluguian (eds) *Business as Usual: The Roots of the Global Financial Meltdown*, New York: NYU Press, pp. 137–157.

Ghani, Ashraf (1995) "Production and Reproduction of Property as a Bundle of Powers: Afghanistan 1774–1901", draft discussion paper, Agrarian Studies Program, Yale University, New Haven, CT.

Latour, Bruno (2005) *Reassembling the Social: An Introduction to Actor-Network Theory*, Oxford: Oxford University Press.

Meek, Charles Kingsley (1938) *Land Law and Custom in the Colonies*, London and New York: Oxford University Press/G. Cumberlege.

Polanyi, Karl (1944) *The Great Transformation: The Political and Economic Origins of Our Time*, Boston, MA: Beacon Press.

Povinelli, Elizabeth A. (2002) *The Cunning of Recognition: Indigenous Alterities and the Making of Australian Multiculturalism*, Durham, NC: Duke University Press.

Schumpeter, Joseph A. ([1942] 1994) *Capitalism, Socialism and Democracy*, London: Routledge.

Sikor, Thomas and Christian Lund (2009) "Access and Property: A Question of Power and Authority", *Development and Change* 40(1): 1–22.

Acknowledgements

This book grew out of a research project, "Conflicts and Cooperation in Resource Governance", funded by the Japan International Cooperation Agency Research Institute (JICA-RI), a newly established institute devoted to the study of development and foreign aid. The project started in September 2008 together with the launch of the institute. I wish to thank Professor Keiichi Tsunekawa of the Graduate Research Institute for Policy Studies, the founding director of the institute, for endorsing this project. Various staff members of the JICA-RI, Ichiro Adachi, Koji Noda and Yukiko Aida along with local staff of JICA in case study countries have assisted with the fieldwork and logistical matters.

The project members also wish to extend their gratitude to workshop participants at various stage of the project. As the project came to a close I asked Bill Ascher, an outstanding scholar on resource governance based in Claremont McKenna College, to contribute a chapter on Latin America, to which he kindly agreed. I also requested Eri Saikawa of Emory University and Andrew Cock of the University of Tokyo to write papers on China and Cambodia respectively. Thanks to their valuable contributions, the book was able cover important parts of the world, from China, Japan and Southeast Asia to Africa and Latin America. Dealing with an extensive range of natural resources, from water, forests, land and fisheries to oil and copper, the book will provide readers with an idea of the central role of human agency in resource governance around the globe.

Original project members and new contributors are all experienced "fieldworkers" who have full command of local languages to carry out their research. Aspects of what were previously largely unknown subjects are now accessible to an English-language audience. We sincerely hope that this book will serve as a useful beginning for much-needed attention and debate in the field of natural resources politics all around the world.

Jin Sato
Tokyo

List of abbreviations

AAC	Anglo American Corporation
AQSIQ	General Administration of Quality Supervision, Inspection and Quarantine (China)
BSAC	British South Africa Company
CATARC	China Automotive Technology and Research Centre
CNOOC	China National Offshore Oil Corporation
CNPC	China National Petroleum Corporation
CO	carbon monoxide
DENR	Department of Environment and Natural Resources (Philippines)
DIW	Department of Industrial Works (Thailand)
ERRI	Environmental Regulatory Regime Index
ESSF	Economic and Social Stabilization Fund (Chile)
FAO	UN Food and Agriculture Organization
GDP	gross domestic product
HC	hydrocarbon
IMF	International Monetary Fund
IPRA	Indigenous Peoples Rights Act (Philippines)
JICA	Japan International Cooperation Agency
JVTC	Jinan Vehicle Test Centre (China)
KTO	Kalanguya Tribal Organization (Philippines)
MAFF	Ministry of Agriculture, Forestry and Fisheries (Japan)
MEP	Ministry of Environmental Protection (China)
MUZ	Mineworkers Union of Zambia
NCCM	Nchanga Consolidated Copper Mines (Zambia)
NCIP	National Commission on Indigenous Peoples (Philippines)
NDRC	National Development and Reform Commission (China)

NGO	non-governmental organization
NIPAP	National Integrated Protected Area Programme (Philippines)
NIPAS	National Integrated Protected Area Systems Act (Philippines)
NO_x	nitrogen oxide
PAMB	Protected Area Management Board (Philippines)
PC	YRC Preparation Committee (Japan)
PCD	Pollution Control Department (Thailand)
PDVSA	Petroleos de Venezuela S.A.
PEMEX	Petroleos Mexicanos
PRK	People's Republic of Kampuchea
RCM	Roan Consolidated Mines (Zambia)
RFD	Royal Forest Department (Thailand)
RIPP	Research Institute of Petroleum Processing (China)
RST	Rhodesian Selection Trust
SEPA	State Environmental Protection Administration (China)
SAC	Standardization Administration Committee (China)
SAP	structural adjustment programme
SBQTS	State Bureau of Quality and Technical Supervision (China)
UN	United Nations
UNDP	UN Development Programme
UNTAC	UN Transitional Authority (Cambodia)
WTO	World Trade Organization
YRC	Yodo River Committee (Japan)
ZCCM	Zambia Consolidated Copper Mines

Introduction

Towards the dynamic analysis of resources

Jin Sato

Visions of resources

On 23 February 2005 earthquake scientist Katsuhiko Ishibashi testified in front of the Budgetary Committee of the House of Representatives in Japan. He warned his influential audience that the Japanese archipelago had entered a particularly active geophysical period of the earthquake cycle, and if an earthquake came, it would almost certainly destroy large portions of the infrastructure which had been constructed based on naïve assumptions nurtured during the post-war "earthquake-dormant" period. In his passionate speech, he touched upon the possibilities of a total collapse of the safety systems integral to the operation of nuclear power plants (House of Representatives, 2005).

Six years later, his prediction was so tragically fulfilled. My concern now is not so much why many politicians failed to take his advice seriously. I am more concerned about the fact that we are still failing to take Ishibashi's message to heart even *after* the 2011 disaster that took 20,000 lives. Here, I am referring mainly to the social disaster that magnified the number of casualties caused by the nuclear disaster in Fukushima. Ishibashi problematized the dominant "ethic of development" that gave priority to efficiency, capital accumulation and city-biased resource allocation in post-war Japan. The industrial structure of the northeastern region of Japan has been developed historically to serve the needs of the nation, more specifically Tokyo, by supplying raw materials and energy (Okada, 2012). The general public not only endorsed nuclear power in

Governance of natural resources: Uncovering the social purpose of materials in nature, Sato (ed.),
United Nations University Press, 2013, ISBN 978-92-808-1228-2

past decades as a clean, self-sufficient source of energy, but also promoted tsunami-prone seashores as suitable places to live and build their factories. Having entered into the "earthquake-active period", Ishibashi argued for an alternative ethics: decentralized, self-sustaining, small-scale and safety-first development by making the best use of natural resources available in rural areas.

Ishibashi is right. We should question the ethics and the vision, or the lack of it, which fundamentally supported a post-war resource policy in a way that led to the present magnitude of disaster. The particular vision of "natural resources" nurtured for the past 50 years has exacerbated the negative effects of the disaster. Since the 1960s natural resources have been conceptually equated with raw materials such as iron ore and oil, which were increasingly imported from abroad and rendered into sale-able goods in Japan's highly developed seaside ports. This particular con-ception of resources invaded the realm of "renewable" as well. The way scholarly communities and policy experts divide up natural resources into categories such as forest, water, land, minerals, etc. has produced a per-sistent system of bureaucracy and academic disciplines that hinders mutual communication and holistic understandings. Soil fertility may de-pend on the use and depletion of phosphate mineral deposits. Agricul-tural products cannot be separated from soil, and thus from other resources such as water and forests that help maintain soil condition. Wil-liam Ascher in Chapter 2 refers to the indivisible connection between water and mines development. One without the other not only leads to failure in creating "resources" from nature, but also hinders effective con-servation of such resources.

Because the primary motivation for natural resource management is the development and production of marketable commodities, institutional structures have accordingly been shaped to pursue such goals effectively (see Chapter 1). But an attempt to make resources "legible" to the state (Scott, 1998) has its own limits in establishing locally appropriate institu-tions. In Cambodia's Tonle Sap, for example, the fields and forests are under water for half the year and function as a terrestrial landscape dur-ing the other half. The lot owner of the fishery will have the "property" right in relation to fish during the flooded season, but a different individ-ual, the landowner, is customarily entitled to cultivate his or her land in the dry season. Not only are the resources multilayered, but the resident population rely on multiple income sources depending on the season, availability of various resources and other conditions such natural haz-ards that shape their opportunity sets. This kind of local practice does not fit well with the unidimensional resource planning often carried out by departments of fishery, environment, tourism and local administration based on maps and zoning. People on the ground live in mobile and flexible ways that escape any of these static apprehensions.

Perhaps we should reconsider the very concept of resources, and how we view them. This is because a vision defines the range of constituents in a particular issue area, and plays a critical role in invoking public support. Thus vision forming can be more critical, in the long run, than specifying a particular causal mechanism through some type of scientific procedure. Renowned economist Joseph Schumpeter (1954) referred to "vision" as a "pre-analytic cognitive act" that defines what will subsequently become raw material for analysis.[1] His insight reminds us that our vision of resources needs to be understood as a product of history, influenced by societal needs and available technologies. For instance, coal and petroleum were not considered major resources until the seventeenth and mid-nineteenth centuries, respectively. Likewise, rubber did not become a resource until Charles Goodyear discovered the vulcanization process in 1839, which allowed it to be rendered light and flexible (Ponting, 2007). Before the revolution in physics at the start of the twentieth century, uranium was seen as a useless by-product of other mining operations. South Africa, in particular, produced up to 40 per cent of the world's uranium as a by-product of its gold mining. Erich W. Zimmermann (1933: 15) stated: "Resources are not; they become." What he meant in his masterly book, *World Resources and Industries*, was that resources are not fixed things that merely exist, but that their meaning and value emerge as humans appraise their worth and develop the technical and scientific knowledge to make possible their practical use. Thus, according to him, the importance of resources depends upon "cultural appraisals". Chapters in this book confirm this claim but add another dimension: perception of resources constitutes the relations between "stakeholders" that constitute the society.

While many theories have been developed to explain the general connection between people and natural resources, few have ventured into the socio-political dynamics mediated by natural resources and environment. In the eighteenth and nineteenth centuries, Europeans observed that the abundance of life-supporting resources such as fruit trees and sago palms in tropical regions made for lazy people and resulted in the absence of civilization (Alatas, 1977). The abundance of resources, according to this theory, deprives people of the stimulus to work to expand their livelihood prospects. This line of thinking was very much endorsed by scholars of geographical determinism, who placed much emphasis on the stimulating (and impeding) role of climate in the level of civilization (Huntington, 1901). After the Second World War, when countries poor in natural resources, such as Japan and Singapore, rose economically, the meaning of resources was re-examined. Since then, the focus of attention has shifted from the existence of natural resources as such to the human and institutional dimensions that facilitate the deployment of resources to further developmental goals.

Although technological improvements in the twentieth century made the material foundation (i.e. land) of civilization less important, energy security and a stable supply of raw materials continued to be major geopolitical concerns for most governments. Even resource-rich countries in the Middle East have started to seek agricultural land in Southeast Asia as a means of food security, while Chinese investments in the resources sector in Africa are becoming a much-examined theme in relation to African development (Brautigam, 2009). Climate change, another issue of rising global concern, is now commonly accepted by scientists as being of anthropogenic origin. However, social consensus is still distant from the scientific consensus.[2]

Increased politicization of the environment and an apparent need for social adaptation to environmental change have shifted the spotlight to the institutional dimension, i.e. issues regarding people and their political associations through nature; not simply people versus nature. Also, in social science communities from the 1990s, economically valuable resources such as oil and minerals have increasingly been treated as a "curse", in the sense of being seen to invite corruption, conflict and economic stagnation (e.g. Ross, 1999; Dinar, 2011). The first decade of the new century, however, saw various criticisms and revisionist arguments that sought to highlight the positive contributions of natural resources to economic development. Dunning (2008), for example, claimed that reliance on natural resources can invite either authoritarianism or democracy, depending on the size of the rent and the structure of the economic elite. Recently there have been more case studies focusing on the "success" that some political entities have had in defying the resource curse (Hertog, 2010).

Most studies, however, take "resources" and more importantly the "state" and "people" as given units of analysis, without critically investigating the dynamics within each category. For example, much of the literature on natural resources tends to treat the state as an uncontested institutional structure, and as a consequence fails to grasp how business interests, civil society movements and intra-bureaucratic politics influence policy outcomes. Human perception transforms aspects of nature into resources, and legitimizes the use of particular technologies (both hard and soft) that justify certain ways of exploitation. Similarly, the main agents in natural resource development, such as state agencies, business enterprises and proximate communities, are also going through dynamic changes.

Thus resources and society must be conceived as co-constitutive of an interactive framework.

Endlessly dissected "disciplines" that provide the scholarly homes of most so-called experts often blind us to the interdependent nature of this system. As a consequence, one must revisit the basic concept of the "resource" to appreciate its original meaning and reach. In an often-cited article in *Science*, "Tragedy of the Commons", Garrett Hardin (1968) pointed out that there is a class of problems called the "no-technical solution problems". Population expansion is one such, according to him. While diffusion of contraceptives and education might offer a technical solution in the sense of assisting parents to reduce the number of children they choose to have, those who deny the value of contraceptives and arguments for limiting family size will probably always outnumber prudent couples. In this way, we see that technological improvement in the absence of changing moral values does not necessarily bring about fundamental change.

If institutional change is more fundamental in bringing about needed transformations, if cooperation among key stakeholders over natural resources moves us towards sustainability, we should strive to adopt concepts that are flexible enough to accommodate the various stakeholders of the present and future generations. In this spirit, we define "resources" as bundles of possibilities that are made to serve societal needs. Natural resources are those resources that exist in nature, but they need to be discovered, transformed and utilized through human labour. This is what distinguishes resources from raw materials (such as oil and coal) *per se* which are already processed for specific use values. Zimmermann's (1933: 7) classic text on natural resources captures the essence:

> The word "resource" does not refer to a thing or a substance but to a function which a thing or a substance may perform or to an operation in which it may take part, namely, the function or operation of attaining a given end such as satisfying want.

Characterizing resources as a "bundle of possibilities" allows us to focus on the human dimension. Because different people discover possibilities that are not identical, they prioritize according to their interests and positions. If the priorities are the same, competition to obtain control over the particular resource may result. Because many of the important resources cannot be tapped and utilized by a single stakeholder and require the close cooperation of related agents, struggle over a particular "bundle" becomes a political issue. This is particularly so in poorer countries where rural livelihoods directly depend on natural resources, while governmental industrial needs for such resources are also intensely pursued under the pretext of promoting economic development. From the perspective of a researcher, investigating why a particular choice was made surely must become a crucial entry point for producing a credible analysis.

"Resource governance" is therefore an activity primarily organized by governments to invoke the various potentials in nature and arrange them in a peaceful manner so that resource use will be fair and sustainable.[3] Technologies, institutions and culture that define the general relations between human society and nature mediate this process. Governmental institutions play a central part. Although governments are usually not the sole actor in these interactions, they play a critical role in defining what is to become a resource and what is to circulate in the specific social environment: money, commodities, raw materials, labour, etc. Healthy circulation secures the perpetuation of the economic system, and thus meets the interests of the governing body.[4]

Anatomy of state and society

While environmental policy tends to focus on the technical aspects of the problem at the end of the pipe, resource policy determines the historical and underlying distribution of natural resources, which makes disciplines such as history, politics and area studies critical for investigation. Understanding the resource context, after all, determines the sustainability of environmental conservation, since the two are intertwined.

One of the distinctive features of this volume is that it treats neither states nor societies as unitary and static decision-making bodies. Instead, they are treated as having multiple layers that contain the seeds of change. State leaders face conflicting goals in addressing resource problems, and it is important to understand the nature of their dilemmas and the reasons why states regularly fail to take timely action to conserve resources and protect the environment (Chapter 1). Decision-making is also often influenced by international conditions and particular bureaucratic cultures (Chapter 3). Unlike studies that deal with "conflict and cooperation" based on states as fixed agents, we treat states as dynamic, mutable institutions, particularly regarding their relations with society.

Society, on the other hand, is also dynamic and should not be treated as fixed in terms of its interests and perspectives *vis-à-vis* resources. Perhaps some of the most neglected dimensions of resource governance are the innovations that people carried out by themselves. Because many of the most valuable resources of the global market economy such as oil and gas tend to be controlled by the state or state-owned companies, the role of people has attracted little attention until recently. Elinor Ostrom, who won the Nobel Prize for Economics in 2009, is an outstanding scholar who attempted to uncover the "people's logic" in regard to sustainable resource use (Ostrom, 1990). While there has been a proliferation of literature on communal resource management techniques, many of them are still anchored to a static notion of resources. These analyses tend to treat forests, water, etc. as separate entities without much investigation into their connections. This volume includes case studies of how people *create* resources or sometimes *cross over* resources to restore lost connections among various parts of the natural world. The tree-planting activities by fishermen that began in Tohoku, Japan, are one such local innovation that is attempting to recover the lost connection between the forest and the sea (Chapter 9). Cases of local people from agricultural communities creating and transforming resources such as tourism in order to revitalize themselves are also reported (Chapter 8).

These examples point to the conclusion that resource governance can be an insightful concept to capture the dynamic relationships people establish with nature. Unlike commonly used conceptions such as "environmental governance", which tend to emphasize particular agents or mechanisms (e.g. market actors, states, non-governmental organizations, local communities) as being most effective (Lemos and Agrawal, 2006; Bridge and Perreault, 2008), we treat resources as catalysts that constantly form the constituents surrounding them. Marx (1976: 283–284) was perhaps one of the first to analyse this process explicitly in his ruminations on labour process as synthesis between man and nature:

> But what distinguishes the worst architect from the best bees is that the architect builds the cell in his mind before he constructs it in wax. At the end of every labour process, a result emerges which had already been conceived by the worker at the beginning, hence already existed ideally. Man not only effects a change of form in the materials of nature; he also realizes his own purpose in those materials.

Reversing Marx's formulation, we attempt to read the social "purpose in the materials" from inside out. In other words, we interpret various meanings and practices related to how materials in nature become resources and thus obtain social meaning in different parts of the world.

While scholars of natural resources tend to focus on environments as material objects based on a sectoral mindset (e.g. water, forests, minerals), the idea of resource governance brings the focus closer to the human and economic dimension, where people negotiate and interact with each other over the utilization of nature. If resources are "bundles of possibilities", resource governance becomes a governance of possibilities, which can shrink or expand based on the technologies, perception and most importantly the politics among relevant stakeholders.

Although the challenges thrust upon human society by nature – from the scarcity of specific natural resources to the inexorable deterioration of the biophysical systems – are worldwide phenomena, tremendous diversity exists in how societies govern these challenges. Some governments and peoples are quick to respond, while others are much slower or fail to respond altogether; some governments respond in a systematic fashion by creating internal bodies to address the challenges, while others respond more on an *ad hoc* basis. While it is tempting to ask what brings about these differences, the answer is not immediately apparent. At the very least, we can hypothesize that any kind of "success" in natural resource and environmental management requires a *fit* between the problem and the institutional arrangement that has been put into place to address it – this is precisely why a study of resource policy should expand its scope to that of "resource governance", which emphasizes the *relationship* between actors and knowledge. In this volume, Ascher's chapter on Latin America convincingly demonstrates this point.

However, there are several possible obstacles that can prevent this "fit" from occurring. The first is a temporal disjuncture. Conditions of natural resources change rapidly and often unexpectedly, while bureaucratic changes and institutional innovations happen much more slowly because various legal steps and administrative procedures must be completed prior to any kind of large-scale response. The second obstacle is a tendency to downplay socio-economic pretexts in which a particular resource policy produces effects, possibly leading to unfeasible or socially unacceptable responses. The ease of dividing resources into sectors (e.g. water, forests, energy) allows certain types of actors to render them "technical". Much effort, then, goes into the science and technology associated with treating resources as material objects, while the social and institutional foundations of these technologies are left behind. The third obstacle is an entrenched bureaucratic sectionalism that resists efforts to derive a concerted response to resource problems on both social and environmental levels. These three forces work differently in different settings, creating a variety of institutional responses to natural resource issues.

Distribution of social scientific focus

If the study of resource governance depends on the ways various "actors" perceive possibilities, negotiate and come to undertake collective action, and if the resulting distribution of benefits and costs depends so much on institutional arrangements that shape how knowledge is gained and shared, resource problems surely fall within the realm of social scientific inquiry.

Indeed, social scientific studies of natural resources have, since the 1990s, grown vastly in number. Yet studies in the past have put too much focus on resources that have a significant impact on revenue (e.g. oil, gas, minerals) and on countries in which these resources are abundant (Rudra and Jensen, 2011). There is also a tendency to limit the focus to the economic contribution of resources, such as to growth and income. Studies that look at the micro-foundations of more mundane resources (such as forests) tend to be sector-focused and fail to convey a general argument that covers people's perspectives of resources or even the changing appreciation of resources by the state and its leaders.

Contributions that link natural resources with social science themes, like democratization, focus much of the discussion of resource governance on the means, such as public versus private (Sikor, 2008) or centralization versus decentralization (Ribot and Larson, 2005). However, it is not the resources and environments themselves that require interventions. A more foundational level is the way in which people associate with each other through the environment and natural resources, which then influences how people interact with the resources. The study of resources must therefore employ social science tools and approaches in addressing how parts of nature are extracted as resources and distributed within a society.

Figure I.1 represents a framework to classify natural resource social science, which highlights the political aspects of resource governance in recent years. With two axes – characterization of actors and proximity to power – we develop a palette of resource-related studies to locate how

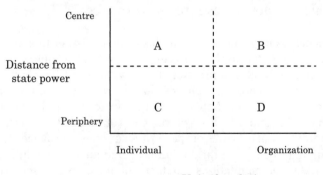

Figure I.1 Distribution of research focus on resource governance

researchers have positioned their focus. First, because governance is a relational concept that is greatly influenced by the distribution of power, the "centre/periphery" axis demonstrates the location of the research in terms of power relations. Second, because some authors place explicit emphasis on particular individuals as units of analysis, while others focus more on organizational or collective action aspects, we have the X axis as "individual/organization" to denote the distribution of the units of analysis.

Quadrants A and C have "individuals" as units of analysis; some focus on elite influence in the corruption of resource control at the political centre (Ascher, 1999), while others focus on people's everyday resistance to state policies (Scott, 1985). Elinor Ostrom (1990) is an outstanding example of a scholar in the D quadrant, where she examines communal institutions of resource management. Although these works successfully capture local context and resistance, very few attempts have been made to investigate the evolution of the government itself in relation to natural resources, the environment and the often-hidden contestation that regularly occurs within governmental bodies (B). Most studies have treated government as a monolithic entity, offering little room for explaining how it changes, expands or shrinks.[5] More specifically, almost no research is available on how state interests change pertaining to natural resources and the environment, or the mechanism of such change. Not only states but "people" also tend to be treated as a monolithic category. We find, however, that their relations with resources tend to change their relations among themselves, often in an innovative ways that go beyond state planning. In sum, the collection of chapters contained in this book aims to fill this gap, by providing the reader with a more dynamic analysis/ understanding of natural resources.

Emerging themes in resource governance

Four specific themes emerge from this volume. These themes have seldom been highlighted in the conventional study of resource governance, and the book is structured precisely to draw them out. The first highlights the vast diversity and hierarchy of power *within* the state, and in this regard Chapter 1 by Jin Sato shows that historical understandings can provide a useful guide to how power can (or cannot) be shared among governmental agents for the purpose of resource governance. A deficient understanding of the general direction of bureaucratic evolution will invite "policy recommendations" that are doomed to be ignored or suppressed by the very people responsible for implementing them. Owing to increased awareness of the finiteness of natural resources and contestation over the use of the environment, there is an increased incidence of the use of resources for overtly political purposes, particularly by the governments of developing countries. As Ascher convincingly claims in Chapter 2, decentralization itself is not a panacea to solve all issues of the environment, especially since local capacities to manage natural resources vary so much depending on the availability of human and financial resources. Appropriate leadership at the political centre of the relevant sovereign community must also support local practices. This first theme calls for the deployment of more sophisticated tools to analyse the "politics" of decision-making.

The second theme is the crucial role of business interests and their co-evolution with state bureaucracy. Saikawa's case study of China's policy on regulating vehicle emissions (Chapter 3) is an effective piece that bridges the first and second themes: she carefully examines the internal workings of the state, and finds both liberal and limiting institutions residing together which allow some standards to be adopted in a stringent form while letting others lag behind international norms in this issue area. Saikawa's piece is also unique in the book since it deals with the quality of resource (i.e. oil) and how it might affect the relationship of stakeholders. Andrew Cock (Chapter 4) offers a quite different perspective on the role of business entities. Drawing on extensive field experience in Cambodia, he demonstrates the mutual dependency of state, business and foreign aid communities in the forestry sector which often downplay the role of "residual" non-timber forest products, inviting negative consequences for much of the rural poor.

The third theme focuses on the critical role of history in shaping people's perception of the institutions as well as the distribution of costs and benefits related to the particular type of institutions governing natural resources. Michiko Ishisone undertook fieldwork in the copper belt of Zambia, and describes the historical sequence of resource governance since colonial times (Chapter 7). By challenging the conventional studies of "resource curse" based on macro-statistical data, Ishisone questions the distributional mechanism of resource wealth based on contextual data. Horita and Allasiw focus on the conflict coping mechanism (Chapter 5). Unlike the conventional approach to "how" we could solve a given problem, they highlight the very mechanism via which we deal with conflicts and argue for an appreciation of ambiguity and pluralism in decision-making. This claim adds another dimension to the study of resource governance. Resource governance is not only about governing particular resources; it must, by definition, include the governing of decision-making *about* those resources. In this theme, Naruhiko Takesada (Chapter 6) reminds us of an often-forgotten dimension of resource governance: how people on the ground live through changes in resource use and attach meanings to these changes. Instead of evaluating a resettlement project over the time span of a few years, Takesada attempted to take a lifelong view of a dam project and how the resident population devoted their lives to pros/cons of the dam and lived through the whole process of debate struggling to find meaning to their cause. Through his effort to dig out insider views, Takesada convincingly demonstrates the pitfalls of "participatory governance" and how democracy might invite marginalization and diluted stakes.

Finally, the fourth theme is how people can overcome resource deterioration and abandonment without relying on the state. This theme will loom large not only in economically advanced nations such as Japan, which is now experiencing "post-growth" issues such as ageing, but also in developing countries where state governance is still weak. Naofumi Suzuki (Chapter 8) traces the process of how an aged, thinly populated village in rural Japan has made innovative use of communal resources to revitalize its community. Based on detailed fieldwork in Kochi, in the Shikoku region, he finds a community transforming abandoned former rice fields into a symbolic "resource" that successfully facilitated the growth in the number of people actively participating in communal activities in a seriously depopulated region. The process of using land abandoned as private rice fields in gaining new life as a communal asset is an eloquent manifestation of why we need to adopt more dynamic conceptions of resources. Tomohiro Oh, in Chapter 9, echoes Suzuki by demonstrating not just people's ability to respond, but also to take initiative in a manner that crosses sectoral divisions (in his case, the division between fishery and forestry). By simply asking why fishermen plant trees, he uncovers their logic and sources of motivation. The "forests as lovers of the sea" became one of the most famous cases demonstrating innovative resource management initiatives of local people in Japan.

Despite the book's extensive geographical coverage, from Africa to Latin America and Asia, and the range of resources examined, the reader will find a surprising level of commonality between many regions in the world. The commonality across regions is not the central claim of this book, yet it does demonstrate that the subject of resource governance deserves attention on its own terms as the key political issue of our time. In this regard, our book is by no means an encyclopaedic treatment of the subject, but an invitation to engage in an exciting field that is of scholarly and real-world importance.

Notes

1. According to Schumpeter (1954: 41), "In order to be able to posit ourselves any problems at all, we should first have to visualize a distinct set of coherent phenomena as a worthwhile object of our analytical efforts. In other words, analytical effort is of necessity

preceded by a preanalytic cognitive act that supplies the raw material for the analytic effort. In this book, this preanalytic cognitive act will be called Vision."

2. A recent survey in the United States revealed that those who are doubtful, or even dismissive, of the climate change threat increased from 2009 to 2010 despite wide consensus among scientists that climate change is a real issue derived from anthropogenic sources (Hoffman, 2012).

3. This definition relies very much on the Foucauldian notion of governmentality, where states are placed as privileged regulators of a "milieu, which involves not so much establishing limits and frontiers, or fixing locations, as making possible, guaranteeing, and ensuring circulation: circulation of people, merchandise, and air, etcetera" (Foucault, 2007: 29).

4. Circulation of knowledge is the key, since the way knowledge is combined with human interest determines what aspects of nature come to be resources.

5. See Bryant and Bailey (1997) for a cursory survey of the role of states in natural resource management.

REFERENCES

Ascher, William (1999) *Why Governments Waste Natural Resources*, Baltimore, MD: Johns Hopkins University Press.

Alatas, Syed Hussein (1977) *The Myth of Lazy Native*, London: Frank Cass.

Brautigam, Deborah (2009) *Dragon's Gift*, Oxford: Oxford University Press.

Bridge, G. and Tom Perreault (2008) "Environmental Governance", in Noel Castree, David Demeritt, Diana Liverman and Bruce Rhoads (eds) *A Companion to Environmental Geography*, Oxford: Blackwell Publishing, pp. 475–497.

Bryant, Raymond and Sinead Bailey (1997) *Third World Political Ecology*, London: Routledge.

Dinar, Sholomi (ed.) (2011) *Beyond Resource Wars: Scarcity, Environmental Degradation, and International Cooperation*, Cambridge, MA: MIT Press.

Dunning, Thad (2008) *Crude Democracy: Natural Resource Wealth and Political Regimes*, Cambridge: Cambridge University Press.

Foucault, M. (2007) *Security, Territory, Population: Lectures at the Collège de France 1977–1978*, New York: Picador.

Hardin, Garrett (1968) "Tragedy of the Commons", *Science* 162 (3859), pp. 1243–1248.

Hertog, Steffen (2010) "Defying the Resource Curse: Explaining Successful State-owned Enterprises in Rentier States", *World Politics* 62(2), pp. 261–301.

Hoffman, Andrew (2012) "Climate Science as Culture War", *Stanford Social Innovation Review* (Fall), available at www.ssireview.org/articles/entry/climate_science_as_culture_war.

House of Representatives (2005) "Record of the Public Hearings of the Budgetary Committee of February 23, 2005", Session No. 162, Vol. 1, available at www.shugiin.go.jp/index.nsf/html/index_e.htm.

Huntington, Ellsworth (1901) *Civilization and Climate*, New Haven, CT: Yale University Press.

Lemos, M. C. and A. Agrawal (2006) "Environmental Governance", *Annual Review of Environment and Resources* 31, pp. 297–325.

Marx, Karl (1976) *Capital*, Vol. 1, Harmondsworth: Penguin Books.

Okada, Tomohiro (2012) "Tohoku (Northeastern Region) as a Stepping Stone", in Rural Culture Association Japan (ed.) *The Cause of Denuclearization* (*Datsu Genpatsu no aigi*), Tokyo: No Bunkyo, pp. 17–26 (in Japanese).

Ostrom, Elinor (1990) *Governing the Commons*, Cambridge: Cambridge University Press.

Ponting, Clive (2007) *A New Green History of the World*, London: Vintage Books.

Ribot, Jesse and Anne Larson (eds) (2005) *Democratic Decentralization through a Natural Resource Lens*, London: Routledge.

Ross, Michael (1999) "The Political Economy of the Resource Curse", *World Politics* 51(2), pp. 297–322.

Rudra, Nita and Nathan Jensen (2011) "Globalization and the Politics of Natural Resources", *Comparative Political Studies* 44(6), pp. 639–661.

Schumpeter, Joseph (1954) *History of Economic Analysis*, New York: Oxford University Press.

Scott, James (1985) *Weapons of the Weak: Everyday Forms of Peasant Resistance*, New Haven, CT: Yale University Press.

—— (1998) *Seeing Like a State: How Certain Schemes to Improve Human Conditions Have Failed*, New Haven, CT: Yale University Press.

Sikor, Thomas (ed.) (2008) *Public and Private in Natural Resource Governance: A False Dichotomy?*, London: Earthscan.

Zimmermann, Eric (1933) *World Resources and Industries*, New York: Harper & Row.

1

State inaction in resource governance: Natural resource control and bureaucratic oversight in Thailand

Jin Sato

Introduction

Southeast Asia's natural environment has suffered severe damage over the past four decades. Development of infrastructure such as dams and major roads has contributed to the destruction of animal and plant life, especially around the Mekong River. Thailand, the focus of this study, has lost more than half its forest cover in the past 40 years, and air pollution measured in terms of NO_2 and SO_2 increased drastically between 1990 and 2000. In terms of the concentration of particulate matter, Bangkok and Jakarta continue to rank among the world's most polluted cities, and CO_2 emissions are increasing in the region as a whole (ESCAP, 2008). Theories on ecological modernization, such as the environmental Kuznets curve, predict that successful economic growth in Southeast Asia will soon at least alleviate, if not eliminate, the region's environmental problems (Grossman and Krueger, 1995; Selden and Song, 1994). Indeed, Southeast Asian countries have some of the world's most advanced environmental legislation and extensive support from international donor agencies such as the World Bank (Goldman, 2005; Hicks et al., 2010). Despite these positive trends, however, environmental quality continues to deteriorate.

We must look for an explanation for this lack of improvement, or rather for its sluggishness, particularly in the case of such an advanced country as Thailand. Compared to other countries in the region, Thailand is well equipped with the institutional resources necessary to address this

Governance of natural resources: Uncovering the social purpose of materials in nature, Sato (ed.), United Nations University Press, 2013, ISBN 978-92-808-1228-2

issue, often with strong support from the city-based middle class. In fact, environmentalism propelled by the country's middle class has been strong enough to drive popular movements that have contributed to re-gime changes since the 1970s (Forsyth, 2004). And yet, despite these fa-vourable conditions, environmental quality continues to deteriorate and the rate of improvement is slow.

Based on a case study of Thailand, this chapter argues that the continu-ing failure of the state with respect to environmental governance is not so much the result of inappropriate actions taken by the responsible agencies in addressing policy problems, but rather the result of the way bureaucratic structures have evolved to limit their policy choices. The state, whether effective or not, continues to dominate in determining the use (and non-use) of natural resources in many parts of the world, and any analysis of environmental policy needs to begin from an examination of bureaucracy and the structure of power.

In Thailand, state-owned land consisting mainly of forest accounts for roughly 40 per cent of total land area, providing refuge to more than a million "illegal" encroachers (Sato, 2003). Strict forest conservation policies have created a class of landless people who are forced to en-croach on to state land to earn some sort of subsistence. Environmental impact assessment regulations are just one mechanism of the state to ex-ercise its power.[1] Note, however, that resources such as forests, land, water and minerals are not managed by "the state" through a single co-herent decision-making unit, but through the state's multilayered min-istries and departments whose individual interests often collide. These intra-governmental relationships can play a critical role in executing a timely policy.

Given the complexity of the bureaucracy surrounding environmental policies, criticizing the poor performance of those agencies is not enough. Instead, a plausible approach is to determine what prevents environ-mental departments from performing better: to transform the environ-ment from being a mere target of exploitation to becoming a long-term reservoir for sustainable development.[2] It is not enough to blame govern-ments for not fulfilling their responsibilities; rather, we need to go further and explain why they fail to do so. In other words, state impact must be examined not only in terms of state action, but also with regard to inac-tion or delayed action.

The problem of state inaction has only recently attracted scholarly at-tention. Environmental management highlights the lack of enforcement, but the problem of inaction goes further back in history.

In the 1960s, when economic growth in Japan was as fast as it is in Thailand today, Minamata and other notorious incidents of pollution were often characterized as the unavoidable side-effects of rapid industrialization. However, a closer examination reveals that the Japanese government had previously suppressed a 1949 draft recommendation from the Resources Council, an inter-ministerial advisory board, urging stricter enforcement of regulations controlling water discharge. The recommendation had included innovative policies such as establishing total emission control standards, but these were not formalized until 1970 (Hirano, 2003). It is worth noting that this recommendation was drafted in the late 1940s, when Japan's prospects for economic recovery were dim and no expert could have predicted the remarkable economic growth that was to come. If the government had adopted it, Japan could have avoided, or at least minimized, the subsequent nationwide environmental damage.

The Resources Council was unable to push the original draft through because of strong opposition from the mining industry and the Ministry of Trade and Industry. Forces favouring increased production even at the cost of the environment made the original draft toothless, and this allowed status quo industry activities to continue. Furthermore, a group of scientists who had received considerable funding from a chemical company played a complicit role in obscuring the ultimate cause of Minamata disease and responsible parties, a cover-up that helped to delay the resolution.[3] It was not until April 2010, more than 60 years after initial identification of the real cause of Minamata disease, that the Japanese government finally decided to compensate the victims fully.

Such policy inaction often further exacerbates social and environmental damage and is difficult to remedy, since inaction is generally the outcome of definite intention, not ignorance. Costly inaction is frequently attributed to the lack of social forces (e.g. middle class, media, non-governmental organizations – NGOs) that would engage in adversarial politics to press governments to swift action, or to the absence of a democratic system that would facilitate such movements (Sonnenfeld, 1998). However, almost no attention has been given to the intra-governmental dynamics and historical roots that have facilitated such inaction by the state. Thus the purpose of this chapter is to analyse the historical evolution of Thailand's bureaucratic structure that formed the foundation of persistent inaction by the state.

The chapter begins with an assessment of the relevant literature, with a brief summary of the situation before the Thai state institutionalized resource governance. I then discuss the ways in which state bureaucracies were formed in the context of modern Thai history for governing resources. In particular, I examine the early years of resource governance when territorialization of land-based resources began through politics among local chiefdoms, European resource companies and the central government in the late nineteenth century. This historical understanding reveals a surprising pattern that extends to the present-day practices of resource departments. Understanding the historical roots of resource governance will influence pragmatic policy advice today: what to avoid so as not to repeat policy failures.

Theories and approach

Literature

The recent shift in emphasis from government to governance (de Loë et al., 2009) has brought a wider understanding of the relevant stakeholders in the study of politics. Harrington, Curtis and Black (2008: 200), for example, defined government as "the formal, centralized and vertical exercise of power and authority, such as through regulation or market based instrument", while in governance "power and authority are horizontally decentralized and devolved to broader members of society". This distinction has the implicit misunderstanding that government is singular and governance is plural in terms of the agents involved. But it is true that, with a notable rise of non-state actors such as NGOs and civil society organizations in the environmental sector, the government is no longer the sole decision-making authority in many parts of the world.

Nevertheless, this shift should not blind us to the actual effects of government policies. Here I refer not only to the ministries directly responsible for the environment as a sector, but also to all other state apparatuses whose policies may have an impact on the environment and natural resources (e.g. energy, transportation, trade). State capacity to authorize and permit the operations of private industries is another area where it exercises its control of natural resources. If we assume that governance connotes collective horizontal decisions that affect the environment, then we must first examine governance within state structures.

Unlike the typical critique of the state that laments shortages of financial and technical means for natural resource and environmental conservation, a new set of theories appeared in the 1990s that identified abundance rather than shortage of resources as the problem – the "resource curse" hypothesis. Originally proposed by Auty (1993), the "resource curse" was widely popularized by an often-cited paper by Sachs and Warner (2001) that examined the statistical correlation between resource dependence and economic growth, and concluded that dependence on the export of natural resources tends to retard growth. From a more political perspective, Ross (1999) argued that resource dependency diminishes the state's incentive to collect taxes and therefore be accountable to its citizens. Rich natural resources, like foreign aid, can easily be transformed into cash for a privileged few while destroying the opportunity for democratic development (Moor, 2001). A revisionist argument has also emerged, claiming that resource abundance can facilitate a democratic regime; it points to the importance of mechanisms in setting up a particular regime type (Dunning, 2008).

Regardless of whether resources are considered as positive or negative elements in economic development, the dominant approach to the study of resource governance has been primarily aggregative, relying on cross-national comparisons of environmental indicators based on regression analysis (Dasgupta et al., 2001). A few exceptions with a more nuanced contextual approach stand out. James Scott (1998), for example, in *Seeing Like a State*, argued that the art of government is geared primarily towards making its subjects more legible so they become easy targets for taxation, conscription and various other means of exploitation that are empowered by the central authority. Scott made his case by tracing the history of the simplification of forests and landscapes in the European context.

In a non-Western context, Agrawal (2005) examined the process of how local people in northern India who originally were against state conservation policies ended up supporting and participating in them. Agrawal observed how decentralization of forest management has influenced people to cooperate willingly with state policies. His work was considerably informed by Foucault's (2007) concept of governmentality, defined as the "art of government" in which governments try to produce citizens who are best suited to fulfil the governments' policies. Jones, Jones and Woods (2007: 174) rephrased this as "the techniques and strategies by which a society is rendered governable".[4] Strongly influenced by Foucault, this recent theory of governance does not simply rely on a dichotomized framework of the state versus the people, but more on the co-evolution of both to serve the interests of power.

The main problem with Scott and others critical of the state is that they tend to treat it as a monolithic and abstract entity: "monolithic" in the sense that the state is treated as a self-contained body with almost no internal diversity or conflicts, and "abstract" in that scant attention is paid to observable variables such as numbers of staff, budgets, legal mandates and technologies mobilized within the state to promote its interests. Disruptions to the state system are often expected to originate from non-state forces, such as civic movements, NGOs and international organizations that pressure the state to change. Although these works have undoubtedly introduced a new dimension to the study of natural resources, they require further refinement from the perspective of public administration. This chapter attempts to pursue this line of thinking.

Approach

Natural resource governance is embodied with distinct features, and it is important to be aware of these before any analysis is conducted. First, there is often a gap between the pace of changing resource needs and the ability of society to supply them effectively. While institutional transformation takes place slowly, resource situations may change rapidly due to sudden, unexpected social or natural causes. Second, natural resources are typically extracted in remote areas which subsequently have limited exposure, making it difficult for civil society and the media to identify damage and act as corrective forces. Third, because the evaluation of natural resources usually pre-dates any capital or labour investment, capturing control *per se* is more than half the economic/political battle. Fourth, policy-makers have a tendency to downplay any existing socio-economic condition in which a particular resource policy could produce effects that might possibly lead to unfeasible or socially unacceptable responses. Because natural resources have conventionally been subdivided into environmental sectors (e.g. water, forests, energy) that are often characterized as "technical", much effort has gone into the science and technology of resources as material objects. The social and institutional foundations of these technologies are often neglected.[5] These forces work differently in different settings, creating a variety of institutional responses to natural resource issues.

To accommodate these characteristics, this chapter goes beyond the investigation of a single sector to develop a cross-sectoral view of the way agencies in the environmental field intersect and interact. I observe the sequence of departments established for particular functions and analyse their activities. More specifically, by listing the purported responsibilities of each agency chronologically, I explore their interrelations from a historical perspective.

I collected data from archival sources on the early years of government and official reports, such as annual reports, gazettes and commemorative volumes published by ministries. Information on the organizational structure of departments is particularly helpful in identifying the scope of the state's interests and the responsibilities assigned to them. My own experience as a policy adviser to the Office of Natural Resources and Environmental Policy and Planning from 2004 to 2005 underlined the importance of this topic and gave me access to the relevant documents. Various informal interviews conducted during my year in the government are used to develop my argument.

To understand the particular relationship that a state develops towards resources and the environment, a historical review of a particular context can be helpful, as uncovering the chain of events may reveal the causal mechanisms involved. As the introduction of this volume articulates, the very definition of "resources" has changed over time, as have the technologies of resource control and utilization.[6] As we shall see, the general policy trend that emphasized production has left little room for the newly arriving conservation practices to achieve legitimate status and influence. Unlike statistical studies, historical case studies such as this can help to establish agency (Rueschemeyer and Stephens, 1997), which then allows us not only to explain causality but also to identify the point of leverage for policy change.

This method of investigation presents several challenges. Publicly articulated "responsibilities" in official documents do not necessarily reveal the agencies' actual mode of operation. Furthermore, official responsibilities may change over time, making it difficult to study the "evolution" of government activities and responsibilities. It is true that organizational mandates do change in response to different needs and resources available for addressing governance issues. However, a cursory observation of the evolution of resource administration reveals that shifts in emphasis are more common in the state's interests than in its range. Publicized duties thus serve as a measure, however imperfect, of the extent of interaction between state agencies, nature and society.

Case study of Thailand

Rich resources and scarce population

Why study Thailand? There are several reasons why this country deserves closer attention. Until the 1997 financial crisis, Thailand was the engine of growth in mainland Southeast Asia, a region currently facing serious environmental damage. Rapid economic growth has brought about severe environmental depredation, but Thailand has taken a proactive stance in responding to these issues, as exemplified by the comprehensive environmental laws in 1975 and the creation of a new, more progressive Ministry of Natural Resources and Environment in 2002; no other country in Southeast Asia has such a comprehensive ministry covering both aspects. Unlike its less developed neighbours, Thailand has the human and financial resources necessary to address environmental issues. Finally, it is the only country in the region to have escaped direct colonization, and thus can expect a more indigenous process of institutional development. These conditions make Thailand an interesting case study.

Although abundant in natural resources, including water, land and forests, it was not until the late nineteenth century that the government of Thailand (known as Siam until 1939) started to manage aspects of nature as "resources". At that time the country's high infant mortality rate had resulted in a relative scarcity of labour, and preserving the nation's man-power was one of the government's chief objectives. Wales (1934: 10) observed that this scarce labour hindered the government from developing its resources to their full potential.[7] With forest cover of over 60 per cent until the 1950s, abundant mineral resources such as tin, and rice produced for export in the fertile delta, Thailand was ideally endowed for economic development. Interestingly, because of the abundance of natural resources, the state made no attempt to administer the peripheral areas until the late nineteenth century. Controlling labour to utilize the land and resources was more important to the governing elites than control of the land *per se* (Ingram, 1971). Tapping natural resources in the periphery would have been impossible without adequate labour.

Until the mid-nineteenth century valuable resources such as minerals and timber were managed by feudal lords (known locally as *chao*), many under royal patronage, with whom foreign companies signed individual trading deals on a case-by-case basis. It was not until the late nineteenth century that European companies began large-scale enterprises in Siam for natural resources exploitation (Falkus, 1989). Why was state regulation of natural resources necessary when the country's resources were plentiful? It was the interest of Western countries such as Britain and France in mineral and forest resources that prompted the Thai government to establish a centralized administrative system to avoid internal discord within the country, which was perceived to provide these foreign forces with an opportunity to intervene. Thus the need for governance did not originate from the state of the resources as such, but from the perception of external threats to these resources.[8]

Original formation of resource bureaucracy: Mining and forestry

How did Thailand create the space in which environmental administration was later founded? Resource administration in Thailand evolved hand-in-hand with state leaders' concern for the scarcity of a particular resource, and this prompted intervention from the political centre. A closer look at two of the oldest governmental organizations, the Royal Mines and Geology Department and the Royal Forest Department (RFD), demonstrates how this process unfolded in the beginning.

The Royal Mines and Geology Department (later renamed the Department of Mines) was established in 1891 with two advisers, one German and one British, who later came to head the department. Thailand had a long history of metal production, but capital-intensive development began with Chinese enterprises around the mid-nineteenth century. In the past, people living in the tin-producing areas in the south had paid their taxes with tin (Wales, 1934: 200) and tin became the first royal export monopoly to boost the Siamese economy. However, most mineral resources known to have existed in the late nineteenth century were not exploited until the arrival of the British. Herbert Warrington Smyth, a British geologist appointed as one of the first directors of the Royal Mines and Geology Department, wrote in his memoir, *Five Years in Siam*:

> There were a dozen or so big mining concessions in existence, covering in some cases a hundred square miles, a weariness of the spirit of their owners, on which, for the most part, no rents had been paid and no work had been done. They had been mostly granted to men of the concession-hunting type, whose sole objective was to sell their concessions as soon as possible for the highest price to some gullible company. (Smyth, [1898] 1994: 33)

Among the first tasks of the new Royal Mines Department, therefore, were to begin geological surveys and to draft a code of mining regulations to help the government secure tax revenue. The political effects of resource centralization, however, should not be overlooked. As Loos (1994: xvi) keenly observed in her introduction to Smyth's *Five Years in Siam*, "Scientific knowledge, in the form of cadastral and mineral surveys of the areas, was a necessary step in the broader centralization and commercialization processes."

Area surveys and map-making have had lasting effects in Thailand and have prepared a path to contemporary turf battles over legitimate jurisdiction among the land-based departments. Different laws and maps administered by various departments have made the issuance of land titles problematic (Werachai and Kasemsun, 2010). The so-called "Re-Shape" programme, initiated in 2005 by the government to clarify the agencies' overlapping jurisdiction, revealed that despite increasingly sophisticated map-making technology, the state had not been able to solve the problem. The forestry and mining departments were among the first resource agencies to use maps to demarcate their properties.

The Royal Forest Department was established in 1896, with H. Slade as the first conservator of forest (*chao krom pamai*) and a staff of 16 Europeans and nine Siamese (Slade, 1901). The near exhaustion of teak forests in Burma, despite tightened conservation measures and growing British demand for the wood, facilitated Siam's centralized control of its forests (Ministry of Interior, 1952). The RFD's main responsibilities in its early years involved survey work and inspections in collaboration with the Royal Survey Department, including supervision of the operations of dominant timber firms such as the Bombay Burmah Trading Corporation to prevent damage to the forest and a decrease in the government's source of revenue (Slade, 1901). To achieve this objective, marking timber, fixing boundaries of leases and settling disputes were among the

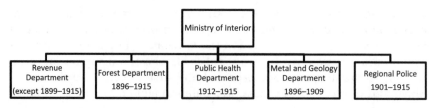

Figure 1.1 Organizational structure of Ministry of Interior, circa 1900
Source: Bunnag (1990).

most important RFD tasks. As shown in Figure 1.1, two resource agencies were under the jurisdiction of the Ministry of Interior, giving an indication of the significance of natural resources as a key governance issue during this period.

It is also worth noting that the threat of European colonization was used to justify the centralization of resource control within the government: "After a short time a regular Forest Department was established, the Siamese Government justifying the step to the chiefs by representing that in this way the Europeans would be kept in order" (Macauley, 1934: 60). The Siamese government skilfully used British and French intimidation to push for centralization, a move that otherwise would have been difficult. Through the control of timber rents, the RFD gradually expanded its sphere of influence from actual timber areas to areas of potential yield, as the label "forest reserves" indicates. At this stage the word "forest" had clearly become political (Peluso and Vandergeest, 2001).[9]

The basic structure of resource governance was founded during this period, and was partially based on the assumption that local inhabitants, particularly the hill people who tended to be beyond state control, were an impediment to sustainable exploitation. Slade (1901: 7) highlighted the key tasks for the department in its initial stage:

> As soon as sufficient staff, both controlling & executive can be established, it is most important that attention be paid to the following: taking up reserves, fire-protection, planting, creeper-cutting, clearing of teak samplings, girdling, preparation of working plans and regulation of hill-clearing.

Slade continued by characterizing the agricultural practices of the hill people as "wasteful", and emphasized that "this last is most important and until some definite policy has been determined on, it will be impossible to estimate the teak areas at the disposal of the government" (ibid.). At that time it was clearly seen that forest protection necessarily involved control of not just the forests themselves but also the people interacting with them, particularly those local inhabitants who were perceived to have a negative impact on the resource base. Implementing these ideas on the ground marked a clear beginning of Siam's "territorialization" and thus the governance of nature (Vandergeest, 1996).

Governance extended beyond the resource sector to include transportation (e.g. how best to transport logs to market), communication (e.g. how to secure effective translators in remote areas) and the division of authority between central government (i.e. the Ministry of Interior, to which the RFD was originally affiliated) and the RFD, its headquarters located in Chiang Mai under the control of the British conservator.[10] The initial period of land-based resource governance set the stage for the division of public and private wooded areas, with most of the underutilized forests falling into the former category, making it clear that all resources in the public domain belong to the state. It is on this colonial legacy that subsequent environmental administration was to build.

From natural resources to environmental governance

After policies controlling mining and forests, state influence was extended to water and fish, and the 1920s saw an acceleration of state intervention in water use. Down to the reign of King Chulalongkorn, canals had been dug and maintained by conscripted labour. The abolition of the corvée ended the maintenance of canals, which had harmful consequences for agriculture (Siffin, 1966: 85). Establishment of the Royal Irrigation Department was partly a response to this largely socio-political crisis. In any event, central government had discovered a new avenue for extending its influence throughout the country with yet another natural resource.

The great depression in the 1930s and the subsequent world war linked natural resources closely with security; this time not so much in extending state influence towards the periphery but more tapping natural resources as a revenue source. Transfer of the RFD and Mines Department to the newly established Ministry of Economic Affairs was an event representative of this trend. Instead of the long-term planning initially envisioned, the emphasis on production was further strengthened in the war years.

The late 1950s saw yet another political use of resources: the debate that led to the establishment of national parks at the initiative of a nationalistic leader, Prime Minister Salit Thanawat. In contrast to the earlier forest legislation, national parks and wildlife sanctuaries established the strict and exclusive right of the state to control vast tracts of territory, home to numerous farmers prior to this legal designation (Sato, 2003). In the 1970s forests once again became the centre of political attention when communist insurgents used them for protective cover during their campaign against the government. State control of land under the pretence of conservation and development laid the groundwork, at least partly, for the rise of popular movements in the 1970s (Hirsh, 1993).

With the introduction of various "environmental" agendas as targets for public policy, the post-Second World War emphasis on "planning" opened up a new stage for state development. Thailand's first five-year economic and social development plan, launched in 1961, made it necessary for the first time to coordinate ministerial interests in a coherent national plan, although explicit recognition of the environment as part of a policy agenda did not come until the mid-1970s, when the Enhancement and Conservation of National Environmental Quality Act of 1975 was passed. The new act was largely a response to the Mae Klong River pollution controversy caused by sugar-mill owners in 1971 and the 1973 scandal over the abuse of Tung Yai Wildlife Sanctuary by senior government members (Stubbs, 1981). Administratively, it facilitated the creation of the National Environment Board, the first overarching decision-making body on environmental issues, with a supporting secretariat housed in the Prime Minister's Office. This organization gave birth to the environmental division (i.e. pollution control, environmental education, planning and policy), later to be upgraded to departments within the Ministry of Science and Technology and housed more recently in the Ministry of Natural Resources and Environment. Thus state interests extended beyond land-based resources to include fish, soil, air, water quality and public perceptions of the environment.

Table 1.1 depicts the series of new departments established to assume responsibility for various aspects of the environment and natural resources. I focus on "departments" rather than other organizational units in the government since they are the most cohesive units with considerable discretionary power given to their directors-general. Central mandates are based on the legal stipulation that justifies the existence of each department. The departments are vested with legal authority not only to carry out policies but also to deploy technical and organizational technologies (e.g. mapping, surveying, harvesting, accounting) that would be most effective in achieving policy goals. Mandates listed here are based on the *current* objectives outlined in official documents such as annual reports. Note that they have not remained consistent over time.

The evolution of the resource bureaucracy reveals a general trend. The state's interests have shifted from production and revenue collection to conservation, from land-based resources to mobile assets and then to broader environmental protection issues, including public awareness. These new interests were overlaid on previous government structures, making the state bureaucracy more complex. It is true that the newer departments are more aligned with resource and environmental conservation than production and revenue collection, but two facts must be

Table 1.1 Sequence of departmental establishment and their mandates

Department (year established)	Overseeing ministries	Central mandates
Department of Mineral Resources (1891)	Interior (1891–1901) → Agriculture (1901–1932) → Interior (1932–1933) → Economic Affairs (1933) → Agriculture (1933–1941) → Economics (1941–1942) → Industry (1942–1963) → National Development (1963–1973) → Industry (1973–2002) Natural Resources and Environment (2002–present)	Develop policies and plans; enforce compliance with law; conduct exploration and research; specify standards
Royal Forest Department (1896)	Interior (1896–1920) → Agriculture (1921–1932) → Interior (1932–1933) Economic Affairs (1933–1935) → Agriculture (1935–2002) → Natural Resources and Environment (2002–present)	Control, regulate and protect forest; conduct studies on afforestation; promote afforestation; limit forest usage; conduct research
Department of Land (1901)	Agriculture (1901–1932) → Interior (1932–1933) → Economic Affairs (1933–1935) → Agriculture (1935–1941) → Interior (1941–present)	Operate activities based on Land Act; coordinate and evaluate land works (including statistics); develop land management
Department of Fisheries (1926)	Agriculture (1926–present)	Enforce acts; conduct research; explore; analyse; conduct research on fishing grounds; promote cooperation with fisheries; promote and develop occupations relating to fisheries
Royal Irrigation Department (1933) (originally established as Department of Canals in 1902)	Agriculture and Commerce (1928–1933) → Economic Affairs (1933–1935) → Agriculture (1935–1963) → National Development (1963–1971) → Agriculture (1972–present)	Control and build small/ mid-sized reservoirs; operate irrigation systems; maintain departmental property; address water shortages; develop measures against inundation; conduct research; share water information technology

Table 1.1 (cont.)

Department (year established)	Overseeing ministries	Central mandates
Land Development Department (1963)	National Development (1963–1971) → Agriculture (1972–present)	Conduct soil surveys and classification; perform soil analysis; carry out land-use planning; conduct land development experiments; assist farmers in soil and water conservation practices and soil improvement; seed production; transfer technology for soil development and soil science
Office of National Environment Board (1975) (later to be part of Ministry of Science and Technology)	Office of Prime Minister (1975–1991) → Science, Technology and Environment (1991–2002) → Natural Resources and Environment (2002–present)	Design policy and planning; conduct environmental impact evaluations; set environmental quality standards; promote environmental information and education
Pollution Control Department (1992)	Science, Technology and Environment (1992–2001) → Natural Resources and Environment (2002–present)	Form policies and plans for pollution control; establish standards; monitor environmental quality; investigate public complaints
Department of Environmental Quality Promotion (1992)	Science, Technology and Environment (1992–2001) → Natural Resources and Environment (2002–present)	Promote, compile, develop and disseminate environmental data; act as national environmental information centre; support public participation; coordinate and formulate plans and measures; conduct research on environmental management and technology

Table 1.1 (cont.)

Department (year established)	Overseeing ministries	Central mandates
Office of Environment and Natural Resources Policy and Planning (2002)	Science, Technology and Environment (1992–2001) → Natural Resources and Environment (2002– present)	Formulate and coordinate policies and plans for natural resources; environmental conservation and administrative management; conduct research; monitor performance on implementation of policies and plans; appraise environmental impact assessment reports; manage Environmental Fund; propose policies and give advice on development; facilitate international cooperation
Department of Water Resources (2002)	Natural Resources and Environment (2002– present)	Prepare master plan on raw water resources; conduct research, development, conservation and rehabilitation; promote and support community participation; implement, monitor and evaluate work
Department of Groundwater Resources (2002)	Natural Resources and Environment (2002– present) (separated from Department of Mineral Resources in the past)	Manage artesian well resources, including research, planning, evaluation and other support
Department of National Parks, Wildlife and Plant Conservation (2002)	Natural Resources and Environment (2002– present)	Conserve and preserve national parks, wildlife and plants; restore ecology; monitor national parks; conduct research; establish standards
Department of Marine and Coastal Resources (2002)	Natural Resources and Environment (2002– present)	Form policies and plans on marine and coastal resource conservation; monitor, research and conserve marine and coastal resources

Source: Author.
Note: Names of the departments are those that are currently used. Departments dealing directly with agriculture (e.g. rice) and bureaux dealing with general affairs of the ministry have been excluded. Also, departments within the Ministry of Energy (2002–) are excluded from this list.

acknowledged: environmental agencies are becoming narrower in scope as well as increasingly more technical, applying advanced monitoring technologies and hiring better-trained staff with more PhDs with technical knowledge; and some of the newer departments lack a legal basis, which weakens their inter-departmental position with regard to budget negotiations and jurisdiction. Unlike the Fishery Department, which was established on the basis of the Fishery Act, neither the Water Resources and Marine Department nor the Coastal Resources Department, for example, has its own legal backbone. One could argue that the newer departments have managed to secure a niche for themselves, but viewed from a larger perspective this trend has helped only to compartmentalize the already overly fragmented environmental policy.

The early emphasis on demarcating state property for increased production set the basic tone of subsequent trends in resource governance, while mandates of the newer departments were increasingly squeezed into the web of already established vested interests. Departments were created in the early 1990s to take responsibility for "environmental regulation", mainly to monitor and clean up environmental damage that had already occurred, while the production systems that had caused such damage continued to operate unhindered.

The important point here is that even though the older departments' key mandates are outdated, they manage to survive by simply modifying their role to fit current circumstances without compromising bureaucratic authority. The growing staff and budget of the forestry departments, despite considerable forest loss, are a case in point.[11] Losing their original aim of ascertaining effective production, both mining and forestry departments have now shifted their emphasis to tourism, research and conservation and have not had to face a serious organizational downgrade.

We also find that some of the older departments have been transferred repeatedly among the different ministries. Over the past 100 years the RFD, for example, has been affiliated with four ministries, a reflection of the changing attitudes in each period to what aspects of a "resource" were worthy of attention, and therefore required governance. For example, during the 1920s' economic recession, both mines and forestry were housed in the newly established Ministry of Economic Affairs to maximize each department's contribution to stabilizing the state's revenue. This demonstrates that state expectations for resources can vary depending on the circumstances and technologies available.

State governance has progressed from viewing resources simply as commodities with international trade value to the development of resource infrastructure (e.g. irrigation) for improving productivity, and finally to establishing reserves for underground water, air and ecosystems (e.g. national parks). Exclusive state control of these resources often con-

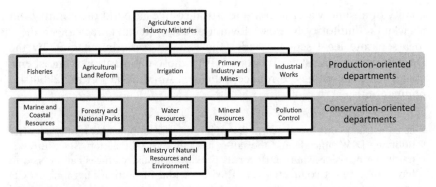

Figure 1.2 Parallel departments as of 2002
Source: Author.

flicts with issues related to property, health and access to public goods by local people. It can be said that the state, by viewing the environment as various natural resources, has continued to find new avenues through which to influence people.

Creating new departments, however, does not mean that all the entities enjoy equal importance in policy implementation. To see the effects of environmental administration, one must understand the structure of environmental bureaucracy. Figure 1.2 is one attempt to parallel the conservation-oriented departments with the traditional production-oriented departments in the same sector.

As Figure 1.2 demonstrates, new departments under the jurisdiction of the Ministry of Natural Resources and Environment are mostly conservation-oriented agencies with the primary mission of conducting research and planning. Most of these have a parallel body within the production sector, often with *de facto* veto power to block actions. The RFD and the National Parks Department are the only exceptions, since they hold significant tracts of land where certain production activities (such as plantations and tourism) take place. The mechanism of non-cooperation among these departments helps to explain why elaborate provisions for environmental improvements often fall short of their target.

Inter-departmental oversight

Next, we examine how the present form of bureaucratic division of labour can harm the environment and society. Under the Enhancement and Conservation of National Environmental Quality Act B.E. 2535, the mandate of the Pollution Control Department (PCD) is to monitor the quality of air and water at non-industrial sources around the country, but it lacks the authority to close down a polluting factory. Factories adhere to a separate legal scheme under the Factory Act administered by the Department of Industrial Works (DIW), whose cooperation is indispensable if the state wishes to reduce pollution. As Mingsarn et al. (2008: 45) pointed out:

> as industrial plants are concerned, a pollution control official can only act after notifying DIW officials and the latter has failed to take action. Since there is hardly an occasion where DIW or its provincial industry offices can be said to have failed to act completely, the Environmental Inspection Division of PCD and its provincial arms, the provincial natural resources and environmental offices ... and the regional natural resources and environmental offices ... have little power over the monitoring of industrial pollution in practice.

A similar relationship exists between the Royal Irrigation Department and the Water Resources Department; the former has authority for all irrigation projects, including large-scale dams, while the latter's mandate is limited to water resource planning and research in general. Since the most important water sources in the agricultural sector are in the hands of the Irrigation Department, the Water Resources Department has no direct leverage to enforce its plans in the rural areas where the majority of the population reside.

Mining is another area where inter-departmental conflicts are triggered, typically in favour of the investor and developer. Salt and potash extraction, for example, has become a major business in northeast Thailand. Industrialization needs "salt", an indispensable component for the food industry and fertilizer production. The Minerals Act was amended in 2002 to allow the state to mine rock salt underground at depths of over 100 m without prior permission from the landowner. The problem is that fertilizer production uses more than five times the domestic demand of the other salts accompanying potash (*Green Line*, 2011). So far, departments within the Ministry of Natural Resources and Environment have not found an effective way to curb the side-effects of potash exploitation, although the impact on the environment is obvious.

Conservation-oriented agencies are not necessarily always the underdog. For example, the RFD, whose original mission was timber production to supplement state revenue, has transformed its role to forest conservation and often vetoed the measures of the Agricultural Land Reform Office, which is mandated to redistribute agricultural land to the landless poor (Sato, 2000). Despite the ban on commercial forestry since 1989, the RFD still holds roughly 40 per cent of Thailand's total area as "forest reserve", a legacy of the original state monopoly on forests. As land for redistribution can only be found within these "reserves", the two agencies are often in conflict with each other (Werachai and Kasemsun, 2010). As the RFD was the first legal "custodian" of the reserves, it has the stronger voice in negotiating which lands are to be handed over for land reform.

When the government's reach surpasses public tolerance, the general public become organized and may resort to court action. The Mab Ta Put industrial estate on the eastern seaboard is a case in point. Here, based on the 2007 constitution, the administrative court gave its initial decision to halt 76 new investment schemes. The eastern seaboard development programme has been a national economic priority for Thailand since the 1980s, yet air quality in the region has been allowed to deteriorate due to a high concentration of petro-industrial factories, despite citizens' protests against these. Because the DIW is responsible for oversight of industrial estates, the PCD has little control over the environmental impact of factories within the estate. The continued environmental deterioration in the area confirms the fact that industrial estates, despite existing environmental rules and regulations, were safe havens over which national pollution control agencies had little direct influence.

The recent emphasis on public participation in resource governance has helped to create non-state constituents for resource planning agencies. For example, the Water Resources Department, in drafting the Water Act (Unger and Siroros, 2011), consulted with more than 3,000 individuals – both citizens and experts. While increased public participation in resource policy is a welcome move, the politicized nature of the water agenda polarized the public, with both camps beyond the control of the department, inducing a stalemate in policy-making. Consequently the Water Act, like the Community Forestry Act, has been off the table too long, despite the issue having received sufficient awareness and public participation.

In short, the new departments not only enhanced the state's "already substantial capacity to manage and degrade the environment, but also led to increased intra-state tensions over the state's development and stewardship roles" (Bryant and Bailey, 1997: 68). These intra-governmental oversights and conflicts have resulted in *ad hoc* ministerial agreements or cabinet resolutions that can only help to put out the fire temporarily.[12] Unger and Siroros (2011: 224), who reviewed the legislative process of creating community forest and water acts, concluded that despite elaborate participation procedures, "Diverse interests seem not to converge to deliberate and compromise, but to identify targets of opportunity for derailing policy initiatives in a sequential policy process susceptible to a host of informal vetoes." Polarization of the public also gives bureaucrats the opportunity to let civil society and NGOs represent their interests.

Intra-governmental oversight is not limited to the central government. Since the Decentralization Act of 1999, local authorities consisting of elected members have increasingly been given authority to control natural resources. As of 1999, environmental policies are to be analysed with explicit attention to local government, i.e. the Tambol Administrative Authorities. However, governors being nominated by the central Ministry of Interior, as well as the reluctance of departments to hand over key responsibilities to local authorities, has meant that local environmental politics has become another domain of state inaction: local authorities are forced to confront various environmental problems with the limited power and few resources transferred from central government. If conducted properly, the transfer of management rights to local authorities will encourage area-based planning that would reflect the needs and demands of the local population. In practice, however, decentralization has not resulted in any actual devolution of power. Except for a few local authorities with sufficient financial and human resources, most communities are under the sway of provincial governors who are not publicly elected, but assigned by the Ministry of Interior.

The increasing layers of the decision-making process initiated by the government have restricted the ability to implement policies at the national level. The present system can work where capable municipalities and industrial estates exist. However, prioritizing infrastructure development and income-generating projects over long-term conservation has been the common practice, particularly among local politicians. Decentralization, where effective, seems to have come with a cost of its own.

Conclusion and policy options

Why did it take more than 17 years for Thailand to legalize a community forest bill giving the right to local people to manage forests that had been used by such people for ages? Why does the Water Act have to be subjected to an informal veto at the final stage even though an elaborate process of public hearings had been carried out? This chapter, by examining the historical evolution of the state agencies of Thailand, has given partial answers to these perplexing issues that have frustrated many observers.

The conclusion can be summarized in two points. First, the interdepartmental conflicts have historical roots that have shaped the present policy environment. New mandates and responsibilities are continuously being added to existing policy space. Because the Thai government established vested interests in production in its formative period in order to expand commercial activities and generate revenue, the more recent mandates for resource conservation were left with little room for manoeuvre. The newly established departments are often harnessed to mandates that limit their role to research and planning, with scant authority to enforce regulations. This asymmetric division of labour not only induced policy inaction among departments that dared not encroach on the domain of other departments, but also created a safe haven for production-oriented departments.

Second, bureaucratic competition is often controlled by pre-existing veto players within the government – i.e. those who are currently associated (and those originally associated) with the production sector and have strong vested interests in maintaining the status quo. It is not these pre-established organizations that manifestly exercise veto power; rather, the restriction to any progressive move made by the conservationists tends to originate from the legal structure and the resulting culture of bureaucratic turf battles.

The way in which bureaucratic division of labour occurs can provide some insight as to why innovative institutions perform poorly. Environmental projects that ultimately aim to regulate production must identify the key veto players and strategically incorporate these from the outset if a project is to achieve its objective. The simplistic but popular argument that we can "grow rich and clean up later" can be a convenient excuse for governments to delay any politically challenging reform that may not necessarily provide rents to constituents. Evidence has started to emerge that many countries do not follow the environmental Kuznets curve (Ruoff, 2009). The layers of institutional interest that accompany economic growth make it difficult to achieve an *ex post* clean-up of pollution or more sustainable use of resources. Building a coalition with veto players at an early stage is certainly challenging, but it is the only way around the problem.

Although these conclusions are drawn from a case study of a single country, I believe the implications are far-reaching and extend to countries now in the process of integrating environmental concerns into their development policies. Thailand is a middle-income country still struggling to meet basic infrastructure needs, and its experience can usefully be applied to countries in early and middle stages of economic advancement. For countries in the early stages of development, such as Laos and Cambodia, Thailand's case highlights the importance of integrating conservation concerns from the outset as an organic part of the legislation related to economic policy and the bureaucracy involved. Thailand's lessons suggest that middle-income countries like Indonesia face severe challenges and limitations on what can be achieved by relying solely on state policies that are structured for and dominated by production-oriented sectors. Evidence from complementary studies carried out in other locations is needed before one can assess to what extent the results from Thailand are part of a broad systematic pattern.

The central question for the future of environmental management in Thailand is whether policies can be shifted from an emphasis on functional division within the government to regional implementation at provincial and inter-provincial levels. This shift, in line with the decentralization initiative evolving since the late 1990s, will undoubtedly give more discretion to the Ministry of Interior and the provincial governors who are well connected with development-oriented industries in each location. Theories aside, various obstacles do exist in promoting decentralization in the field of environment. As Chapter 2 highlights in the context of Latin America, the potential to revoke previous policy often erodes the foundational trust on which any policy requiring sustainable commitment must stand. Uneven distribution in the capacities of personnel and finance severely limits the space for local municipalities (Garden, Lebel and Chirangworapat, 2010). Conflicts within departments and communities are common (Kijtewachakul, 2010). Nevertheless, the key is to shift the focus from the national policy level to the local level, where real inter-departmental cooperation is needed for problem solving. Growth-oriented, production-oriented institutions are hard to reform quickly. Local initiatives, no matter how scattered and small, are the remaining areas for hope.

In the past many policy instruments have been recommended for improving environmental quality in Thailand, but there has been very little follow-up or implementation. Generally, this was not due to a lack of awareness or shortage of funds, but rather the paucity of resource governance: the societal ability to invoke, nurture and combine appropriate means to realize its goals. It is not enough simply to strive to propose better policy options; we also need to try to understand why similar attempts have failed in the past. This could help to reduce all kinds of transaction costs. Analysis of cases where veto players have been successfully bypassed in order to promote conservation policies is a possible subject for future research.

Acknowledgements

The author would like to thank Rujirat Vinitphol for her effective research assistance and Minpei Ito of JICA Thailand Office for his logistical support. The main part of the research was funded by the JICA

Research Institute. The author wishes to extend his gratitude for the Scientific Research Grant by the JSPS under the project led by Professor Tomoya Akimichi during 2012 and the Research Institute for Nature and Humanity Feasibility Study Grant for partial funding of this project. An earlier version of this chapter appeared as a JICA Research Institute working paper in 2010.

Notes

1. It is impossible to ignore the impact of international investments in environmental programmes, ranging from tree plantation projects to climate change interventions. Although there are many private initiatives, major funding still comes from governments and multilateral banks. According to the latest statistics compiled by the OECD (2012), a total of US$25.4 billion of foreign aid was spent with a focus on environment.
2. Indicators of sustainable development as used here include whether or not a country has enforced mechanisms such as the polluter pay principle to internalize the cost of environmental damage, legal arrangements to punish those who damage the environment or national plans based on sustainable yields for renewable resources, and governmental units to monitor and publicize the results.
3. A critique of the negative role played by scientists is powerfully provided by Ui (1968). The role of science in justifying inaction is well documented around the world (Ascher, 2004).
4. Foucault (2007) highlighted the "arrangement of things" as the original form of governmentality, where "things" included not substances or materials but the relationship between people and materials. He noted that the contemporary mode of government is not characterized by the state's encroachment on the liberties of society, but rather by a link between techniques that assure coercion and those processes by which free individuals themselves modify or construct a self. This notion is very close to our definition of resources, although "resource" tends to connote a positive utilization of materials, ignoring the negative aspects such as inequality, exploitation and natural hazards.
5. This is perhaps the very reason why environment policy, when depriving locals of access to vital resources such as land and forests, can become a harmful weapon against people, even if it is less obvious as such (Peluso, 1993).
6. The concept of "renewability", which constitutes an important element in the definition of what resources are, is intimately linked to the human dimension of time as measured in terms of seasons and decades (Bankoff and Boomgaard, 2007: 2).
7. In other words, under conditions of abundant natural resources, people "had few real wants that the state could usefully have attempted to relieve, and until comparatively recent times it formed no part of the programs of Siamese kings to raise the standard of living of their subjects" (Wales, 1934: 226).
8. These international interactions, as well as the fact that Europeans established extractive industries only in locations with relatively low mortality rates, demonstrate that resource development is built on layers of socio-political foundations (Bankoff and Boomgaard, 2007: 11).
9. Interestingly, this present interpretation is in stark contrast with the contemporary view. Prince Damrong, who took the lead in forming the Ministry of Interior, pointed out that the establishment of the RFD allowed "taking forestry issues out from politics" (Ministry of Interior, 1952: 54). He meant to say that Burmese timber traders who occasionally

had contract problems with their Siamese counterparts often relied on the British diplomatic channel to solve them; this in turn gave the British an opportunity to intervene in the domestic politics of Siam which Damrong tried to fence off.

10. In reflections on his first five-and-a-half years of service as conservator of forest, Slade (1901) highlighted this tension and the limited discretion given to the conservator as major obstacles to effective resource governance in the field.

11. As of 2007, forestry departments (the RFD and the National Parks, Wildlife and Plant Conservation Department) alone account for 63 per cent of the total budget allocated to the 10 departments in the Ministry of Natural Resources and Environment (Mingsarn et al., 2007).

12. One must not forget the important influence of donor communities in developed countries, which often facilitate the creation of new units to take care of projects they bring in from outside. Climate change (a unit now included in the Office of Natural Resources and Environmental Policy and Planning) is a typical area where new funding is increasingly becoming available.

REFERENCES

Agrawal, Arun (2005) *Environmentality: Technologies of Government and the Making of Subjects*, Durham, NC: Duke University Press.

Ascher, William (2004) "Scientific Information and Uncertainty: Challenges for the Use of Science in Policymaking", *Science and Engineering Ethics* 10, pp. 437–455.

Auty, Richard (1993) *Sustaining Development in Mineral Economies: The Resource Curse Thesis*, London: Routledge.

Bankoff, Greg and Peter Boomgaard (eds) (2007) *A History of Natural Resources in Asia: The Wealth of Nature*, Basingstoke: Palgrave Macmillan.

Bryant, Raymond and Sinead Bailey (1997) *Third World Political Ecology*, London: Routledge.

Bunnag, Piyanart (1990) "Politics among Governmental Organizations: A Case Study of Major Conflicts among Ministries during the Reform Period, 1892–1910", PhD dissertation, Chulalongkorn University (in Thai).

Dasgupta, Susmita, Ashoka Mody, Subhendu Roy and David Wheeler (2001) "Environmental Regulation and Development: A Cross-Country Empirical Analysis", *Oxford Development Studies* 29(2), pp. 173–187.

de Loë, R. C., D. Armitage, R. Plummer, S. Davidson and L. Moraru (2009) "From Government to Governance: A State-of-the-Art Review of Environmental Governance", final report prepared for Alberta Environment, Environmental Stewardship, Environmental Relations, Rob de Loë Consulting Services, Guelph, ON.

Dunning, Thad (2008) *Crude Democracy*, New York: Cambridge University Press.

ESCAP (2008) *Statistical Yearbook for Asia and the Pacific*, Bangkok: United Nations.

Falkus, Malcolm (1989) "Early British Business in Thailand", in R. P. T. Davenport-Hines and Geoffrey Jones (eds) *British Business in Asia since 1860*, Cambridge: Cambridge University Press, pp. 117–156.

Forsyth, Tim (2004) "Industrial Pollution and Social Movements in Thailand", in Richard Peet and Michael Watts (eds) *Liberation Ecologies: Environment, Development and Social Movements*, 2nd edn, London and New York: Routledge, pp. 422–438.

Foucault, Michel (2007) *Security, Territory, Population: Lectures at the Collège de France 1977–1978*, New York: Picador.

Garden, Po, Louis Lebel and Charunee Chirangworapat (2010) "Local Government Reforms as Work in Progress", in Chusak Wittayapak and Peter Vandergeest (eds) *The Politics of Decentralization: Natural Resource Management in Asia*, Chiang Mai: Mekong Press, pp. 137–160.

Green Line (2011) "Mineral Mining: Bonanza of Bust", *Green Line*, January–April.

Goldman, Michael (2005) *Imperial Nature: The World Bank and Struggles for Social Justice in the Age of Globalization*, New Haven, CT: Yale University Press.

Grossman, Gene M. and Alan B. Krueger (1995) "Economic Growth and the Environment", *Quarterly Journal of Economics* 110(2), pp. 353–378.

Harrington, Chris, Allan Curtis and Rosemary Black (2008) "Locating Communities in Natural Resource Management", *Journal of Environmental Policy and Planning* 10(2), pp. 199–215.

Hicks, Robert, Bradley C. Parks, J. Timmons Roberts and Michael J. Tierney (2010) *Greening Aid? Understanding the Environmental Impact of Development Assistance*, Oxford: Oxford University Press.

Hirano, Takashi (2003) "The First Draft of the Environmental Law in Postwar Japan", *Ryukyu University Law Journal* 36(1), pp. 1–71 (in Japanese).

Hirsh, Philip (1993) *Political Economy of the Environment in Thailand*, Manila: Journal of Contemporary Asia Publishers.

Ingram, James (1971) *Economic Change in Thailand: 1850–1970*, Stanford, CA: Stanford University Press.

Jones, Martin, Rhys Jones and Michael Woods (2007) *An Introduction to Political Geography: Space, Place, and Politics*, New York: Routledge.

Kijtewachakul, Nitaya (2010) "Local Politics and Decentralization", in Chusak Wittayapak and Peter Vandergeest (eds) *The Politics of Decentralization: Natural Resource Management in Asia*, Chiang Mai: Mekong Press, pp. 161–178.

Loos, Tamara (1994) "Introduction", in H. Warrington Smyth, *Five Years in Siam from 1891–1896*, Vols 1 and 2, Bangkok: White Lotus, pp. i–xix.

Macauley, R. H. (1934) *History of the Bombay Burmah Trading Corporation Ltd, 1814–1910*, London: Spottiswoode, Ballantyne.

Mingsarn, Kaosa-ard, Benoit Laplante, Kobkun Rayanakorn and Sakon Waranyuwattana (2008) "Capacity Building for Pollution Taxation and Resources Mobilization for Environmental and Natural Resources, Phase II", report submitted to the Asian Development Bank, Manila.

Ministry of Interior (1952) "Anuson Nuang naigaansong wanthiraluk sapapana Krasuwang Mahathai Krop Roop 60 pii boribun", Ministry of Interior, microfilm at National Library, Bangkok (in Thai).

Moor, Mick (2001) "Political Underdevelopment: What Causes 'Bad Governance'", *Public Management Review* 3(3), pp. 1–34.

OECD (2012) "Aid in Support for Environment, Statistics Based on DAC Members' Reporting on the Environment Policy Marker, 2009–2010", Creditor Reporting System Database, OECD, Paris.

Peluso, Nancy (1993) "Coercing Conservation? The Politics of State Resource Control", *Global Environmental Change* 3(2), pp. 199–217.

Peluso, Nancy and Peter Vandergeest (2001) "Genealogies of the Political Forest and Customary Rights in Indonesia, Malaysia, and Thailand", *Journal of Asian Studies* 60(3), pp. 761–812.

Ross, Michael (1999) "The Political Economy of Resource Curse", *World Politics* 51, pp. 297–322.

Rueschemeyer, Dietrich and John Stephens (1997) "Comparing Historical Sequences: A Powerful Tool for Causal Analysis. A Reply to John Goldthorpe's Current Issues in Comparative Macro-Sociology", *Comparative Social Research* 16, pp. 55–72.

Ruoff, Gabriele (2009) "Grow Rich and Clean Up Later? International Political Integration and the Provision of Environmental Quality in Low- and Middle-Income Countries", paper presented at Midwest Political Science Association 67th Annual National Conference, Chicago, 2 April.

Sachs, Jeffrey and Andrew M. Warner (2001) "The Curse of Natural Resources", *European Economic Review* 45, pp. 827–838.

Sato, Jin (2000) "People in Between: Conservation and Conversion of Forest Lands in Thailand", *Development and Change* 31(1), pp. 155–177.

—— (2003) "Institutional Basis of Community Forestry in Thailand", *Journal of Southeast Asian Studies* 32(2), pp. 329–346.

Scott, James (1998) *Seeing Like a State: How Certain Schemes to Improve the Human Condition Have Failed*, New Haven, CT: Yale University Press.

Selden, Thomas M. and Daqing Song (1994) "Environmental Quality and Development: Is There a Kuznets Curve for Air Pollution Emission?", *Journal of Environmental Economics and Management* 27, pp. 147–162.

Siffin, William (1966) *The Thai Bureaucracy*, Honolulu, HI: East-West Center Press.

Slade, Herbert (1901) *Report of the Royal Forest Department*, National Archive of Thailand, Bangkok, R5 M16/3.

Smyth, H. Warrington ([1898] 1994) *Five Years in Siam from 1891–1896*, Vols 1 and 2, Bangkok: White Lotus.

Sonnenfeld, David (1998) "From Brown to Green? Late Industrialization, Social Conflict, and Adoption of Environmental Technologies in Thailand's Pulp Industry", *Organization & Environment* 11(1), pp. 59–87.

Stubbs, R. (1981) "Environmental Administration in Thailand", Research Paper No. 5, East-West Environment and Policy Institute, Honolulu, HI.

Ui, Jun (1968) *Politics of Pollution*, Tokyo: Aki Shobo (in Japanese).

Unger, Daniel and Patcharee Siroros (2011) "Trying to Make Decisions Stick: Natural Resource Policy Making in Thailand", *Journal of Contemporary Asia* 41(2), pp. 206–228.

Vandergeest, Peter (1996) "Mapping Nature: Territorialization of Forest Rights in Thailand", *Society and Natural Resources* 9, pp. 159–175.

Wales, H. G. Q. (1934) *Ancient Siamese Government and Administration*, London: Paragon Books.

Werachai, Narkwiboonwong and Chinnavaso Kasemsun (2010) "Conflicts and Cooperation in Resource Governance: State Control of the Public Domain and the Role of Local People in Thailand", report prepared for JICA, Bangkok.

2

Natural resource governance in Latin America

William Ascher

Introduction

Latin American nations have experienced a host of weaknesses in natural resource governance, resulting in widespread problems in resource exploitation practices. Defining governance as the allocation of decision-making authority and resultant institutions that exercise this authority, virtually every Latin American nation has suffered from weak governance in determining the degree and manner in which natural resources are developed, extracted, processed and exchanged. However, several nations have demonstrated the potential for improvement, as they have established relatively stable and sound governance over crucial resources.

It is important to specify at the outset what it means to "improve" natural resource management and practice. The objective of material prosperity calls for the criteria of effectiveness and efficiency in resource exploitation. A corollary is that sound knowledge must be incorporated into the formulation of resource policies and practices. The objective of socio-economic justice calls for the criterion of fair distribution of the benefits of resource exploitation. The objective of maintaining environmental amenities, species and habitats calls for the criteria of strong environmental protection and conservation. The goals of maximizing human dignity and avoiding violence and disruption call for the criterion of peaceful resource development involving the least possible coercion. Improvements in resource management – and therefore resource governance – must show progress in one or more of these criteria without undue sacrifices in

Governance of natural resources: Uncovering the social purpose of materials in nature, Sato (ed.), United Nations University Press, 2013, ISBN 978-92-808-1228-2

the others. Finally, the stability of sound governance arrangements – as long as they are truly sound – is a great virtue, and crucial for the analysis here.

This chapter argues that Latin America's decentralization and privatization efforts, which have received the bulk of attention in natural resource governance, must be far more nuanced than they have been thus far. While the enthusiasm for wholesale decentralization is often rooted in a laudable pursuit of greater democratic participation, this enthusiasm needs to be tempered by several limitations and drawbacks of decentralization in some contexts. Devolving responsibility to subnational governments or user groups without adequate financial resources, expertise or authority risks the effectiveness of resource management and regulation. Local control can undermine incentives to limit negative externalities that damage other areas. Domination by local elites may reduce the access of marginal people to resources. Decentralization is sometimes a cynical strategy for national governments to shed responsibility for degraded ecosystems. Finally, when national leaders decide that the wealth from resource extraction is worth retaking, the disruptions and uncertainty emerging from recentralization can be very costly.

This chapter also argues that the multiplicity of motives government leaders pursue through natural resource extraction is responsible for contradictory governance mandates that often can be found at all levels, from local to national. These contradictory motives frequently undermine transparency, so that more challengeable motives can be pursued at low political cost. Therefore making sure that institutions involved in resource governance have straightforward mandates, whether in extraction *per se* or regulating the process, is a crucial challenge.

Natural resource decisions in Latin America range from sweeping governmental policies, such as the banning of all tree harvesting or nationalization of oil and mining industries, to the most micro-decisions of the farmer who has the discretion to plant trees or the mine operator deciding how much ore to extract today. At each level, governance is exercised within the span of effective authority defined by the discretion held by each decision-maker, backed by power or the recognition of rights on the part of others. Thus a quite complex set of potential decision-makers must be examined to see where pivotal decisions are made and what their consequences will be.

Understanding resource governance in Latin America

However, the argument of this chapter is that Latin American national government leaders are almost universally the key architects of natural resource governance. This is not to argue that what national leaders do is the sum total of relevant factors. They face the obstacles of embedded arrangements (e.g. some constitutional guarantees of user rights of others), limited financial and administrative capacity, resistance from other actors and conflicting objectives that sometimes relegate sound resource management to secondary status. In addition, national governments are by no means monolithic: different institutions within any government have conflicting mandates and interests. Nevertheless, the actions of national leaders in reshaping natural resource governance loom very large.

In part this is due to the fundamental dominance of the national government over resource user rights, which holds in all world regions. Insofar as government is the ultimate protector of property rights, it is the ultimate arbiter of these rights as well. When a government is unwilling or unable to defend property rights, the decision scope of the ostensible resource owners is greatly curtailed. For example, in the 1980s and 1990s the Brazilian government did not extend protection to many of the Amazonian ranches with formal government-granted titles, leaving many exposed to encroachment by squatters (Schneider, 1995). In addition, regulation is a central facet of governance, and government is the primary formulator and enforcer of regulations. Environmental regulations limit what resource exploiters can do with the resources to which they have access. Less obviously, government's economic activity restricts the scope of what other resource exploiters can profitably do. For example, when the Honduran government created state monopolies for marketing timber, it essentially drove much of the profit out of timber extraction.

These governmental responsibilities and privileges are typically stronger in Latin America than in developed countries. Growing out of the colonial legacy, the formal state control over subsoil assets and the weakness of private and communal property rights in the face of coercive governments, national leaders have largely dictated resource governance arrangements. Roughly three-quarters of South America's forests are publicly owned (UN Food and Agriculture Organization, 2010: xxv). The bulk of oil exploitation is formally controlled by state-owned oil companies. Minerals rights are all under the formal control of the state, and although the infrastructure may be owned by private firms, government expropriation has been very common. Other actors generally lack effective constitutional protections to fend off national government's imposition of authority. Latin America countries have not enshrined these protections in constitutional provisions such as the US takings clause, which protects property owners from outright expropriation. Moreover, only four Latin American nations have federal systems (Argentina, Brazil, Mexico and Venezuela), which means that in all other countries the national government is *the* government. In a unitary system, no powers are unalterably reserved to subnational governments – the national government has the power to rescind subnational government authority.

Thus understanding governance arrangements first requires understanding how national leaders strive to pursue their objectives. Going beyond this truism, I argue that national leaders' governance decisions reflect their efforts to manage the tensions among three chronically conflicting overarching goals. The most obvious one is to secure the means to actualize the economic potential of the natural resource endowment. National government leaders sometimes find themselves without the means needed to accomplish this, whether financial (e.g. investment capital to develop resource extraction infrastructure) or political (e.g. the capacity to convince local people to conform to sound resource exploitation practices).

A somewhat less obvious meta-goal is to maximize their discretion over the rate and manner of resource extraction and the allocation of benefits from that extraction. Maximizing discretion is a meta-goal in that it encompasses control over both the exploitation process itself and the selection of beneficiaries. Discretion over the rate of exploitation obviously helps to set the level of revenues. We shall see how important this has been in national government decisions on dealing with international companies. For example, government leaders must decide whether international companies should be brought in because of their access to capital, and whether to take over their operations when the companies are reluctant to invest and extract. The discretion to provide access to resource assets at below the competitive bid price will encourage extraction and channel higher profits to the producers. Discretion over domestic pricing of fuel, water, etc. allows national leaders to benefit consumers, on whom many of the leaders depend politically. Similarly, leaders' discretion over supplies and prices of raw materials, water and energy allows them to benefit producers reliant on these inputs. Discretion over channelling revenues can serve a range of distributional objectives for the leaders, from personal aggrandizement to the general welfare of the population. Directing benefits to particular locales and groups can elicit support, adding to the political standing of those held responsible, especially if yet others are unaware of the advantages enjoyed by the targeted beneficiaries. Therefore in many instances it is just as politically compelling to control the distribution of benefits derived from resource extraction as it is to receive the benefit.

The least obvious but no less important meta-goal is to minimize negative accountability when resources deteriorate or are squandered. National leaders must address the risks of losing political support or economic cooperation, domestically or internationally. Forest degradation, mine pollution, oil spills, unwise expenditure and confrontations with displaced local populations all erode the standing of the national government if various actors, domestic or international, perceive it as being in control.

Second, understanding governance arrangements requires appreciating that the most common response to these problems has been to delegate authority to other entities, but generally in unstable and contentious ways. This reflects the instability of domestic politics, the cycles of international markets and the changing status of the resources themselves. Latin American resource governance has seen the proliferation and evolution of various forms of *provisional* decentralization. In fact, the predominant focus of recent policy analysis and promotion of resource governance has been on decentralization, either to subnational governments or to non-governmental community groups. This reflects the general trend of decentralization throughout Latin America, of which governance over natural resources is but one element, as well as the establishment of communal resource control.[1]

However, national government leaders retract delegated authority quite often as conditions alter, typically making wholesale changes in the governance of the resource in question. This, in turn, undermines the certainty of user rights, deters investment and provokes suboptimal resource practices. Only a few Latin American nations – Brazil, Chile and Costa Rica – have achieved the political maturation and economic security to maintain a stable general governance framework for most resources that still affords sufficient flexibility to address the leaders' needs.

The delegation has five major targets: agencies within the national government, state-owned enterprises formally under national government control, subnational governments, local communities or user groups, and domestic or foreign private firms. Delegating to each can help national government leaders to pursue some of their objectives, but inevitably the interests of these other entities diverge, to a greater or lesser degree, from those of the national leaders. When these divergences become too great for national leaders to accept, the leaders try to alter the governance arrangements, often by reversing the delegation. This disruption of expectations and operations is one of the reasons why natural resource practices in Latin America have been so problematic.

Three further clarifications are useful. First, it is important to note that to some extent, delegation is unavoidable. Because the highest level of government officials – presidents, prime ministers, legislators – cannot possibly make all the specific decisions on how natural resources will be regulated and managed, government ministries and agencies necessarily take on some control. Each of these national entities has its own mandate and institutional interests – typically to enhance its resources and jurisdiction. Similarly, state-owned enterprises, even if fully owned by the central government and formally controlled by top-level national leaders through their appointed boards and managers, typically have considerable discretion, due to their greater mastery over relevant information and their technical expertise. Moreover, even if the national government lays claim to complete control over a resource – as in the case of the Honduran government's 1973 appropriation of all trees – the lack of monitoring and enforcement capacity means that non-governmental resource exploiters maintain some degree of control. The assertion of central government control over surface resources, declared through national laws such as the expropriation of all trees, has often been more formal than effective. Nevertheless, it gives the government the discretion to assert its authority when national leaders deem it desirable. In short, natural resource control is always distributed to a certain degree, even though top national leaders shape this distribution.

Second, even when actors other than national leaders hold an apparently broad range of resource user rights, resource practices will reflect the expectations that governmental action may threaten these rights. Godoy, Kirby and Wilkie (2001) note that one cause of deforestation by Bolivian farmers is the fear that without land clearing, their property claims would be void. Pichon (1997) found a similar pattern in Ecuador. More generally for Latin America as a whole, Jaramillo and Kelly (1997) highlight that "Traditional policies that required land clearing to obtain title have been strong promoters of deforestation." To a certain degree, these practices simply reflect vestiges of earlier attitudes towards the forest – even in conservation-minded Costa Rica, a traditional term for forestland is *tierra sucia* (dirty land).

Third, in Latin America resource control has never been fully – i.e. irreversibly – *devolved*. Rondinelli (1981) usefully distinguishes among three decentralization categories. "Deconcentration" entails relocating government personnel outside the capital area(s). "Delegation" entails provisional transfers of authority to other – typically lower – levels of decision-makers. "Devolution" entails permanently ceding authority to lower levels of decision-makers. Government officials may claim they are engaging in devolution – that they are permanently recognizing the rights of other entities to control natural resource exploitation. In some world regions the authority of these entities, whether private or governmental, is sufficiently protected through constitutional provisions, entrenched law, political power or custom. In Latin America, in contrast, the history of reversing delegation, and even reversing what was presented as devolution, demonstrates that no natural resource decentralization is totally immune from reversal or modification by national leaders, whether it is formally presented as decentralization or devolution. Thus the key insight for understanding how Latin American resource governance evolves is to appreciate the flexibility of delegation from the central government to the various other actors, driven by the efforts of national government officials to pursue their multiple and varying objectives.

This perspective conforms with the insights of a growing literature that emphasizes the importance of interactions among different levels of decision-making, as the entities that assume provisional control are nested within higher levels of decision-making, with the top-level national government leaders at the apex. This literature argues that "the study of political systems needs to consider the degree and forms of nestedness of political actors within larger political systems. The patterns of interaction and outcomes depend on the relationships among governance actors at different levels and the problems they are addressing" (Andersson and Ostrom, 2008: 73).

These considerations lead to the key prescriptive argument of this chapter. Top national officials require – and can gain – some degree of adaptability in resource governance, even if delegated to subnational governments or private actors, to cope with political demands and economic challenges. *If this adaptability can operate within a broader, stable and sound institutional framework, the criteria for appropriate resource policy, management and practices can be met.*

Clarifying the problems and the goals of reform

The concern over natural resource governance in Latin America stems from a basically poor record of resource management throughout the region, despite some exceptions. With respect to forests, three South American countries, Brazil, Bolivia and Venezuela, were among the 10 countries worldwide that lost the most forest cover in absolute terms from 2000 to 2010; Brazil lost more than four times as much forest cover as Australia, the second biggest loser. Brazil and Bolivia have been losing roughly 0.5 per cent of forest cover per year, and Venezuela 0.6 per cent per year (UN Food and Agriculture Organization, 2010: 21). From 1990 to 2010 South America as a whole lost forests at a rate of 0.45 per cent a year, although the trend has decreased slightly over the past five years, reflecting Brazil's modest decline in its rate of deforestation (ibid.: 17–18).

Water policies and practices are also problematic in many Latin American countries, in terms of both economic use and the quality of water for personal consumption and health. Although Latin America is blessed with more than its share of freshwater resources (31 per cent of the global total, compared to only 8 per cent of global population[2]) and enormous hydropower potential (currently 68 per cent of all electricity generation, compared to the global average of less than 16 per cent), the failure to build the infrastructure to sequester water and manage the current systems during droughts has contributed to reduced electricity production in Argentina, Brazil, Chile, Ecuador, Peru and Venezuela. Water shortages have become a constraining factor in Chilean and Peruvian mining. In terms of agrarian water uses, shortages led to the loss of 1.5 million head of cattle and half the wheat crop in Argentina in 2008; Guatemala and Mexico suffered comparable losses in 2009.

Water quality for consumption and health maintenance in Latin America suffers because of inadequate wastewater treatment and residential access to water. Roughly 85 million Latin Americans (nearly 15 per cent of the total population) lack piped water in their homes, and the poor quality of this water has led to a tripling of bottled water use over the first decade of this millennium; for many low-income families, bottled water is much more expensive than the charges for piped water. Roughly 115 million Latin Americans (nearly 20 per cent) lack adequate sanitation. More than 80 per cent of wastewater goes untreated. These quality problems lead to 38,000 annual deaths of children under the age of five from diarrhoea, in addition to high incidence of other water-borne diseases. Because of the scarcity of residential water meters, residential piped water usage is twice as much as in Germany and three times the volume in China. Mexico City and Caracas have recently had to ration water because of wasteful overuse. In a number of Latin American countries the abortive efforts to privatize potable water systems in order to secure sufficient capital to expand the coverage and quality of the system have foundered on the resistance of users to paying the full operating and maintenance costs and the unwillingness of the government to subsidize the lowest-income families. Underpricing is a policy instrument that governments often use to gain political favour, but private enterprises have to recoup their costs and secure a profit.

Regarding subsoil resources, Latin America's oil and gas sector is dominated by state-owned companies, whose efficiency is dramatically lower than that of private international companies. According to an analysis by Eller, Hartley and Medlock (2007), the technical efficiency of generating revenues from employees and oil and gas reserves for the five national oil and gas companies of Brazil, Colombia, Ecuador, Mexico and Venezuela during the 2003–2004 period ranged from $506 per employee for Mexico to $1,985 for Venezuela (prior to the dramatic operational deterioration that the Venezuelan company PDVSA suffered in the second half of the decade), and from $0.66 per barrel of oil equivalent reserves for Venezuela to $4.01 for Mexico. The five largest international oil and gas companies[3] have revenues that average $2,865 per employee and $15.28 per barrel of oil equivalent reserves; for 42 smaller international oil companies, average revenues are $1,629 per employee and $11.24 per barrel of oil equivalent reserves. Undoubtedly many factors are responsible for these ratios,[4] but the differences between the national companies and the international firms are so great that the operational inefficiencies of the state companies cannot be easily explained away. Underlying these inefficiencies are notoriously glaring problems: Mexico's state oil company Petroleos Mexicanos (PEMEX) is universally acknowledged to be woefully undercapitalized and bloated with redundant employees. Venezuela's Petroleos de Venezuela S.A. (PDVSA) is equally notorious for having plummeted from its early reputation as one the world's few efficient national oil companies to its current state of mismanagement, lack of competence in the spheres it has been required to work in (ranging from shipbuilding to agriculture) and lack of transparency.

Domestic fuel pricing, an important factor for increasing the volume of oil and gas exports, has also been highly problematic for the Latin American countries that depend most heavily on these exports. According to a recent study by the German aid agency GTZ (2008), the median price of high-octane gasoline worldwide was roughly US$1.15 per litre. While the Brazilian price was US$1.26, reflecting in part the government's efforts to promote ethanol use, the price in Venezuela was 2 cents, Ecuador 51 cents, Bolivia 68 cents and Colombia US$1.04. The greater domestic fuel consumption induced by these low prices not only reduces the crude oil and gas available for hard-currency-earning exports, but also induces more driving, the retention of older vehicles and therefore more pollution.

Latin America's environmental protection, an essential aspect of resource governance not only in terms of conservation but also because clean air and water are themselves resources, is problematic in many respects. In light of the multiple dimensions involved as well as the highly divergent economic and physical conditions across countries, the overall effectiveness of environmental protection institutions and policies is very difficult to gauge. However, some benchmarking measures are useful even if they are not fully up to date. The Environmental Regulatory Regime Index (ERRI) (Esty and Porter, 2001) combines scores on environmental regulatory stringency, structures, subsidies and enforcement, based on judgemental evaluations gathered through questionnaires solicited from respondents in business, government and non-governmental organizations. Esty and Porter (ibid.: 93) report the ERRI scores for 71 countries: 28 "low-income" countries with per capita incomes less than US$6,500, including 13 Latin American countries; 25 "middle-income" countries (per capita incomes of US$6,500–$23,000), including six Latin American countries; and 18 "high-income countries". Table 2.1 shows the relative scores of 19 Latin American countries, with a few non-Latin American countries for benchmarking purposes. It should be noted that only three sub-Saharan African countries (Nigeria, South Africa and

Table 2.1 Environmental Regulatory Regime Index

Rank		
1	*Finland*	*2.303*
2	*Sweden*	*1.772*
3	*Singapore*	*1.771*
14	*United States*	*1.184*
17	*Japan*	*1.057*
25	Chile	0.177
27	Uruguay	0.059
34	Jamaica	–0.037
35	Brazil	–0.077
36	Costa Rica	–0.078
42	Panama	–0.242
44	*China*	*–0.348*
46	Colombia	–0.416
48	Mexico	–0.602
50	Peru	–0.722
51	Argentina	–0.732
53	Bolivia	–0.743
60	Dominican Republic	–1.014
61	Venezuela	–1.079
62	Nicaragua	–1.164
63	El Salvador	–1.215
64	Honduras	–1.300
69	Guatemala	–1.532
70	Ecuador	–1.616
71	Paraguay	–1.743

Note: Countries in roman type are those on which this chapter focuses; all other countries are in *italics*.

Zimbabwe) were included in the study, so it may very well be that lower scores on regulatory effectiveness would have been present if the coverage were much broader. Nevertheless, the table reveals that while a few Latin American governments have decent environmental regulatory effectiveness in light of their overall economic levels[5] (Chile, Uruguay, Jamaica, Brazil and Costa Rica), the rest do quite poorly and six Latin American countries are among the 10 worst. To some degree, the poor performance is due to differences in wealth within Latin American nations and among nations of other regions. However, eight of the 13 Latin American countries in the under-$6,500 per capita income bracket were in the bottom half of those countries; and four of the six Latin American countries in the middle-income range were below the median score of environmental regulatory effectiveness. The relatively good performance of Costa Rica, Jamaica and Uruguay reflects the crucial importance of tourism, attracting expatriate residents, or both. While one should not minimize the accomplishment of these countries in safeguarding their eco-tourism or expatriate residence potential, the more remarkable cases are Brazil and Chile. Both are well above the median for countries of their broad per capita income levels.

However, an important and perhaps obvious qualification is necessary for Brazil. While its regulatory effectiveness is high, this has not stopped the conversion of forests to other land uses. The forest conservation regulations, largely under the control of state governments in Brazil's federal system, are not nearly as strong as the Brazilian conservation movement wishes them to be. State governments in the Amazon lack strong incentives to conserve forests when the pressures of settlement and the economic inducements of expanding ranches and farms grow stronger.[6]

Finally, an indicator of problematic resource management is the prevalence of violence over the exploitation of forests, hard minerals, oil and water. Violence related to forests has been endemic in Bolivia, Brazil, Colombia, Ecuador, Guatemala, Honduras, Mexico, Nicaragua, Peru and Surinam. Conflicts over oil and mineral exploitation have been particularly acute in Brazil, Bolivia, Colombia, Ecuador and Venezuela.

Another perspective on the problematic nature of resource governance in Latin America rests on the policy failures that underlie poor practices and resource conflicts. One pervasive problem is the underpricing of access to or consumption of resources. Where national or subnational governments set electricity and water rates, users rarely pay enough for full cost recovery. This limits the capacity of the electric infrastructure to expand coverage, leaving 26 per cent of rural Latin Americans without electricity (International Energy Agency, 2010: table 1). Similarly the inadequacy of residential water provision and sanitation can be directly traced to insufficient cost recovery (the revenues brought in from water charges in relation to the costs of providing the water), which averages only 50 per cent for Latin America as a whole (Inter-American Development Bank, 2009). As mentioned, where governments of oil-exporting countries set domestic fuel prices, these are typically below the appropriate border price. Because state oil and mining companies are not required to pay royalties directly tied to the in-ground value of the resource, the differences between revenues and costs are not meaningful business profits, and the companies lack incentives to perform efficiently or limit extraction to economically sound rates. In essence, these companies underpay for access to the nation's resources, which undermines their efficiency and prompts overextraction. Access to forest resources is also underpriced in many cases, whether for state or private exploiters.

A second pervasive problem is the uncertainty of user rights. Unstable arrangements create additional uncertainty; uncertainty provokes overly hasty extraction by those who fear losing their access to resources. When the rights of landowners or tenants are unclear, as in the case of Nicaragua (Bandiera, 2007), or when farmers feel compelled to clear trees to secure their rights, as in the case of Bolivia (Godoy, Kirby, and Wilkie, 2001), resource practices are likely to be shortsighted. This is such an endemic problem because of the almost continual changes in resource control and user rights in many Latin American nations.

A third problem is the subordination of sound resource exploitation to the pursuit of other objectives. Underpricing to gain political favour from beneficiaries is widespread, and the risks of proper pricing are often great – as demonstrated by the fuel price riots in the oil-producing nations of Bolivia, Ecuador and Venezuela. Some of the problems of the Mexican oil company PEMEX and the Venezuelan PDVSA mentioned earlier can be traced to their history of providing off-budget funding for national leaders' favoured projects. The severe undercapitalization of PEMEX is due in large part to heavy taxation that forces PEMEX into high levels of international borrowing, in effect extending the government's international credit ceiling. The goal of income redistribution is often pursued through price controls on resource-based products ranging from firewood and charcoal to food.

A fourth problem is governmental corruption in regulation and access charges. Of course, governments often impose regulations and establish restricted areas, typically invoking conservation and environmental protection. Yet each restriction opens the possibility of illegal payments to regulators or protected-area guards, to allow illegal activity. Even in Costa Rica, widely regarded as one of the most advanced Latin American nations in terms of conservation, illegal logging permitted by corrupt officials is a significant problem (Miller, 2011).

A fifth problem grows out of the aforementioned jurisdictional competition among government agencies. Often the leaders of agencies involved in resource governance are understandably motivated to rush to promote resource exploitation within their mandate. For example, land reform agencies push people into forested areas, and agricultural ministries "extensify" agriculture by assisting in draining of marshes, converting forests into pasture, etc. This competition provokes agencies to establish conflicting rules in an effort to secure their control. An obvious governance problem is that several Latin American countries, as diverse as Costa Rica and Peru (see Mainhardt-Gibbs, 2003; Ascher, 1999), have had conflicting land-use classifications established by different national government agencies, leading to insecure property rights and a scramble to occupy forested areas under whichever classification is most lenient regarding rapid resource extraction.

In light of the policy failures and the manifestly poor natural resource management in many Latin American nations, it is important to examine resource governance to see where and how to make improvements. Understanding the technical aspects – whether decisions are being made at levels where useful and comprehensive information is available, where externalities can be soundly addressed, etc. – is crucial for assessing *what* improvements ought to be made. Yet in order to identify *how* to improve resource governance, it is equally important to understand *why* suboptimal governance structures exist.

One obvious reason is that institutional inertia has left governance structures that are no longer appropriate for the resource management tasks at hand. Yet this diagnosis, even if correct in some circumstances, begs the question of why obsolete governance persists. I begin to answer this question by briefly reviewing the historical and contemporary trends in resource governance.

Historical and contemporary trends

Surface resources

Some of the factors still relevant for natural resource governance in Latin America date back to the early colonial period. At the beginning of the sixteenth century the Spanish Crown granted jurisdiction – but not formal ownership – to Spanish soldiers, administrators and a few of the indigenous elite. These *encomiendas* entailed a form of guardianship over indigenous people, who were formally wards of the *encomenderos* yet in reality were indentured servants, relegated to sharecropping or plantation labour. The Portuguese colony of Brazil was more direct in its enslavement of the indigenous people – slavery was not fully abolished in Brazil until 1888.

The *encomenderos* in Spanish America effectively governed the land and people under their control, often abusively. The system was abolished at the beginning of the eighteenth century, but by then the *encomenderos* and others of Spanish ancestry had secured ownership of much of the quality cropland. Unlike other world regions, much of the cropland was thereby consolidated into very large landholdings (*latifundios*); over time the land owned by indigenous, mixed-race or downwardly mobile Spanish farmers came to be divided into progressively smaller holdings (*minifundios*). Land hunger, reflecting the economic impoverishment of the landless and the *minifundio* owners, exacerbated by generally rapid population growth and the fact that many *latifundios* were underexploited, has long provoked demands for land reform, frequently resulting in violence.

Those indigenous people in both Spanish America and Brazil who were not exterminated during the many revolts, or tied to the *encomenderos* as low-wage agricultural labourers, were pushed into the highlands or jungles. Formal titling was overwhelmingly the exception rather than the rule. The only claim that local people could make to defend their use of farmland, pasture or forest resources was that they had customary rights based on generations of use without challenge by authorities.

For most of the twentieth century Mexico was a special case, resulting in community control of roughly 80 per cent of forestlands. Following the bloody Mexican Revolution (roughly 1910–1920), landless peasants were given inalienable rights to land confiscated from the owners of *latifundios* and plantations for communal exploitation. These *ejidos* were self-governing in several respects, yet a crucial user right – the right to sell the land or put it up for collateral – was prohibited by the inalienable status of the land. The Mexican government's exertion of control was to keep the *ejido* governance arrangement intact. This came at the long-term cost of denying *ejido* members the opportunity to borrow capital for investment to improve their productivity. The impoverishment of the *ejidos*, combined with the rising economic liberalization climate, led eventually to the elimination of the inalienability restriction in the early 1990s.

The forestry sector has been characterized by the greatest discrepancy between formal and actual control. For centuries the very locations of forests in relatively remote areas permitted local populations to engage in low-intensity harvesting of timber and non-timber extractive resources. Farmers harvested trees on their land or in uncultivated areas that were essentially open access. However, the weakness of formal user rights left the forests vulnerable to more extensive logging by commercial firms as well as clearing to extend large agricultural holdings. These incursions led to significant conflict between local people and logging companies and large estates, still acute in Brazil, Colombia, Honduras, Mexico and Peru. Other forests gave way to expanding cities. Forests in areas experiencing high population growth, such as the Atlantic forests in Brazil, shrunk dramatically.

A complex combination of revenue generation, conservation considerations, foreign assistance opportunities and venal interests led to a wave of forest nationalizations beginning generally in the 1960s. In some cases the explicit motive was to put logging rights into the hands of the state, to secure the profits of harvesting for the government. For example, the aforementioned Honduran expropriation of all forest assets resulted in the dominance of a state forestry enterprise, the Corporación Hondureña de Desarrollo Forestal, in harvesting and marketing timber. In other cases conservation, whether for its own sake, to promote eco-tourism or to ensure sustainable forest product extraction, was the primary motive. As international non-governmental conservation organizations and foreign assistance agencies became interested in supporting forest reserves, many government leaders found the establishment of forest reserves to be a compelling means of gaining both more assistance and a reputation for being conservation-minded. The threat to the livelihoods of local people posed by their exclusion from some forestry activities sometimes prompted policies to create income-earning opportunities, such as serving as guides or forest guards, but often these efforts have been feeble compared to the economic damage done to the local populations. The venal motive has been reflected in the awarding of logging concessions, or simply wilfully ignoring illegal logging, in exchange for bribes. A mid-2000s estimate of the proportion of illegally harvested logs was roughly 12 per cent for Brazil and 20 per cent for the rest of Latin America (World Bank, 2006: 12).

Latin America has had its share of "paper parks" in which illicit logging, burning for shifting cultivation and other formally illegal encroachments proceeded despite restrictions, reflecting inadequate efforts at enforcement. The IUCN World Conservation Union (1999: 1) asserted that "A survey of 10 key forest countries showed that only 1 per cent of forest protected areas were regarded as secure and many were already suffering from serious degradation and loss."

As central governments were roundly criticized by both national and international actors for incompetence, corruption and disinterest in maintaining forest cover in general and forest reserves in particular, the option of reducing accountability became increasingly attractive. Thus the major contemporary trend in the forestry sector has been the decentralization of management to subnational governments, particularly municipalities, as well as non-governmental forest user groups. To be sure, this serves other objectives as well. As the general trend of decentralization proceeded in most Latin American countries over the past two or three decades, subnational governments acquired the authority to collect logging royalties to pay for the services they were required to provide. On the other hand, the entity with the new privilege to control forest exploitation has also had to take on the costs and risks of doing so.

Ceding governance to local communities has the potential to ingratiate the national government to those communities – as in the case of the Colombian *resguardos* (guardianship reserves) in areas facing guerrilla threats (Ascher, 1995). One can also argue that local governance may elicit more compliance than a remote national government would be able to secure. Nevertheless it is striking that decentralization can reduce both the reputational risk and the financial responsibility of the national government.

Entities acquiring decentralized authority over surface assets often find that the resource base has already been severely degraded. Frequently decentralization reflects the national government leaders' judgement that revenue capture, political credit through channelling the benefits and credit for good resource management are no longer sufficient incentives to retain control. High-value timber stands are often "mined" by the time the national government cedes control to local users or subnational governments.

Subnational government officials given delegated authority over natural resources face a set of risks and opportunities comparable to that of the national officials before delegation. The advantages of directing the benefits of resource exploitation are balanced against the burden of managing the resource, often with inadequate capacity, and bearing the accountability of poor performance (Gibson and Lehoucq, 2003; Larson, 2003; Larson and Soto, 2008).

The incentives for sound decentralized subnational management are often lacking. Local authorities are sometimes in a position to receive pay-offs for permitting formally illegal resource extraction to proceed. Even so, Andersson, Gibson and Lehoucq (2006: 577) note: "The problem is often that local governments bear substantial costs associated with environmental protection, but reap only a small part of the benefits. This collective-goods dilemma raises an important question: Why would local politicians be interested in forest governance?" However, their study, based on comparisons of 200 municipalities in Bolivia and Guatemala, concludes that municipal authorities do use effective governance, particularly in Guatemala, when they "reap political and/or financial rewards from doing so" (ibid.: 580). They base this on the finding that Guatemalan mayors respond to greater devolution of political, regulatory and fiscal powers (ibid.: 590). Without these incentives, resource governance is more of a burden than a privilege. For Bolivia, Ribot, Agrawal and Larson (2006: 1875) note that:

> though local governments in Bolivia have greater powers in forest management than ever before, forestry decentralization has been a top-down process that has left little room for local discretionary decision making. The central government still controls key decisions, such as the definition of forest resources rights and regulations, the allocation of concessions, and tax collection for forest uses. Local people and governments have had no input into the forest regulations themselves, which many claim are biased against them. Funding for UFMs [municipal forestry units] is limited, and local governments have no say over the remaining 80% of public forests. The central government's priority appears to be large-scale concessionaires, who perceive local governments as unfavourable to their interests.

It is also important to note that generally the decentralization of governance over forest resources is still at least formally reversible at the discretion of national leaders. Any national government has many formal means to deny other actors the opportunity to harvest forest products profitably, from requiring an onerous process of filing harvesting plans to eliminating any profit by monopolizing the marketing network. Furthermore, the formal devolution of governance often has a caveat. For instance, the legislation establishing the Colombian *resguardos* requires *resguardo* communities to continue to practise traditional production methods; presumably if more modern methods are adopted that permit more intensive extraction, the Colombian government could annul the *resguardo* rights (Ascher, 1995).

In such cases, national government leaders can constrain delegated resource governance by imposing immediate constraints or posing the threat that delegation can be withdrawn. Thus central government can maintain some degree of control without exposing itself to direct accountability. This state of affairs is one reason why the decentralization of natural resource governance has not met the expectations of either the local recipients of control or the advocates of more sustainable forestry practices.

One natural resource subsector in which devolution to resource users has been notably successful is irrigation, particularly in the case of Mexico. In the early 1990s, following a decade of severe deterioration of the irrigation system and strong farmer resistance to raising water charges, the national government established local user groups that had both control over the irrigation districts and far more responsibility for financing maintenance of the system. Within four years cost recovery increased from 57 per cent to 80 per cent (Gorriz, Subramanian and Simas, 1995: 13). This reform changed the national government's political-economy logic from seeking political support by undercharging for water, at the expense of a badly deteriorating irrigation system, to delegating governance at the water district level and gaining political credit for improving the volume and reliability of the water supply. Comparable successes in establishing administration by local user groups have been documented for Colombia (Plusquellec, 1989) and Peru (Hunt, 1990).

Subsoil resources

Labour was the limiting factor of production in colonial Latin American mining. The initial strategy of those with access to exploit the resources was to enslave or indenture indigenous people. The infamous mines of Potosí in what is now Bolivia were producing silver for the Spanish Crown by the mid-sixteenth century, first through the adoption of the Inca institution of *mit'a* (corvée) of forced labour, and then through open slavery, including importation of African slaves because of the high mortality from mercury poisoning and general poor working conditions.

Subsoil rights were, from the very beginning, the property of the Crown. While some mining concessions gave *de facto* ownership to the companies that developed the infrastructure to exploit resources, access was available through concessions granted by the state, not as a matter of formal private ownership. Orihuela (1996: 32–33) notes:

> Generally, all Latin American countries from Mexico to Argentina follow the principle of state ownership of all continental and maritime underground land within their territorial boundaries. Hence, in Latin America, mining rights granted to private interests are not a grant of an ownership interest in the mineral in place. Rather, the rights are concessions or licenses that merely provide a right to attach the minerals and reduce them to ownership upon separating them from the reserves. Moreover, the concessions or licenses are considered separate property from the real estate where they are located.

Despite this formal principle, by the twentieth century *de facto* control over mining sites and the nascent oil industry was in the hands of the private sector, whether domestic or international. Early on, when mining was relatively labour intensive, local magnates controlled some of the most important mining operations. In Bolivia, for example, two of the three twentieth-century "mining barons", Patiño and Aramayo, were Bolivians by birth; the third, Hochschild, resided in Bolivia as long as he could in the face of physical threats. Yet other early-twentieth-century mining operations were controlled by foreign entrepreneurs, such as the Guggenheims in Mexico and Chile.

By the mid-twentieth century the challenges were the shortages of capital and expertise. Mining required increasingly expensive infrastructure; the emerging oil industry required very costly exploration as well as the infrastructure and technologies for production, refining and transport. This called for foreign capital, accompanied by foreign expertise and marketing networks. The international companies founded largely by the American mining magnates partnered with major financial companies such as J. P. Morgan and consolidated into worldwide mineral corporations such as ASARCO, Kennecott and Anaconda.

Because of the desperate need for capital, until the policy changes of the 1960s Latin American governments offered extraordinarily attractive terms to international companies. Knakal (1984: 4–5, cited in UN Conference on Trade and Development, 1997: 10) describes the pre-1960s situation:

> On the one hand, the mining codes held that the minerals in the soil and the subsoil are the property of the State, but on the other hand a system of very advantageous concessions was instituted for investors which gave them the

right to use, enjoy and freely dispose of the product of their activities in the areas given to them under concession for a practically indefinite length of time (50 years or more), with guarantees of tax and exchange stability. The investors paid a very small land rent which enabled them to maintain large areas indefinitely without being exploited, as part of their world reserves for possible exploitations, while the host state, in practice, lacked the capacity to question or annul a concession ... the taxation of profits was excessively low (between 6% and 25% of the taxable amount), while the effective rate of tax was even lower because of various types of deductions and exemptions.

The oil industry in Latin America was pioneered in the 1920s by American and British companies. With virtually no domestic experience in the petroleum business, Latin American countries needed foreign firms for production for both the domestic market and the growing export industry. Yet the presence of foreign firms in control of the oil industry aroused considerable resentment and presented the temptation to expropriate their assets, as indicated by three acts of nationalization by Argentine governments from 1922 to 1930, followed by nationalizations in Uruguay (1931), Chile (1932) and Bolivia (1937) (Berrios, Marak and Morgenstern, 2011). While these were not major oil or gas producers, the 1938 Mexican nationalization of the sector proved to be a major milestone, as Mexico still has enormous proven and prospective oil potential. It is also significant that Venezuela, comparably rich in oil as well as unconventional oil resources,[7] did not experience state takeovers of the oil industry until the mid-1970s.

By the second half of the twentieth century the widely fluctuating world prices for both hard minerals and hydrocarbon fuels had created high volatility in the profitability of exploration and extraction. The North American and Western European oil and mining companies held back on production and investment during the price downturns. Moreover, when production in other, more prospective, regions expanded, the investment of the international firms was redirected to other areas, such as the Middle East and Southeast Asia.

Governments of oil- and mineral-exporting countries were thus exposed to wide fluctuations in royalties and taxes, as well as increasingly militant labour unions demanding more stable employment and higher wages. The formation of powerful unions in the extractive industries has been in many respects easier to accomplish than unionization in other industries, because of the concentration of workers on extraction sites and the potential for severe economic consequences if they successfully strike. In contrast with the virtually enslaved miners of the colonial period, unionized mine workers in most Latin American countries have become a "labour elite". Among the oil-exporting countries, oil workers' unions have played a particularly large role in shaping policy in Colombia, Mexico and Venezuela (Lahn et al., 2007: 24). The miners' unions in Bolivia and Chile played major roles in the nationalization of their mining industries in 1952 and 1971 respectively. Because modern mining and petroleum exploitation are capital intensive, oil and mining companies are typically motivated to pay a reasonably sized workforce a handsome wage in comparison with the bulk of the workforce, especially those in the informal sector, to avoid strikes and retain experienced workers. Even so, organized labour in the large-scale subsoil extractive industries has typically taken radical pro-statist positions, in large part out of concern that private firms would shed excess labour. The Mexican state oil company has long been an egregious case of overemployment, and the Venezuelan state enterprise, once quite efficient, has been following in this path.

The motive to maintain high levels of production, employment and state revenues (through royalties and taxes), combined with the allure of windfall economic gains and the political gains of nationalistic populism, often resulted in expropriations. The earliest major nationalization supported by the doctrine that the state should directly and exclusively undertake resource extraction was Mexican oil in 1938, leading to the formation of PEMEX; and the Bolivian "Revolution of 1952" led to the nationalization of the mining industry. From an economic perspective, the idea was that the revenues from resource extraction would be able to finance expanded operations.

In many cases of nationalization, expropriation without full compensation was justified through accusations of prior "excessive profits" gained by companies. The incidence of very high profits has reflected three factors: the uncertainty of the richness of deposits, the limited use of concession contracts that would provide the government with graduated royalties for higher-than-anticipated yields, and (in some instances) corruption in making concession arrangements. Expropriation without full negotiated or arbitrated compensation has often made nationalization the source of international political-economic conflict. In addition, given the possibility of expropriation, the bids that international extractive industry firms are prepared to make for concessions are often lower than what government officials estimate as fair, because the private firms need to build in a cushion against the expropriation risk. The disillusionment towards international oil companies, combined with the political advantages of the nationalist appeal, has left most of Latin America's oil reserves in state hands (Bremmer, 2010).

Despite the frequent gulf between government and private sector assessments of the value of deposits, nationalizations have often been reversed by inviting the private sector back into resource exploitation. This pattern reflects the frequently linked phenomena of Latin American governments coming under control of less radical-nationalistic leaders, and economic downturns that starve state enterprises of capital and make financial gains from the sale of state assets more compelling. In some instances this was done under the political cover of formalizing arrangements as "service contracts" with state companies or the government, yet the economic consequence of a foreign firm receiving a negotiated proportion of the value of oil sales is hardly different from the royalty and tax arrangements that would pertain if the company held concessions.

What we see in the very brief history outlined above is that effective control of extractive industries in Latin America has undergone a clearly cyclical pattern. Chang, Hevia and Loayza (2010: 5) note:

> Partly as reaction to the Great Depression, nationalizations became quite frequent and extensive in the 1930s. After World War II, a second tide of privatization occurred, only to be reversed under the populist regimes of the 1960s and 70s. Two decades later, in the early 1990s, the pendulum fluctuated back to privatization, which ... occurred in [sic] a massive scale ... [and] nationalization-privatization cycles tend to occur more often in the natural resources and utilities sectors.

In Brazil and Chile, currently Latin America's most economically successful nations, the pattern is quite different, in highly illuminating ways. In Brazil the enormous Companhia Vale do Rio Doce (now renamed Vale), the world's second-largest mining company and largest iron producer, was privatized in 1997, but with *de facto* control by the national government. Other companies are permitted to operate in the mining sector, while Vale has expanded rapidly internationally. Periodic demands to renationalize Vale were deflected even by leftist leader President Luis Ignácio Lula da Silva. Yet this does not mean that the government eschewed heavy influence over the company. Through its own minority share[8] and those of the state development bank BNDES and state pension funds, the government controls a majority of shares, as well as having a "golden share" that gives it the power to demand or veto a change in control. Although technically the government is not to interfere in strategic decisions, in fact it has pressured Vale to reduce lay-offs and invest more in Brazil. By the same token, the Brazilian government has a stake in the shares of Petrobras; although the huge Brazilian oil company was partially privatized in 1997, the government holds a majority of voting stock and recently took a majority share of Petrobras common stock. Other oil companies operate in Brazil, often but not exclusively in partnership with Petrobras. Many observers believe that the government's backing of Petrobras gives the company an advantage over others.

Chile's situation is more straightforward. The fully state-owned Corporación Nacional del Cobre (Codelco) grew out of the nationalization of copper in 1971, taking over the world's largest open pit and underground copper mines as well as other rich ore deposits. However, in 1982 a major change in policy permitted full concessions, tantamount to property rights, for Chilean and foreign firms on an equal footing, guarantees of full compensation in the event of expropriation and long-term commitments on tax rates (Bande and French-Davis, 1989). Thus instead of privatizing Codelco, which has enormous nationalistic and political symbolism in Chile, the government partially privatized the mining sector. International mining companies moved in to develop mines of comparable magnitude.

In both cases, the partial delegation requires a delicate balance. The government's pressure cannot be so onerous as to threaten profitability, deter the markets from maintaining companies' stock value or frighten away needed partners. With the scrutiny that comes along with listings on stock exchanges, the capacity of government leaders to direct benefits surreptitiously to particular targets at the expense of a company's profitability is much diminished, as is their capacity to support national projects at the company's cost. The trade-off is greater access to capital versus the usefulness of the company as a non-transparent off-budget mechanism for maintaining discretion over allocating resource wealth.

Another stabilizing mechanism with direct bearing on the incentives to exploit resources on an appropriate optimal time path is the sovereign wealth fund, pioneered by Chile and very recently initiated in Brazil. A sovereign wealth fund is a state-operated investment fund designed to manage a portion of government revenues to increase their value and stabilize the level of revenues available for government spending. These are often referred to as stabilization funds, because of their potential to limit revenues available for spending during boom times and augment spending when revenues are low. The Chilean government established the Copper Stabilization Fund in 1985 (renamed the Economic and Social Stabilization Fund – ESSF – in 2007), to moderate the amount of copper revenues the national budget could draw on each year. The ESSF's independence is protected quite effectively by the fact that the financial committee responsible for its operations is appointed by the independent Central Bank. Over the years the fund, currently holding over US$20 billion, has not only dramatically smoothed out the Chilean national budget, but as a consequence has reduced the pressures on Codelco to extract and sell more copper when world prices are low. The Sovereign Wealth Fund Institute (2010b) gives the ESSF its highest ranking on transparency.

In 2009 the Brazilian government established the Sovereign Fund of Brazil, with a target of US$20 billion. One of its goals, like that of Chile's ESSF, is to stabilize Brazil's national budget by sequestering some portion of government export-derived revenues during commodity booms, and to release some portion of the funds when export-derived revenues are low. However, unlike the ESSF, another goal of the Sovereign Fund is to "assist Brazilian firms to increase trade and expand abroad" (Sovereign Wealth Fund Institute, 2010c). The governance of the fund gives the Brazilian president more influence than in the Chilean case, moderately reducing the Brazilian fund's capacity to safeguard revenues and thereby neutralize the temptations to extract resources too hastily to make up for possible unsound investments.

It is significant that beside Brazil, Chile and Trinidad and Tobago, no other substantial and successful stabilization funds exist in Latin America. Extensive evidence worldwide demonstrates that a stabilization fund can only be effective if the nation's executive permits it to be so (Davis et al., 2001; Moreen, 2007). A World Bank analysis indicates that of the five natural resource stabilization funds with the potential to insulate revenues during the commodity boom beginning in 2002, Chile and Trinidad and Tobago were quite successful; Ecuador and Venezuela essentially abandoned the discipline of their funds; and Mexico's fund was so modest that it "did not result in sufficient savings to finance a strong counter-cyclical package" (Synott, Nash and de la Torre, 2010: 45). Venezuela still has a relatively minor fund, with assets of less than US$1 billion; it was established in 1998 and is so dominated by President Hugo Chavez that the Sovereign Wealth Fund Institute (2010a) gives it the lowest possible rating for transparency. If one governance strategy is self-hands-tying[9] to insulate natural resource revenues from the government's own temptations to overspend, very few Latin American nations have succeeded in this respect.

Understanding the dilemmas

Resource governance predominantly shaped by national government leaders presents several dilemmas. First, the flexibility that national leaders reserve to alter the governance arrangements undermines the certainty facing resource exploiters, thereby eroding the incentives to exploit resources soundly. For example, the cyclical nature in the treatment of international companies in the oil and mining sectors has reduced the investment levels these companies are willing to devote to exploration and infrastructure development, or to extract at the rate optimal for the country, or both. Moreover, private (particularly foreign) oil and mining companies have to underbid for concessions to hedge against expropriation risk or reneging on royalty arrangements. Timber harvesting, whether undertaken by foreign or domestic firms or by people living in or near the forests, is similarly subject to the logic of hasty extraction while the opportunity to do so still exists. Local governments fiscally stressed by unfunded or underfunded regulatory mandates opt for overexploitation to bring in more revenues.

Second, the national governments that are most dependent on natural resource extraction tend to be the poorest performers in terms of adopting sound long-term extraction strategies. It is no accident that the most notorious cases of poor oil management are Venezuela and Mexico, where national leaders have eroded the investment funds of the state oil companies either directly or by driving them into heavy indebtedness through taxes far beyond what other companies are required to pay.[10] Very high dependence provokes more shortsighted efforts to capture greater revenues, whether through changes in user rights, greater rates of extraction or other manoeuvres.

Third, the potential virtues of decentralization are offset by serious problems in many circumstances. The potential virtues are greater accountability (insofar as constituents have more direct control over who becomes a local official), greater efficiency (insofar as officials and others participating in decision-making are more knowledgeable about the local context and preferences), greater compliance and democratic participation for its own sake. In some instances, decentralized government enhances equity insofar as local leaders recognize the interests of the relatively deprived segments of the community, and these people have a voice in decision-making. Yet subnational government officials are often less educated, and hence less expert. Local government institutions are less well funded. Local officials are beholden to the local elite rather than to the community as a whole. Even when subnational governments faithfully reflect the interests of their constituents, conflicts arise between these interests and those of other parts of the country. This is illustrated in federal systems, in which the resources the national government can control or regulate (basically the subsoil assets) will reflect the economic agenda of that government, but the governance of other natural resources (primarily the surface resources) reflects the agendas of the next level of government, whether states (Brazil, Mexico, Venezuela) or provinces (as in Argentina). This compromises the capacity of the national government to regulate negative externalities (such as water pollution from one state affecting downstream states) or limit excessive resource depletion for the good of the country as a whole.

Finally, formal protection of resources, such as creating forest preserves or banning extraction of particular types of resources, increases the opportunities for corruption. As mentioned earlier, restriction of resource use by government entities gives rise to the opportunity to avoid the restriction through bribes to officials. In many instances conservation measures attractive to international donors and non-governmental organizations have proven to be both corrupt and ineffective in reducing extraction, thereby undermining trust in government.

Conclusions and recommendations for improving natural resource governance

The history of Latin American resource governance demonstrates how complex and varying the challenges and responses have been. Anyone who may have expected resource governance to settle into a single, sound and stable form would be disappointed. However, it is possible to point to progress in some countries, especially with regard to the extraction of major subsoil resources.

Addressing challenges to the extraction of major subsoil resources

First, in light of the problems that emerge from mixed mandates, separation of roles has been achieved in many Latin American countries with the establishment of separate cabinet-level environmental ministries and extraction oversight agencies that have significant regulatory authority over other government entities. Nevertheless, an obvious recommendation is to encourage elevating the standing of environmental ministries in their battles with both private and state resource extractors. This is an effort to which the international community can contribute impressively, through technical assistance to arm these ministries with the capacity to make more compelling analyses of the societal and even economic costs of unsound resource extraction and polluting practices in general.

Second, although *partial* governmental ownership of major resource extraction enterprises may not seem like a "clean" solution to the state versus private ownership choice, and raises the risk of conflicting mandates, in some prominent cases such as Brazil it may be the best and most stable compromise for addressing the national government's insistence on the continuity of production. As Brazil's Vale demonstrates, market responsiveness and business discipline can live fairly comfortably with some government influence. Moreover, this mixed form has the promise of breaking the cycle of privatization and renationalization that has created uncertainty and opportunities for corruption, and discouraged investment.

Sound non-renewable resource governance entails the national government overseeing a mixed state and private resource sector, combined with a politically insulated stabilization fund. The rationale for the state to play a role, as opposed to the government simply collecting royalties, does not rest on the likelihood of corruption. Joseph Stiglitz (2007) and others point to the possibility of corruption in the privatization of subsoil resource exploitation, but there is no basis for assuming that state enterprise resource exploitation in Latin America has been less corrupt, and the transparency to detect corruption has been even more lacking. Rather, the rationale for a role for state enterprises in oil and mining rests on the different rates of extraction that are best for the nation and preferred by the private resource companies. Stiglitz makes the rather obvious point that the objective of private extractive enterprises to obtain as much of the revenues as possible often clashes with the interests of the nations in which they operate. It may be advisable for the resource wealth to be extracted imminently because of attractive domestic investment opportunities, when the nation's resources at that point in time are insufficiently attractive to interest private extraction or international lending on the strength of future resource wealth. Thus having government involvement in the extractive industry can move the extraction rate closer to the optimal level for the nation. Brazil's Vale, with national government control but the transparency required of a publically traded company, serves this objective. Yet the expertise, capital and infrastructure of international firms should not be dismissed, as long as the national government is institutionally strong enough to conduct transparent concession auctions and maintain the contracted royalty payment arrangements. Chile's mixed mining sector serves the objective of bringing in international companies while maintaining the capacity to inject government capital into the sector when higher extraction is deemed desirable.

For Latin American nations still highly dependent on particular natural resource exports, the stabilization funds in Brazil, Chile and Trinidad and Tobago offer compelling models for reducing the need to diverge from the optimal time path of resource extraction or to undermine the stability of expectations about user rights. More stable revenue streams reduce the pressure on leaders of resource-dependent countries to resort to unsound resource governance. Yet the national government leaders must have the restraint to permit the fund to operate without interference, especially when political pressures for higher spending tempt leaders to raid the fund or engage in excessive borrowing on the strength of it (Moreen, 2007: 73). One approach is for the officials establishing the fund – who presumably are committed to protecting it, at least at that time – to formulate a complicated series of steps that future officials would have to go through to violate the fund's guidelines. Another approach is for these officials to enter into an agreement with an external entity, such as the World Bank or Inter-American Development Bank, to maintain the fund as part of a broader package of policy reforms, thereby tying the hands of government officials. Donor governments' foreign assistance agencies can also play this role by working with Latin American governments to agree on environmental and conservation conditionalities on their grants and loans.

If the need for overriding even a strong fund becomes temporarily a priority – if circumstances become so dire that the fund's constraints would damage the nation – then all parties may reconsider and temporarily loosen the constraints. For example, the Chilean Copper Stabilization Fund contributed beyond its standard transfer to the Chilean budget following the massive 2010 earthquake. Thus even delegation to a strong sovereign wealth fund may be provisional, and yet the Chilean ESSF retains its effectiveness now that conditions have normalized.

Addressing challenges to the extraction of surface resources

A less optimistic judgement must be levied on smaller-scale surface resource governance – forests, fisheries, etc. We have seen that delegation without the support of the national government is fraught with difficulties in many Latin American countries. Subnational governments often exhibit insufficient capacity or motivation to manage forests or water resources, or to protect private land holdings. Communal resource governance often falters when the national government is unprepared to help the communities defend their user rights. To a limited degree, international action can help to protect local user rights and communities' technical capacities to use resources more sustainably, through political pressure (e.g. Elinor Ostrom's (1990) dictum of nesting local community authority within higher and higher levels of alliances that can come to the defence of beleaguered local communities) or by offering expertise and financial resources. Yet international actors clearly must tread carefully to avoid a backlash against perceived foreign interference. Thus national government involvement, whether to guard local prerogatives, regulate negative externalities or strengthen local communities' technical capacities, can rarely be avoided. However, national governments face their own chronic weaknesses, as seen in rapacious state marketing boards, inefficient state timber companies, corruption in forest and land concessions, inadequate irrigation, mispricing and resistance on the part of resource users.

It is very helpful to adopt Dennis Rondinelli's (1981) insight that regulation is a service provided to the public – in principle no different from supplying electricity or policing – and that services can be provided better or worse by different levels of government, or by non-governmental entities, depending on the specific context. In Latin America, *some* aspects of resource governance ought to be devolved to local governments or user communities, but *only if on balance the services of regulating or managing resource extraction would be delivered more efficiently, fairly and sustainably.* While local people may know their ecosystems and their own needs and wants better than remote officials do, higher-level governance may be necessary to ensure technical expertise, greater equity of access and greater discipline regarding harm to other areas. China is certainly not the only nation to see decentralization of environmental protection and conservation to local authorities bent on rapid if short-sighted economic growth strategies. And to devolve governance and then revoke it can wreak havoc on the securing of user rights; this insecurity is often a leading cause of hasty, inefficient extraction.

These contrasting weaknesses call for complementary governance roles across different government levels and governmental and non-governmental sectors. The security of user rights and the local knowledge and accountability of subnational governments must be tempered with the might and ultimate authority of the national government. For local resource users to have sufficient incentive to exploit resources responsibly, they must have sufficient and stable roles in the governance of these resources. Yet, at a minimum, national and subnational governments must play a facilitating role in providing both user rights protection and regulation to reduce negative externalities. Governments and stakeholders must work out stable arrangements of mixed governance, often labelled collaborative governance (Wondolleck and Yaffee, 2000; Conley and Moote, 2003) or "hybrid governance" (Brannstrom, 2009). The irrigation user group arrangements reviewed briefly above provide a good example of mixed governance: national governments of Colombia, Mexico and Peru administer the overall irrigation system; subnational governments are responsible for enforcing environmental compliance; and farmers manage the water districts to agree on the distribution of water and cover the operation and maintenance costs.

However, the balance between central and local authority does not have to be static. As the capabilities of local governments and user communities strengthen, more authority can be shifted to these entities. Foreign assistance agencies can make a very significant contribution by enhancing the technical expertise and professionalization of local actors involved in resource use and regulation.

Overall, we have seen how natural resource governance arrangements can entail effective and relatively stable delegation, as long as the arrangements allow the national government a degree of flexibility without having to negate these arrangements altogether and exacerbate uncertainty. The question is not whether resource governance in general should be decentralized, but rather which aspects of governance ought to be retained by national leaders and which ought to be distributed to subnational, state or private actors to permit the most responsible resource management and regulation.

Notes

1. The International Tropical Timber Organization (2006: 35) reported: "Over the past 10–15 years there has been an important shift towards the ownership of forest by local communities in several countries. Indigenous people now own large tracts of forest in Bolivia, Colombia, Panama and Peru, while more than 100 million hectares of forest in the Brazilian Amazon are indigenous lands . . . Today, about 22.1 million hectares of forest, mostly in the Amazon, are owned by indigenous communities and 5 million hectares, mainly in the Pacific region, by Afro-Colombian communities."
2. See Inter-American Development Bank (2009) for these data and further diagnostic points in this and the following paragraph. Further assessment is found in Organization of American States (2010) and Pan American Health Organization (2008).
3. BP, Chevron, ConocoPhillips, ExxonMobil and Shell.
4. For example, the absolute magnitude, location and extraction difficulty of the oil and gas assets, and the other objectives that the national companies are mandated to attain.
5. Per capita income levels correlate fairly highly with environmental regulatory effectiveness across all 71 nations in the study.
6. Global Environment News (2006) reported "WWF-Brazil says that will only happen when clear, public forest policies are implemented and financial resources are made available to tackle deforestation, stimulate sustainable forestry activities, and encourage state governments in the Amazon region to better cooperate when tackling environmental issues."
7. Oil shale and "tar sands" can yield petroleum, but only at significantly higher costs than conventional liquid petroleum.
8. Although the precise proportion of the government's share varies, it has typically been just over 10 per cent.
9. The logic of self-hands-tying is explored in Ascher (2009).
10. These cases are documented in Boué (1993), Ascher (1999) and Sour, Ortega and San Sebastián (2003).

REFERENCES

Andersson, Krister P. and Elinor Ostrom (2008) "Analyzing Decentralized Resource Regimes from a Polycentric Perspective", *Policy Sciences* 41, pp. 71–93.

Andersson, Krister, Clark C. Gibson and Fabrice Lehoucq (2006) "Comparative Analysis of Decentralization in Bolivia and Guatemala", *World Development* 34(3), pp. 576–595.

Ascher, William (1995) "Community Natural Resource Management Policies in Colombia and Mexico", in John Montgomery and Dennis Rondinelli (eds) *Great Policies: Strategic Innovations in Asia and the Pacific Basin*, Westport, CT: Praeger, pp. 199–221.

—— (1999) *Why Governments Waste Natural Resources*, Baltimore, MD: Johns Hopkins University Press.

—— (2009) *Bringing in the Future: Farsightedness and Sustainability in Developing Countries*, Chicago, IL: University of Chicago Press.

Bande, Jorge and Ricardo French-Davis (1989) "Copper Policies and the Chilean Economy: 1973–88", Notas Técnicas No. 132, CIEPLAN, Santiago.

Bandiera, Oriana (2007) "Land Tenure, Investment Incentives, and the Choice of Techniques: Evidence from Nicaragua", *World Bank Research Observer* 21(3), pp. 487–508.

Berrios, Ruben, Andrae Marak and Scott Morgenstern (2011) "Explaining Hydrocarbon Nationalization in Latin America: Economics and Political Ideology", *Review of International Political Economy* 18, pp. 1–25.

Boué, Juan Carlos (1993) *Venezuela: The Political Economy of Oil*, Oxford: Oxford University Press.

Brannstrom, Christian (2009) "Environmental Governance in Latin America's Modern Agricultural Systems", paper presented at Congress of the Latin American Studies Association, Rio de Janeiro, 11–14 June.

Bremmer, Ian (2010) "The Long Shadow of the Visible Hand: Government-owned Firms Control Most of the World's Oil Reserves", *Wall Street Journal*, 22 May, available at http://online.wsj.com/article/SB10001424052748704852004575258541875590852.html.

Chang, Roberto, Constantino Hevia and Normal Loayza (2010) "Privatization and Nationalization Cycles", NBER Working Paper, June, NBER, Cambridge, MA.

Conley, Alexander and Margaret A. Moote (2003) "Evaluating Collaborative Natural Resource Management", *Society and Natural Resources* 16, pp. 371–386.

Davis, Jeffrey, Rolando Ossowski, James Daniel and Steven Barnett (2001) "Stabilization and Savings Funds for Nonrenewable Resources: Experience and Fiscal Policy Implications", Occasional Paper No. 205, International Monetary Fund, Washington, DC.

Eller, Stacy, Peter Hartley and Kenneth Medlock III (2007) "Empirical Evidence on the Operational Efficiency of National Oil Companies", James A. Baker Institute, Rice University, available at www.rice.edu/energy/publications/docs/NOCs/Papers/NOC_Empirical.pdf.

Esty, Daniel and Michael Porter (2001) "Ranking National Environmental Regulation and Performance: A Leading Indicator of Future Competitiveness?", in Michael Porter, Jeffrey Sachs and Andrew Warner (eds) *The Global Competitiveness Report 2001*, New York: Oxford University Press, pp. 78–100.

Gibson, Clark and Fabrice Lehoucq (2003) "The Local Politics of Decentralized Environmental Policy", *Journal of Environment and Development* 12(1), pp. 29–49.

Global Environment News (2006) "Rate of Deforestation in the Amazon", available at http://vanishingearth.com/environment-news-1/Rate-of-deforestation-in-the-amazon.html.

Godoy, Ricardo, Kris Kirby and David Wilkie (2001) "Tenure Security, Private Time Preference, and Use of Natural Resources among Lowland Bolivian Amerindians", *Ecological Economics* 38, pp. 105–118.

Gorriz, Cecilia, Ashok Subramanian and José Simas (1995) "Irrigation Management Transfer in Mexico", Technical Paper No. 292, World Bank, Washington, DC.

GTZ (2008) "International Fuel Prices, 6th Edition – Data Preview", available at www.gtz.de/de/dokumente/en-int-fuel-prices-6th-edition-gtz2009-corrected.pdf.

Hunt, Robert (1990) "Organizational Control over Water: The Positive Identification of a Social Constraint on Farmer Participation", in R. K. Sampath and Robert Young (eds) *Social, Economic, and Institutional Issues in Third World Irrigation Management*, Boulder, CO: Westview Press, pp. 141–154.

Inter-American Development Bank (2009) "Fact Sheet – Water: A Threatened Resource in Latin America and the Caribbean", available at www.iadb.org/announcements/2009-11/english/fact-sheet-water-a-threatened-resource-in-latin-america-and-the-caribbean-5956.html.

International Energy Agency (2010) "Energy & Development: Access to Electricity", *World Energy Outlook*, available at www.iea.org/weo/electricity.asp.

International Tropical Timber Organization (2006) *Status of Tropical Forest Management 2005*, Yokohama: ITTO.

IUCN World Conservation Union (1999) "Threats to Forest Protected Areas: Summary of a Survey of 10 Countries", November, IUCN, Gland.

Jaramillo, Carlos and Thomas Kelly (1997) "Deforestation and Property Rights in Latin America", December, Instituto del Bien Común, available at www.ibcperu.org/doc/isis/6247.pdf.

Knakal, J. (1984) "The Role of the Public Sector and Transnational Corporations in the Development of Mining in Latin America", paper presented at Workshop on Technical and Economic Co-operation for the Latin American Mining and Metallurgical Sector, Santiago, 19–23 November.

Lahn, Glada, Valérie Marcel, John Mitchell, Keith Myers and Paul Stevens (2007) "Report on Good Governance of the National Petroleum Sector", April, Royal Institute of International Affairs, London.

Larson, Anne M. (2003) "Decentralisation and Forest Management in Latin America: Towards a Working Model", *Public Administration and Development* 23, pp. 211–226.

Larson, Anne M. and Fernanda Soto (2008) "Decentralization of Natural Resource Governance Regimes", *Annual Review of Environment and Resources* 33, pp. 213–239.

Mainhardt-Gibbs, Heike (2003) "The World Bank Extractive Industries Review: The Role of Structural Reform Programs towards Sustainable Development Outcomes", August, World Bank, Washington, DC.

Miller, Michael J. (2011) "Persistent Illegal Logging in Costa Rica: The Role of Corruption among Forestry Regulators", *Journal of Environment and Development* 20(10), pp. 1–19.

Moreen, Amber (2007) "Overcoming the 'Resource Curse': Prioritizing Policy Interventions in Countries with Large Extractive Industries", doctoral dissertation, RAND Corporation, Santa Monica.

Organization of American States (2010) *Integrated Water Resources Management*, Washington, DC: OAS.

Orihuela, Sandra (1996) "Latin America: A New Era for Mining Investment", *International Lawyer* 30(1), pp. 31–56.

Ostrom, Elinor (1990) *Governing the Commons: The Evolution of Institutions for Collective Action*, Cambridge: Cambridge University Press.

Pan American Health Organization (2008) "Situación de salud en las américas: Indicadores básicos", Washington, DC, available at http://new.paho.org/hq/dmdocuments/2008/BI_2008_SPA.pdf.

Pichon, Fransisco J. (1997) "Colonist Land-Allocation Decisions, Land Use, and Deforestation in the Ecuadorian Amazon Frontier", *Economic Development and Cultural Change* 44, pp. 127–164.

Plusquellec, Herve (1989) "Tow Irrigation Systems in Colombia: Their Performance and Transfer of Management to Users' Associations", PPR Working Paper Series No. 264, World Bank, Washington, DC.

Ribot, Jesse, Arun Agrawal and Anne Larson (2006) "Recentralizing While Decentralizing: How National Governments Reappropriate Forest Resources", *World Development* 34(11), pp. 1864–1886.

Rondinelli, Dennis (1981) "Government Decentralization in Comparative Perspective: Theory and Practice in Developing Countries", *International Review of Administrative Sciences* 47(2), pp. 133–145.

Schneider, Robert R. (1995) *Government and the Economy on the Amazon Frontier*, Washington, DC: World Bank.

Sour, Laura, Irma Ortega and Sergio San Sebastián (2003) "Política Presupuestaria durante la Transición a la Democracia en México: 1997–2003", November, CIDE Documento de Trabajo, Mexico City.

Sovereign Wealth Fund Institute (2010a) "FEM", June, available at www.swfinstitute.org/swfs/fem/.

——— (2010b) "Pension Reserve and Social and Economic Stabilization Fund", June, available at www.swfinstitute.org/fund/chile.php.

——— (2010c) "Sovereign Wealth Fund of Brazil", June, available at www.swfinstitute.org/swfs/sovereign-fund-of-brazil/.

Stiglitz, Joseph (2007) "What Is the Role of the State?", in Macartan Humphreys, Jeffrey Sachs and Joseph Stiglitz (eds) *Escaping the Resource Curse*, New York: Columbia University Press, pp. 23–52.

Synott, Emily, John Nash and Augusto de la Torre (2010) *Natural Resources in Latin America and the Caribbean: Beyond Booms and Busts?*, Washington, DC: World Bank.

UN Conference on Trade and Development (1997) "Management of Commodity Resources in the Context of Sustainable Development: Governance Issues for the Mineral Sector", February, UNCTAD, Geneva.

UN Food and Agriculture Organization (2010) "Global Forest Resources Assessment 2010", available at www.fao.org/docrep/013/i1757e/i1757e.pdf.

Wondolleck, Julia M. and Steven L. Yaffee (2000) *Making Collaboration Work: Lessons from Innovation in Natural Resource Management*, Washington, DC: Island Press.

World Bank (2006) "Combating Illegal Logging and Corruption in the Forestry Sector: Strengthening Forest Law Enforcement and Governance", in *2006 Environmental Matters at the World Bank*, Washington, DC: World Bank, pp. 12–15.

3

Domestic politics and environmental standards: China's policy-making process for regulating vehicle emissions

Eri Saikawa

Introduction

China's unprecedented economic growth – with an average real GDP growth rate of 9.7 per cent per year between 1979 and 2010 – has no doubt contributed to making it the second-largest consumer of oil behind the United States. Despite being an oil-exporting country until 1992, half of China's oil supplies currently come from the Middle East and one-third from Africa. Recently, due to expected demand increase in the near future, China has been aggressively exploring new markets, especially in Africa, for all possible natural resources on top of oil (Taylor, 2006; Hanson, 2008).

Observing the policy-making processes in China, it becomes clear that oil is intertwined with vehicle emissions. Oil quality is indispensable for lowering vehicle emissions, but there is a lack of supply and it is costly to refine oil. The dilemma, therefore, is that although oil needs to be refined to lower emissions and enhance advanced vehicle technology transfers from developed countries, there are large costs associated in doing so. Within what appears to be a unanimous decision for oil quest and economic growth, there are many struggles behind the scenes in China's domestic politics. This is especially the case for policy-making processes related to both natural resources and the environment. In this chapter, I illustrate the nexus between the two using vehicle emission regulations as an example.

Governance of natural resources: Uncovering the social purpose of materials in nature, Sato (ed.), United Nations University Press, 2013, ISBN 978-92-808-1228-2

The last three decades have witnessed incessant growth in the number of automobiles in China. The total number of vehicles (cars, buses and trucks) rose from 1.7 million in 1980 to 62.8 million in 2009, and the number of gasoline vehicles expected in 2020 is 22 times more than in 2000 (Saikawa et al., 2011). China's air quality has inevitably suffered due to such a sudden rise in vehicle numbers. One study suggests that 46, 78 and 83 per cent of total nitrogen oxides (NO_x), carbon monoxide (CO) and hydrocarbon (HC) emissions – which contribute to tropospheric ozone formation that is harmful to human health and crops – in Beijing in 1999 originated from vehicles (Hao, Hu and Fu, 2006). In an effort to remedy the situation, the Chinese central government has adopted European standards to regulate vehicle emissions at a rapid pace.

There are three vehicle emission standards in the world (European, American and Japanese), and each accompanies separate fuel quality standards. Fuel quality in this context represents the quality of gasoline or diesel in terms of sulphur content. High sulphur content indicates low fuel quality and vice versa. The European emission standards are named Euro 1 (least stringent) to Euro 6 (most stringent), and the fuel quality standards are similarly named Euro I (lowest quality) to Euro VI (highest).

Fuel quality is essential in regulating vehicle emissions, because high sulphur content damages emission abatement technologies (e.g. catalytic converters) installed in vehicles. As a result, even vehicles with sufficient emission mitigation technologies fail to meet required emission levels. Researchers have conducted studies to examine the impact of fuel quality on vehicle emissions, and found that low-quality fuel leads to more emissions even if vehicles are equipped with technology to meet the required reduction levels (Asian Development Bank, 2003; Liu et al., 2008). Vehicle emission reduction technologies and high fuel quality are both indispensable for successful regulation of vehicle emissions. The Worldwide Fuel Charter, signed by major automobile and engine manufacturers, provides guidelines for fuel quality standards to minimize vehicle emissions and obtain desirable performance (Auto Alliance, 2006). It emphasizes the need to reduce fuel sulphur content (enhance quality), and argues the importance of fuel quality standards being matched to emission standards.

What is puzzling, then, is the fact that although China adopted stringent vehicle emission standards to improve its air quality without any international requirement to do so, its fuel quality standards do not meet the level required for these emission standards. Why did it adopt more stringent vehicle emission standards than fuel quality standards? Why is there this mismatch between the two standards when the government is aware of the consequences?

This chapter analyses China's policy-making process for vehicle emission regulations. I illustrate how the involvement of different actors in policy-making leads to adoption or non-adoption of stringent natural resource and/or environmental policies. The institutional structures differ widely between those for vehicle emission standards and those for fuel quality. Based on interviews with government officials, policy-makers, managers of vehicle manufacturers and scholars knowledgeable in the management of vehicle emissions, I posit that a liberal policy-making process enhances diffusion of standards.

By focusing on policy-making processes in the adoption of the two European environmental standards essential for regulating vehicle emissions (i.e. emission standards and fuel quality standards), the study contributes to the existing literature. It adds to the work on Chinese policy-making and the fragmented authoritarianism model by Lieberthal and Oksenberg (1988), in which they explain the bureaucratic structure within Chinese politics and how that affects policy-making processes as well as policy implementation. There has been research on policy-making within the economy and energy sector (ibid.; Shirk, 1993; Andrews-Speed, 2004; Kong, 2009). How different institutional structures affect policy output, however, has not been sufficiently considered. This study builds on Lieberthal and Oksenberg's (1988) framework as well as recent additions to the model (Mertha, 2006, 2009), focusing on how institutional structures differ depending on issue areas, and the effect of such differences on policy outputs.

The chapter starts with a brief overview of the adoption of European standards for vehicle emission regulations in China and the existing mismatch of the two standards, followed by a discussion of how existing theories might try to explain the mismatch. I illustrate the institutional framework, describing how a liberal policy-making process leads to the adoption of more stringent policies; then I test the framework using the case of vehicle emission regulations in China, and tracing the policy-making process of vehicle emission standards and fuel quality standards, respectively. The final section provides a conclusion.

Adoption of the European environmental standards

Using econometric analysis of vehicle emission standards' adoption over the past 20 years, I find the global diffusion of these standards results from countries' efforts to stay competitive in the international market (Saikawa, 2013). Under the General Agreement on Tariffs and Trade, which later became the World Trade Organization (WTO), vehicle emission standards fall under the Technical Barriers to Trade Agreement, as they are product standards that act as non-tariff barriers. Due to the pressure from importing countries and economic competitors that have adopted stringent emission standards, even developing countries have moved rapidly to adopt rich-country standards.

Field research offers an insight that China also adopted European vehicle emission standards due to some competitive pressure. Adoption of the European standards was not unique to China. Countries had a choice to develop their own or adopt one of the three existing standards (American, Japanese and European) that are of similar stringency levels. In fact, 57 out of 67 countries with regulations have adopted the European emission standards. For fuel economy (standards for regulating fuel efficiency – how many kilometres a vehicle runs per litre of fuel) there were more variations, as countries often developed their own standards. It has thus been difficult to build any sort of international norm to harmonize fuel economy standards, unlike the emissions or fuel quality standards. China adopted fuel economy standards that are similar to the Japanese ones, and this fact shows that the central government takes sufficient control of which standards to be adopted for different regulations rather than blindly deciding on the European ones.

Since China adopted the emission standards created by the Subcommittee on Road Transport of the UN Economic Commission for Europe in the late 1980s, it has been implementing European vehicle emission standards at a rapid pace.[1] China adopted the first Euro 1 emission standards nationally in 2000 for both gasoline and diesel civilian vehicles, and adopted Euro 2 and Euro 3 in 2004 and 2007, respectively, for light-duty vehicles.[2] Vehicle emission standards as adopted in Europe and China are summarized in Table 3.1. Considering that it took over 12 years for Europe to adopt the Euro 4 standards after its adoption of Euro 1, China's fast action while still being a developing country is quite remarkable. Implementation has also been more successfully enforced for the Euro standards than for the pre-Euro standards before 2000.

On the other hand, China's national fuel quality standards are not following the same path. The time lines of the adoption of fuel quality standards in Europe and China are summarized in Table 3.2. China adopted the European standards to match its vehicle emission standards, but there has always been a reluctance to apply stringency in fuel quality. For example, after banning leaded gasoline in 2000, the first gasoline quality standards China adopted were not necessarily the same as the Euro I gasoline standards. As time passed, China adopted the Euro II gasoline standards at the end of 2006 and Euro III standards at the end of 2009. In sum, Euro II and Euro III quality gasoline was only available almost two-and-a-half years after the equivalent emission standards for light-duty gasoline vehicles were adopted. It is also uncertain when the

Table 3.1 Vehicle emission standards' adoption in the European Union and China

	European Union	China	CO	HC	HC + NO$_x$	NO$_x$	PM
Light-duty gasoline (g/km)							
Euro 1	1 July 1992	1 January 2000	3.16		1.13		
Euro 2	1 January 1996	1 July 2004	2.20		0.50		
Euro 3	1 January 2000	1 July 2007	2.30	0.20		0.15	
Euro 4	1 January 2005	1 July 2011	1.00	0.10		0.08	
Euro 5	1 September 2009		1.00	0.10		0.06	0.005
Euro 6	1 January 2014		1.00	0.10		0.06	0.005
Light-duty diesel (g/km)							
Euro 1	1 July 1992	1 January 2000	3.16		1.13		0.180
Euro 2	1 January 1996	1 July 2004	1.00		0.90		0.100
Euro 3	1 January 2000	1 July 2007	0.64		0.56	0.50	0.050
Euro 4	1 January 2005	1 July 2011	0.50		0.30	0.25	0.025
Euro 5	1 September 2009		0.50		0.23	0.18	0.005
Euro 6	1 January 2014		0.50		0.17	0.08	0.005
Heavy-duty diesel (g/kWh)							
Euro 1	1 October 1992	1 January 2000	4.50	1.10		8.00	0.612
Euro 2	1 October 1996	1 September 2003	4.00	1.10		7.00	0.250
Euro 3	1 October 2000	1 January 2008	2.10	0.66		5.00	0.100
Euro 4	1 October 2005	1 July 2011	1.50	0.46		3.50	0.020
Euro 5	1 October 2008		1.50	0.46		2.00	0.020
Euro 6	1 January 2013		1.50	0.13		0.40	0.010

Sources: Walsh (2007); Saikawa et al. (2011).

Euro IV gasoline quality standards will be adopted in order to meet the equivalent emission standards.

For diesel fuel quality, Euro I – adopted in 2002 – was the only compulsory standard until recently. Euro II was recommended, and adopted in 2003, but these were not compulsory regulations, unlike the emission standards. China adopted the Euro III diesel standards in June 2009, but there is no plan for Euro IV diesel quality despite the emission stand-

Table 3.2 Fuel quality standards' adoption in the European Union and China

	European Union	China	Sulphur content (ppm)
Gasoline			
Euro I	1 January 1994	1 January 2000	2,000 (1,500 in China)
Euro II	1 October 1996	6 December 2006	500
Euro III	1 January 2000	31 December 2009	150
Euro IV	1 January 2005		50
Euro V	1 January 2009		10
Diesel			
Euro I	1 October 1994	1 January 2002	2,000
Euro II	1 October 2003	1 October 2003 (voluntary)	500
Euro III	1 January 2000	1 June 2009	350
Euro IV	1 January 2005		50
Euro V	1 January 2009		10

Source: Walsh (2007).

ards' adoption for heavy-duty diesel vehicles in 2011. There is a mismatch of vehicle emission and fuel quality standards at the national level, and this discrepancy is causing problems.

One study suggests that using Euro II level gasoline for vehicles that meet the Euro 3 emission standards produces 28.5, 15.0 and 22.5 per cent more emissions of NO_x, CO and HC, respectively, when compared to using Euro III level gasoline for the same vehicles (Liu et al., 2008). The authors find similar results for other combinations when fuel quality is lower than the vehicle emission standards. On the other hand, when fuel quality is higher than emission standards, the emissions of all pollutants were lower for all vehicles, and significantly so for diesel vehicles. This led to their conclusion that "the best emission control effect can be achieved by completely matching the fuel sulfur requirements with the emission standards" (ibid.: 3147). As this was research assigned by the State Environmental Protection Administration (SEPA – the Ministry of Environmental Protection since 2008), it is clear that the government realizes the problem of low-quality fuel. However, so far it has been difficult for it to tighten national fuel quality standards.

Existing theoretical approaches to standards' adoption in China

This section looks at relevant existing theories to analyse the mismatch of the two standards for regulating vehicle emissions in China. There is a cost-benefit as well as a technical argument. Then I review the fragmented authoritarianism model.

One could argue that the reason for the mismatch is cost. In this explanation, China has more stringent emission standards because it is cheaper to implement these compared to fuel quality standards. Adoption of stringent emission standards usually leads to the need for more advanced control technologies in vehicles. Installing a catalytic converter could increase the cost of a vehicle by several hundred dollars, but this cost is usually passed on to consumers. When introducing the Euro 2 emission standards, the Chinese government created a tax incentive in 2000 for early adopters before national implementation (Gallagher, 2006). By 2003, partly due to this incentive, all new vehicles met the Euro 2 emission standards.[3]

Oil refineries need to be upgraded to produce higher-quality fuel, and the move from Euro II to Euro III level could require the investment of approximately 50 billion RMB (US$7 billion).[4] Other estimates range between 20–30 billion RMB (US$2.6–3.9 billion) (China Oil News Web, 2007) up to as much as US$10 billion (*New York Times*, 2004). Because of fuel price control by the National Development and Reform Commission (NDRC), such costs cannot be passed on to consumers (Kong, 2006). Although the domestic oil price has approached the international market price after a major restructuring of the government in 1998 (Andrews-Speed, 2004) and modifications in the pricing mechanism in 2009 (*Xinghua News*, 2009), the NDRC price control often creates no incentives for oil companies to upgrade refineries. Indeed, as crude prices have risen, refining has suffered low profit margins and sometimes lost money in China (Houser, 2008). Theoretically, the price could increase nationally when fuel quality is upgraded, as it did in Beijing when the city implemented both the Euro 4 emission and Euro IV fuel quality standards in 2008.[5] However, it is not clear if such an increase is feasible at the national level, considering the constant struggle in setting prices for gasoline and diesel in the past.

The mismatch in the stringency of the two standards can therefore be considered as due to the difficulty of upgrading refineries. It is true that there has always been a problem in upgrading fuel quality all over the world. Another possible argument for the mismatch is that some Chinese leaders were opposed to adopting high fuel quality standards. There could be various reasons for this – the most prominent may be that they are worried about energy security (Downs, 2004). This consideration could in theory drive leaders to be against upgrading oil refineries, to emphasize quantity rather than quality. However, nothing indicates that anyone was opposed to the upgrade of refineries. On the contrary, the

Ministry of Environmental Protection (MEP) has been trying to revise the Law of the People's Republic of China on the Prevention and Control of Atmospheric Pollution – the Chinese Clean Air Act – to get control of and tighten fuel quality regulation.[6] Furthermore, other countries realized the need for integrated management, and it has been the international norm to match fuel quality standards with emission standards. Following this logic, China should have delayed the implementation of stringent vehicle emission standards until it was ready to provide the equivalent quality fuel.

Students of Chinese politics have studied bureaucracy within the policy-making process in detail, and a fragmented authoritarianism model has been used for some decades to analyse the process. This framework explains China's policy-making as "disjointed, protracted, and incremental" (Lieberthal and Oksenberg, 1988: 22). It argues that fragmentation within the bureaucracy and conflicts between departments often inhibit efficient policy-making. Mertha (2009) proposed an advancement of this framework by adding plurality: he argues that there has been a lowering of entry to policy-making in China and the degrees of redundancy and consolidation in bureaucracies explain the effectiveness of each policy. Lampton (2001) also argues that there is a trend of "corporate pluralization" in Chinese foreign policy-making. More actors are getting involved in the process, and at the same time there are many more diverse interests for policy-makers to take into account.

These additions to the fragmented authoritarianism model are an important step, as they explain that some policy-making processes succeed in including the voices of more actors, as well as when this inclusion takes place. However, this model is still unclear as to how the number and power of actors involved in policy-making affect the ability to enhance environmental policy effectively. For example, in the case of vehicle emission regulations, adopting vehicle emission and fuel quality standards on different time lines was not effective. We need a better understanding of when and how domestic politics interferes with the natural resource and/or environmental policy-making process.

The institutional framework

I offer an alternative model for understanding China's policy-making process: an institutional framework, which posits that differences in bureaucratic institutions due to the level of liberal policy-making process within the issue area determine how certain policies are strengthened while others are not. The policy-making process within fragmented authoritarianism can vary from liberal to restricted.

The liberal process is defined by two factors: low barrier to entry into policy-making, and less centralization of power in policy-making.[7] The former influences the political diversity involved in policy-making as well as the amount of information that forms the basis for policy. The latter affects the level of bargaining within the process. Most of the time the two correlate with each other, but they are the essential factors to determine how liberal the policy-making process is in an issue area. The institutional framework seeks to answer how different institutional structures affect the ability to strengthen a policy effectively, and it is applicable to environmental regulations in different sectors.

Rather than considering all Chinese policy-making processes to follow one fragmented authoritarianism model, the new framework takes into account the variations in the process. When an issue area has a liberal policy-making process, (i.e. a lower barrier to entry and less centralization of power), there is greater competition among the actors as a larger number are involved and nobody has a strong power to dominate the process. Power here is defined as the ability not only to veto policies but also to shape policy outcomes.[8] More institutions are created to increase the flow of information, which enhances policy coordination (Halpern, 1992). With no politically prevalent actor opposed to stringent standards, lobbying by many equally influential actors with different interests leads to more information sharing. Contrary to the conventional wisdom, I argue that in some cases it is possible that more inputs into policy-making can lead to policy change rather than policy stability.[9]

On the other hand, when an issue area has a less liberal policy-making process (i.e. a higher barrier to entry and a greater centralization of power), there is minimal competition between bureaucracies. Political uniformity leads to less information sharing, and this causes regulatory capture by limited vested interests (Stigler, 1971). The government agency that is responsible for environmental protection becomes unable to control these politically prevalent actors, and thus cannot execute its intended policy. As a result, the interest of the influential actor with most power prevails. This framework expands the fragmented authoritarianism model, as not all policy-making is as fragmented and can vary in its processes.

Bureaucratic politics literature argues that horizontal conflicts abound and horizontal specialization often affects policy outcomes (Egeberg, 1999; Campbell, 1984). Equally important are the preferences and interests of the actors involved in policy-making (Halperin, Clapp and Kanter, 2006). Different actors with conflicting preferences and interests are indeed a reason for intense horizontal conflicts. On the other hand, there is still a lack of study on the impact of organizational structures on policy formation (ibid.; Hammond, 1986).

Explaining the policy-making process using the bureaucratic structure and interests of actors involved is not at all new to political science. For example, taking the US experience during the Cuban missile crisis, Allison (1969) provided three models of decision-making – the rational actor, the organizational process and the governmental politics model. In the Chinese context, Andrews-Speed (2004: 53), for example, argued that "Bargaining occurs horizontally between government Ministries, agencies and state enterprises, as well as vertically between different levels of government." However, it was not clear when there is more negotiation between these actors and when there is not. This chapter highlights the importance of these domestic organizational structures in environmental policy-making.

The barrier to entry into policy-making has a range of low to high, depending on how easy it is for actors to enter a process. I differentiate low and high based on the number of actors that are allowed to draft policies in an issue area. When multiple actors are free to draft a policy for consideration, I define the barrier to entry as low. It also indicates that a larger number of administrative organizations are involved in policy-making. In contrast, when only a designated actor is able to draft a policy, there is a significant lack of participation and political uniformity in the policy-making; here I define the barrier level to be high. Differences in the political diversity taking part in policy drafts influence the flow of information into policy-making. The more actors that are freely able to propose policies, the more transparent the policy-making process is likely to become with more informed government. But when only a designated few actors are able to propose policies, the process is less transparent and there is limited flow of information.

The centralization of power in policy-making affects the level of bargaining. If each actor has equivalent power, there is large bargaining opportunity for each to gain his/her interests. However, when there is a power asymmetry among the actors and a limited few have a large influence on policy-making, there is not much room for bargaining. These two situations are defined by low and high centralization of power, respectively. The institutional framework involves the power struggles not only among the top leaders but also the actors in the periphery within the central government.

In sum, in this framework policy outcomes are due to lobbying and information sharing under a liberal policy-making process, and are determined by a small number of powerful actors under a restricted policy-making process. Important actors that have often been overlooked – industries and state-owned companies – are also included. This framework has the potential to expand to other actors such as non-governmental organizations and media that are becoming increasingly important in Chinese policy-making (Mertha, 2009).

Regulation for vehicle emissions

To test the hypotheses, I use the regulations for vehicle emissions. In the two cases examined here (vehicle emission standards and fuel quality standards), there is a substantial difference in the level of barriers to entry as well as in the executive power actors had for the two policies. Liberal policy-making results in more lobbying and information sharing among different actors involved in the process. This leads to the adoption of a stringent environmental policy. On the other hand, when there is restricted policy-making, the powerful actor dominates the process and it leads to failure in policy adoption.

These cases are specific to China, but the larger claims are generalizable to other countries. This helps us understand why it was difficult to integrate fuel quality and vehicle emission standards in some countries with strong state-owned oil companies. Theoretically, it advances the fragmented authoritarianism theory by creating a framework that includes variations in policy-making processes for different issue areas. Furthermore, this provides a framework to help understand the environmental policy-making process, which lacks study despite the recent increase in interest. I argue that although China is an authoritarian country, its intra-bureau politics is very similar to bureaucratic politics in democratic countries. The difference is a lack of actors' interest in obtaining votes from the public, but these actors support certain policies based on their organizational interests.

In terms of environmental/natural resource management, it is important to gain a better understanding of how China deals with its vehicle emission problems, and how policies are made to alleviate them. The higher the level of liberal policy-making, the more likely it is that China will adopt more stringent environmental policies. As China's involvement in reducing air pollution and climate change gains significance, this research finding becomes all the more important.

Policy-making for vehicle emission standards

The current policy-making process for setting vehicle emission standards is characterized as highly liberal (i.e. low barrier to entry and low centralization of power). This has led to policy-making by lobbying and enhanced information sharing by various research institutions. The outcome has been the adoption of stringent standards at a fast pace. Due to the lower barrier to entry, many actors have been able to comment during the policy-making process and, as illustrated below, diverse institutions created drafts for vehicle emission standards.

Why China chose the European standards

Why did China adopt the European regulations for vehicle emission standards? There were three basic reasons. First, Volkswagen – dominating the market at the time – lobbied the Chinese government to adopt the European regulations at an early stage when China was in the middle of determining what measures to take.[10] It has a specific section called "homologation, standards and lobby" within its technical development division, and was quick to react when it learned of China's regulation on vehicle emissions. Japanese joint-venture companies also demanded that China set the European equivalent standards in the 1990s.[11] It was easier for these foreign companies to manufacture what already existed and produce these goods within China than to use a completely new calibration if the Chinese government introduced emission regulations. Most had experience either producing in or exporting to European countries, and thus following their standards was the most efficient and economically optimal choice. The European Automobile Manufacturers' Association (2009) writes that "Common standards and regulations are essential to the competitiveness of the European automobile sector", and this was true for vehicle emission standards. The automobile manufacturers would not produce high-quality vehicles without standards because of the increased costs and concern about the loss of intellectual property rights, but it was not difficult for them to apply a technology when a regulation was put in place.

The Chinese government waited until it was the right moment to intervene to adopt Euro 1 emission standards.[12] It was important that two key conditions were met to implement stringent emission standards: technological capacity and a stable economy. The central government was aware that technology transfer could be enhanced by the adoption of emission standards. Wanting to make automobiles a "pillar industry", this was a strategic policy – not only to enhance air quality but also to increase China's competitiveness in the global market. But the government was also aware that technologies are costly, and adoption could initially raise the price of a vehicle too high to sustain the industry. When SEPA finally made a decision to adopt Euro 1 standards there was opposition from the local automobile industry (discussed in depth later).

Second, Chinese policy-makers and researchers found that China's driving cycle was much more similar to that in Europe than that in the United States. They came to realize that the average driving speed used to test emissions in the United States (31.4 km/hr) was much faster than that in Europe (18.7 km/hr). Based on similarity in driving speed and population density between China and the European Union as opposed to the United States or Japan, it decided on adopting the European method for both emission and fuel quality standards.[13]

Third, the Chinese government might have chosen the European standards since they were laxer regulations, especially at the earlier stage, than those of the American or Japanese.[14] It is possible that because the European standards were less stringent at the beginning, it allowed China to phase in implementation gradually. Furthermore, China had a vision to increase its diesel usage in the future, and the more diesel-friendly European standards were a better fit in its eyes.[15]

In contrast to the European Union, the United States showed no interest in harmonizing vehicle regulations. This is in line with the argument that "Americans tend to be in a second-mover position more often than Europeans" (Mattli and Büthe, 2003: 42) because European systems "possess organizational modes that easily accommodate the new layer of supranational standardization activity" (ibid.: 40), whereas the American system does not. Although Japan is currently taking the initiative to harmonize to the European standards, the United States has not become involved in this effort. This is most likely why the EU standards have diffused to more countries, including China, whereas the US ones did not.

China's liberal policy-making process

There are four ministries involved in automobile industry policy-making under the State Council in China, but for setting vehicle emission standards the responsibility falls solely on MEP. Because MEP is responsible for national air quality, it has a genuine interest in reducing air pollution, which is why MEP is keen on adopting stringent emission standards as well as improving fuel quality.

In establishing vehicle emission standards, MEP asks for experts' advice and technical support.[16] It consolidates drafts from those interested in being involved. Anyone is able to provide comments, but based on institutional capacities, often those chosen to draft policies are the Environmental Standards Institute, China Automotive Technology and Research Centre (CATARC) and Jinan Vehicle Test Centre (JVTC). When these institutes write drafts, they send them out to key automobile manufacturers for comments. The institution that created the draft reviews these comments, formulates them into a summary and writes a revised draft, which is sent to government departments. This draft is either accepted or rejected by an expert panel composed of government departments and actors involved in policy-making. When the draft is accepted, it is refined to formulate the final version, published by MEP and then sent to WTO member countries and foreign automobile industries. Comments are due in three months: following the Technical Barriers to Trade Agreement, WTO members can state acceptance or rejection of the standards. Drafters again analyse all the comments and suggestions received from the WTO member countries, and ask the governments for final approval of the policy draft. Usually within three months, MEP approves the policy; if not, it gives suggestions and/or recommendations. After standards are approved by the Standardization Administration Committee (SAC) under the General Administration of Quality Supervision, Inspection and Quarantine (AQSIQ), they are issued by both MEP and AQSIQ. The standards are administered by MEP.

It is important to note that there are different interests even within the automobile industry in China. As mentioned, some foreign joint-venture companies were lobbying for the European emission standards. With technologies in hand, they had no problem meeting the requirements. These foreign joint ventures were more worried about technologies being stolen, with little protection for intellectual property rights.[17] Also, there was a concern that the cost increase would affect the sales of automobiles. However, it is possible that these joint ventures realized they were going to be the beneficiaries rather than the local automobile industry when the standards were in place.[18] The local automobile industry was not in favour of adopting standards, because it recognized its lack of technologies compared to foreign companies.[19]

The current automobile industry in China is not institutionally strong enough for each manufacturer to lobby the government effectively, and there is not much collective force involved in the policy-making process. MEP delegates the drafting of policy to a third party in order to tighten vehicle emission standards with the input of multiple interests, and this mechanism has helped change policy outcomes. The automobile industry makes its voice heard at various stages of policy-making, but local manufacturers cannot inhibit the adoption of more stringent vehicle emission standards due to the role of delegated institutions such as CATARC and JVTC in drafting policy.

There was an incentive for the central government to raise its vehicle emission standards. China has made the automobile industry its "pillar industry" since 1986 (Thun, 2006), and it prioritized the industry's development in the Tenth Five Year Plan starting in 2001 (Gan, 2003). In this plan, the government had a clear vision to produce more than 1 million automobiles a year as its immediate goal (Committee on the Future of

Personal Transport Vehicles in China, 2003: 1). It is therefore no surprise that the central government was interested in increasing the technology transfer from foreign company counterparts, and created a policy that only allowed the entry of foreign firms in the automobile industry through joint venture with Chinese companies (Harwit, 1995). China adopted vehicle emission standards to reduce air pollution, but these standards also became a catalyst for enhancing technology transfer. Without the regulation, there was no reason for foreign companies to introduce the technologies in China. When the regulation was in place, the foreign manufacturers "immediately transferred the pollution-control technologies" (Gallagher, 2006: 389). There was no problem for joint ventures to meet the regulation, because they already had these advanced technologies. My interviews also suggest that there was a significant increase in technology transfer after the standards' adoption.[20] This explains why the government was willing to comply when German and Japanese manufacturers lobbied to adopt the Euro emission standards. Furthermore, there was no assertion that any bureaucratic agencies were opposed to the idea of adopting more stringent standards.

Many automobile manufacturers did, however, complain about the lack of high-quality fuel within the country even when the stringent vehicle emission standards were in place. This was especially problematic in adopting the Euro 3 emission standards, due to the damage the fuel does to essential technologies in vehicles equipped to meet the standards. SEPA (before the upgrade to MEP in 2008) was aware of the problem, and a director of the new vehicle declaration department at the Vehicle Emission Control Centre within SEPA made an open remark on 21 June 2007 about the problem of low-quality fuel, stating that it was not an ideal situation to be implementing the Euro 3 equivalent standards nationally when fuel quality was not high enough (*China Industry News*, 2007). So why did this result in higher emission standards? This mismatch of the two standards was possible because even though the automobile industry was able to voice its comments, the drafting institution was well aware of what technologies were available, and the industry – with many divided interests – was not powerful enough to influence the outcome. Using various institutions, the government was able to gather information effectively and overcome the fragmented authoritarianism by enforcing the power of MEP.

Before the liberal policy-making process

What is interesting about the policy-making process in the automobile industry is that it was not always liberal. The hypothesis, however, is also supported for the period when the policy-making process was restricted.

Even though the Chinese government has always sought technology transfer and placed an emphasis on the automobile industry, before 1998 the State Bureau of Quality and Technical Supervision (SBQTS, currently AQSIQ) was responsible for establishing emission standards, just as it has been for establishing fuel quality standards. During this time, the automobile industry agency within the government proposed standards through the National Automotive Standardization Technical Committee, which mainly comprised people from the automobile industry (Chang, 2006: 42). The industry preferred not to have stringent emission standards and only proposed some lax pre-Euro standards (ibid.: 59), which were not only formulated by the automobile industry itself, but also not well enforced. At that time there was no delegation to a research institution to enhance information flow. Also, there were a few powerful automobile industry actors in the policy-making process, and the National Environmental Protection Agency (before its upgrade to SEPA in 1998, it was only a subministry) had little power to be able to overcome that.

In 1997, as China prepared to open its automobile industry to the international market, the first automotive emission testing facility was established at the Chinese Research Academy of Environmental Sciences with some funding from the Japanese government (ibid.: 40). Furthermore, CATARC became an independent research body in 1999. Creation of the liberal market also slowly shifted the policy process from constrained to more liberal.

SEPA's ministerial status shifted its relative power higher than the agency in charge of supervising the automobile industry (State Bureau of Machinery Industry) in 1998. However, some struggles persisted between SBQTS and SEPA, and it took a while for SEPA to be able to propose and issue emission standards by itself. There were, in fact, two conflicting standards between 1999 and 2001. SEPA adopted the Euro 1 standards in 1999 to be implemented in 2000, but at the same time SBQTS was issuing laxer standards, with the plan that Euro 1 would be implemented in 2001 (ibid.). The struggle between ministries issuing different emission standards continued until 2001, but in the end Euro 1 was adopted and SEPA became fully responsible for administering the standards.

In sum, with a low barrier to entry, more actors are involved in the policy-making process for creating vehicle emission standards after 2001. The actors include those within the government and those in the industry. There is also a mechanism that involves discussions with different actors both within China and in WTO member countries and foreign automobile industries. Because of the liberal process, regardless of the large number of actors with diverse interests, the central government was able to adopt stringent emission standards through effective information management and the determination by MEP to execute its political power.

Before 1998, however, the policy-making process was restricted, and a high barrier to entry with centralized power in the local automobile industry inhibited the adoption of stringent standards. The transformation from a restricted to a liberal policy-making process took about three years.

Policy-making for fuel quality standards

The policy-making process for establishing fuel quality standards is characterized as highly restricted (i.e. high barrier to entry and high centralization of power). This has led to policy-making primarily by vested interests of the state-owned oil companies. The policy outcome has therefore been less stringent standards, falling behind the vehicle emission standards. Due to the high barrier to entry, policy-making tends to be more closed and the state-owned oil companies control the overall process. We do not see diverse institutions creating drafts, and even MEP has had little chance to exercise influence over this decision-making. The state-owned oil companies have the highest concentrated power in the process and are powerful actors. The result is restricted policy-making where, despite diverse interests within the government, the regulated industry is able to exercise its power, unlike the case for vehicle emission standards. This policy outcome has led to frustration for many actors which are unable to have any influence in the process.

The strong political power of the three major state-owned oil companies – the China National Petroleum Corporation (CNPC), the China National Petrochemical Corporation (Sinopec) and the China National Offshore Oil Corporation (CNOOC) – has been inhibiting the tightening of the standards. These state-owned oil companies have partially privatized subsidiaries, named PetroChina, Sinopec Corp and CNOOC Ltd, respectively. PetroChina and Sinopec are the key players, as can be seen in the technical committee for deciding fuel quality standards, and the main actors in refining oil. These two companies produce 90 per cent of gasoline, with hundreds of small refineries producing the rest (Downs, 2006: 26).

These state-owned oil companies were government ministries in the 1980s. CNPC was formed from the Ministry of Petroleum Industry in 1988 and Sinopec was created from the downstream (in charge of refining and marketing) assets of that ministry as well as the Ministry of Chemical Industry in 1983. CNOOC was first established in 1982 under the Ministry of Petroleum Industry to form joint ventures with foreign firms. The two companies are no longer government agencies, but are not completely out of the bureaucracy either. Their top officers, for example, are appointed by the Central Committee of the Chinese Communist Party (Downs, 2004: 25), and the general managers of all three companies hold the rank of vice minister in the national government (Downs, 2008: 122). Downs (ibid.: 121) states that "the oil industry has been a powerful interest group" and "the industry has had access to the top leadership and made its voices heard in the policymaking process". Furthermore, these companies employ an overwhelmingly large number of skilled and knowledgeable staff compared to the small number of positions in the government. In 2009 Sinopec had 619,000 employees and a net profit of 579.85 billion RMB (approximately US$84.9 billion) (Sinopec Group, 2009). It was the third-largest refinery company in the world with processing capacity of 3.6 million barrels per day, while CNPC was ranked ninth with 2.44 million barrels per day capacity (Walls, 2010). This resulted in a situation of "an energy regulator forced to rely on the regulated for policy recommendations" (Rosen and Houser, 2007: 18).

For fuel quality regulations, a technical committee (Subcommittee 1 on Petroleum Fuels and Lubricants of National Technical Committee 280 on Petroleum Products and Lubricants of Standardization Administration of China) is in charge of the standards, and consists of 57 personnel, of whom 21 are from Sinopec, 17 from PetroChina and three from CNOOC.[21] Others include two from the army and 10 from various government agencies; only four are outsiders – three from automobile-industry-related institutions and one from a university. The Research Institute of Petroleum Processing (RIPP) – the research institute under Sinopec – provides every specification.[22] The administration of standards for fuel quality is not under MEP, but SAC under AQSIQ. After SAC makes a plan based on the published draft, RIPP does a study and SAC organizes meetings to discuss the proposal. Because administration of this standard lies with SAC, MEP can only recommend stringency, even though it has the remit for national air quality. MEP is responsible only for implementation of fuel quality standards, and although it can recommend some standards, its political status in terms of issuing these standards is and has been relatively weak. The powerful actors both within and outside the government have made a policy change from the status quo extremely difficult.

The involvement of MEP and other actors in fuel quality regulations is significantly different from that for vehicle emission standards. The barrier to entry for fuel quality standards is much higher, and no actors apart from the technical committee have any responsibility for drafting the standards. Because the general secretary of the technical committee is from RIPP, it is argued that the "oil industry can control the fuel quality standards".[23] As explained, the automobile industry has also tried to lobby for higher fuel quality, but to no avail.

In sum, a restricted policy-making process in the energy sector inhibited the adoption of stringent fuel quality standards. The main actors were the powerful state-owned oil companies, and there was minimal involvement of the automobile industry and even MEP. Because the barrier to entry into policy-making was high, and the Chinese oil companies were much more institutionally organized and had an advantage with more expertise and larger numbers of employees, they were able to maintain the lower fuel quality standards that they wanted. The restricted policy-making process inhibited the fuel quality standards matching with vehicle emission standards.

Conclusion

There is a clear link between natural resource management and environmental regulations. In this chapter I illustrate how an environmental problem – vehicle emission regulation – interacts with a natural resource problem – fuel quality standards. The two policy-making processes vary widely due to the differences in the degree of liberality. Thus although a stringent vehicle emission standard is facilitated through a liberal policy-making process, an equivalent fuel quality standard is inhibited by a restricted policy-making process. Overall, this brings a dilemma in regulating vehicle emissions efficiently in China.

The provided framework offers theoretical and empirical contributions to the domestic politics of environmental policy-making and, more specifically, for vehicle emission management in China. First, it provides a new insight into China's environmental policy-making process and the conditions under which stringent policy is or is not adopted. The fragmented authoritarianism described in Lieberthal and Oksenberg (1988) has been a major theory used in describing Chinese politics, but with increasing actors and higher pluralism in place it is important to expand the existing theory. In the case of emission standards, while the restricted policy-making process for the automobile sector before and during the 1990s limited the adoption of stringent standards, the liberal policy-making process that started in 2001 led to the quick adoption of high standards. On the other hand, in the case of establishing fuel quality standards, a highly restricted policy-making process with strong power held by state-owned oil companies resulted in not adopting stringent standards. The two cases produced policy outcomes that departed from the international norm, which is the adoption of equivalent standards for both vehicle emissions and fuel quality. The institutional framework covers some factors that led to this mismatch. The degree of liberal policy-making process – measured by barriers to entry into policy-making and the centralization of power – determines how much the adoption of stringent policies is enhanced.

Second, this framework provides a new way to analyse China's environmental management. The current policy-making process for vehicle emission standards relies more on lobbying, and even includes actors such as foreign automobile manufacturers that have joint ventures with Chinese companies. There are more numerous actors with different interests involved in policy-making, and this research shows that the Chinese central government is not a unitary actor in policy-making. Despite the number of actors, the power is spread equally among them with only one prevalent actor: MEP. It is likely that more actors, including the public and the media, will be involved in the future, and it will most likely augment liberal policy-making, which will enhance environmental regulations.

The policy-making processes for fuel quality standards as well as that for emission standards before 2001 have different dynamics, and stringent standards were not adopted. In contrast to the current policy-making for vehicle emission standards, these processes do not include as many actors and there is not much lobbying. However, there are a small number of actors with much larger political power. The influential actors for fuel quality standards are the state-owned oil companies, and although there are other actors with different interests, it almost seems as if these companies constitute the unitary actor in this case. The automobile industry was very influential before the policy-making process became liberal, and dominated the process. It is hard to say if a more liberal policy-making process will be as feasible for fuel quality standards as it was for vehicle emission standards in the near future, given the existence of such powerful and politically prevalent oil companies.

With increasing interest in understanding the policy-making process and enhanced pluralization in China, this new institutional framework provides a clearer picture of how environmental policy-making is executed based on the bureaucratic structure and the government-business relationship. It tries to disentangle how different actors succeed or fail in influencing environmental policy outcomes. Enhancing a liberal policy-making process, which creates a clear divide between the regulator and the regulated and allows more transparency, is one of the ways in which China could improve its environmental management.

Although this analysis focuses on China, there are large implications for understanding broader policy-making processes in other developing countries. For example, Malaysia is a major energy-producing country and has seen an increase in the number of vehicles since the late 1990s. Consequently, vehicle emissions are becoming an important source of air pollution, and Malaysia is similarly struggling to adopt both emission and fuel quality standards at the same time. More research is needed to test whether lowering the barrier to entry into policy-making and reducing the centralization of power of a specific actor in the process lead to more policy liberalization and more stringent domestic environmental policy-making not only in China but also in other countries.

Notes

1. The UN Economic Commission for Europe, rather than the European Union, was the main regulating body in Europe for air pollution from the road transport sector until the 1980s (Wurzel, 2002).
2. Military vehicles are exempt from these regulations.
3. Interview with Yan Ding and David Vance Wagner, Beijing, 14 July 2008.
4. Interview with Yan Ding, Beijing, 25 February 2009.
5. Beijing's Euro 4 emission standards for light-duty and heavy-duty vehicles went into effect on 1 March and 1 July 2008, respectively. Beijing's Euro IV fuel quality standards went into effect on 1 January 2008.
6. Interview with Yan Ding and David Vance Wagner, Beijing, 25 February 2009.
7. This approach is similar to that of Naoi (2007: 41), who argues that the two "decentralization" factors – the "degree of decentralization in a government's export administration and the degree of geographical concentration of industries" – affect the Chinese government's Sino-Japanese trade dispute settlement choice.
8. Therefore this is not only the veto power, as considered in the veto players' theory. For veto players' theory see Tsebelis (1999, 2002).
9. Veto players' theory suggests that the larger the number of veto players and the greater the ideological differences are among the actors, the more likely the situation is to lead to policy stability (Tsebelis, 1999).
10. Interview with a manager in Chinese automobile industry, Beijing, 15 July 2008.
11. Interview with a manager in Chinese automobile industry, Beijing, 14 July 2008.
12. Interview with a manager in Vehicle Emissions Control Centre, Beijing, 18 July 2008.
13. Interview with Yan Ding and David Vance Wagner, Beijing, 14 July 2008.
14. For carbon monoxide, the standards that are equivalent to Euro 1 required 2.10 g/km in Japan and the United States, whereas the limit for the Euro 1 standards was 2.72 g/km. The same trend was seen for the limits of hydrocarbons and nitrogen oxides.
15. Interview with Professor Tomoo Marukawa, Tokyo, 7 July 2008.
16. The procedure is based on an interview with a researcher, Tianjin, 17 July 2008.
17. Interview with three managers in Chinese automobile industry, Beijing, 21 July 2008.
18. E-mail correspondence with Professor Tomoo Marukawa, 28 May 2008.
19. Interview with a manager of Chinese automobile industry, Hangzhou, 29 July 2008.
20. Interview with managers in the automobile industry and researchers in research institutions, August 2008 and March and July 2009.
21. The names are provided on the website of National Technical Committee 280, available at www.cptcstd.org/Attach/20080904113621375.doc.
22. Interview with a government official, Beijing, 25 February 2009, and with Ying Yuan and Liang Ji, Chinese Academy of Environmental Sciences, Beijing, 29 February 2009.
23. Interview with Yan Ding, Beijing, 25 February 2009.

REFERENCES

Allison, Graham T. (1969) "Conceptual Models and Cuban Missile Crisis", *American Political Science Review* 63, pp. 689–718.

Andrews-Speed, Philip (2004) *Energy Policy and Regulation in the People's Republic of China*, The Hague and New York: Kluwer Law International.

Asian Development Bank (2003) "Reducing Vehicle Emissions in Asia", available at www.adb.org/publications/reducing-vehicle-emissions-asia.

Auto Alliance (2006) "Worldwide Fuel Charter", 4th edn, available at www.autoalliance.org/files/WWFC.pdf.

Campbell, John Creighton (1984) "Policy Conflict and Its Resolution within the Government System", in Ellis S. Krauss, Thomas P. Rohlen and Patricia G. Steinhoff (eds) *Conflict in Japan*, Honolulu, HI: University of Hawaii Press, pp. 294–334.

Chang, Cheng (2006) "Automobile Pollution Control in China: Enforcement of and Compliance with Vehicle Emissions Standards", PhD dissertation, Stanford University.

China Industry News (2007) "State Environmental Protection Administration: Euro 3 Vehicle Emission Standards Cannot Be Delayed", *China Industry News*, 29 June, available at http://auto.sohu.com/20070629/n250823720.shtml (in Chinese).

China Oil News Web (2007) "Fuel Supplies Fail to Meet Emission Standards", China Oil News Web, 4 July, available at http://news.chinaoilweb.com/China/Fuel-supplies-fail-to-meet-emission-standards.798.htm.

Committee on the Future of Personal Transport Vehicles in China, National Research Council, National Academy of Engineering and Chinese Academy of Engineering (2003) *Personal Cars and China*, Washington, DC: National Academies Press.

Downs, Erica S. (2004) "The Chinese Energy Security Debate", *China Quarterly* 177, pp. 21–41.

—— (2006) "China Executive Summary: Grappling with Rapid Energy Demand Growth", Brookings Institution, Washington, DC.

—— (2008) "Business Interest Groups in Chinese Politics: The Case of the Oil Companies", in Cheng Li (ed.) *China's Changing Political Landscape*, Washington, DC: Brookings Institution Press, pp. 121–141.

Egeberg, Morten (1999) "The Impact of Bureaucratic Structure on Policy Making", *Public Administration* 77, pp. 150–170.

European Automobile Manufacturers' Association (2009) "Harmonisation of Rules and Standards", EAMA, 19 May, available at www.acea.be/news/news_detail/international_harmonisation_of_regulation_is_a_high_priority/.

Gallagher, Kelly S. (2006) "Limits to Leapfrogging in Energy Technologies? Evidence from the Chinese Automobile Industry", *Energy Policy* 34, pp. 383–394.

Gan, Lin (2003) "Globalization of the Automobile Industry in China: Dynamics and Barriers in Greening of the Road Transportation", *Energy Policy* 31, pp. 537–551.

Halperin, Morton H., Priscilla Clapp and Arnold Kanter (2006) *Bureaucratic Politics and Foreign Policy*, Washington, DC: Brookings Institution Press.

Halpern, Nina P. (1992) "Information Flows and Policy Coordination in the Chinese Bureaucracy", in Kenneth Lieberthal and David M. Lampton (eds) *Bureaucracy, Politics, and Decision Making in Post-Mao China*, Berkeley, CA: University of California Press, pp. 126–149.

Hammond, Thomas H. (1986) "Agenda Control, Organizational Structure, and Bureaucratic Politics", *American Journal of Political Science* 30, pp. 379–420.

Hanson, Stephanie (2008) "China, Africa, and Oil", 6 June, Council on Foreign Relations, available at www.cfr.org/china/china-africa-oil/p9557.

Hao, Jimin, Jingnan Hu and Lixin Fu (2006) "Controlling Vehicular Emissions in Beijing During the Last Decade", *Transportation Research Part A* 40, pp. 639–651.

Harwit, Eric (1995) *China's Automobile Industry: Policies, Problems and Prospects*, New York: M. E. Sharpe.

Houser, Trevor (2008) "The Roots of Chinese Oil Investment Abroad", *Asia Policy* 5, pp. 141–166.

Kong, Bo (2006) "Institutional Insecurity", *China Security* 2, pp. 64–88.

—— (2009) "China's Energy Decision-Making: Becoming More Like the United States?", *Journal of Contemporary China* 18, pp. 789–812.

Lampton, David M. (2001) "China's Foreign and National Security Policy-making Process: Is It Changing and Does It Matter?", in David M. Lampton (ed.) *The Making of Chinese Foreign and Security Policy in the Era of Reform*, Stanford, CA: Stanford University, pp. 1–26.

Lieberthal, Kenneth and Michael Oksenberg (1988) *Policy Making in China: Leaders, Structures, and Processes*, Princeton, NJ: Princeton University Press.

Liu, Huan, Kebin He, Dongquan He, Lixin Fu, Michael P. Walsh and Katherine O. Blumberg (2008) "Analysis of the Impacts of Fuel Sulfur on Vehicle Emissions in China", *Fuel* 87, pp. 3147–3154.

Mattli, Walter and Tim Büthe (2003) "Setting International Standards – Technological Rationality or Primacy of Power?", *World Politics* 56, pp. 1–42.

Mertha, Andrew C. (2006) "Policy Enforcement Markets – How Bureaucratic Redundancy Contributes to Effective Intellectual Property Implementation in China", *Comparative Politics* 38, pp. 295–316.

—— (2009) "'Fragmented Authoritarianism 2.0': Political Pluralization in the Chinese Policy Process", *China Quarterly* 200, pp. 995–1012.

Naoi, Megumi (2007) "Decentralization, Industrial Geography and the Politics of Export Regulation – The Case of Sino-Japanese Trade Disputes", in Ka Zeng (ed.) *China's Foreign Trade Policy: The New Constituencies*, London and New York: Routledge, pp. 40–58.

New York Times (2004) "China Pays a Price for Cheaper Oil; Sulfur-Laden Fuels Contribute to Growing Pollution Problem", *New York Times*, 26 June, available at www.nytimes.com/2004/06/26/business/china-pays-price-for-cheaper-oil-sulfur-laden-fuels-contribute-growing-pollution.html?pagewanted=all&src=pm.

Rosen, Daniel H. and Trevor Houser (2007) *China Energy – A Guide for the Perplexed*, Washington, DC: Peterson Institute for International Economics.

Saikawa, Eri (2013) "Policy Diffusion of Emission Regulations: Is There a Race to the Top?", *World Politics* 65(1), pp. 1–33.

Saikawa, Eri, Jun-ichi Kurokawa, Masayuki Takigawa, Jens Borken-Kleefeld, Denise L. Mauzerall, Larry W. Horowitz and Toshimasa Ohara (2011) "The

Impact of China's Vehicle Emissions on Regional Air Quality in 2000 and 2020: A Scenario Analysis", *Atmospheric Chemistry and Physics* 11, pp. 9465–9484.

Shirk, Susan L. (1993) *The Political Logic of Economic Reform in China*, Berkeley, CA: University of California Press.

Sinopec Group (2009) "Responsibility Report", available at www.sinopecgroup. com/gsjs/Doc/ResponsibilityReport2009.pdf (in Chinese).

Stigler, George J. (1971) "The Theory of Economic Regulation", *Bell Journal of Economics* 2, pp. 3–21.

Taylor, Ian (2006) "China's Oil Diplomacy in Africa", *International Affairs* 82, pp. 937–959.

Thun, Eric (2006) *Changing Lanes in China: Foreign Direct Investment, Local Government, and Auto Sector Development*, New York: Cambridge University Press.

Tsebelis, George (1999) "Veto Players and Law Production in Parliamentary Democracies: An Empirical Analysis", *American Political Science Review* 93, pp. 591–608.

—— (2002) *Veto Players: How Political Institutions Work*, Princeton, NJ: Princeton University Press.

Walls, W. David (2010) "Petroleum Refining Industry in China", *Energy Policy* 38, pp. 2110–2115.

Walsh, Michael (2007) "Can China Control the Side Effects of Motor Vehicle Growth?", *Natural Resources Forum* 31, pp. 21–34.

Wurzel, Rüdiger (2002) *Environmental Policy-making in Britain, Germany, and the European Union (Issues in Environmental Politics)*, New York: Manchester University Press.

Xinhua News (2009) "China Explains Details of New Oil Pricing Mechanism", *Xinhua News*, 8 May, available at http://news.xinhuanet.com/english/2009-05/08/ content_11339021.htm.

4

People and business in the appropriation of Cambodia's forests

Andrew Robert Cock

When the government sold the forests to let the big companies cut down the trees, it cut the throats of the poorer people in the villages . . . Now, nobody can make a living . . . Big companies come in with automatic tools and can cut down a tree in a very short time, and they use special trucks to lift and carry the logs . . . In the past, people used the trees in the forest very slowly. The big companies use the forest very quickly . . . The money used to go to the people in the village. Now, who gets it? (Kratie forest area resident, quoted in Malcolm, 1998)

I am used to going to the forest whenever I want or need. I am free to decide which day I go. The company will force me to work when it wants. I am a free man. If I need to buy or exchange something, I go to the forest and collect resin. If one morning, I do want to stay at home, I stay. I can do it. I am free. I do not want to become a slave of the company. (Kampong Thom forest area resident, 2004)

Introduction

From the late 1980s Cambodia's forests were heavily logged, with many areas degraded, reduced to scrublands or converted into agricultural schemes of various kinds. As the rate of logging rose in the lead-up to the UN-sponsored peace process and following the formation of a coalition government in 1993, a range of multilateral and bilateral aid organizations engaged in the promotion of forest policy reform. This reform

Governance of natural resources: Uncovering the social purpose of materials in nature, Sato (ed.), United Nations University Press, 2013, ISBN 978-92-808-1228-2

agenda centred on the formal state capture of rents generated through logging operations and the promotion of logging concessions as vehicles for "sustainable forest management". Despite persistent efforts and high levels of foreign aid that some of the most influential of the "external" actors were able to offer in support of reform initiatives, limited headway has been made in preserving Cambodia's forests in the almost two decades since the end of the United Nations Transitional Authority (UNTAC) operation in 1993. Logging at rates well in excess of what was broadly accepted as a sustainable level continued throughout the 1990s, with virtually none of the profits harnessed for public purposes. More recently, land "development" schemes have intersected with logging operations to convert forestlands into plantations. Early 2013 estimates suggested these schemes now cover more than 2 million hectares of Cambodia. These business schemes, aimed at the promotion of agro-industry such as rubber cultivation, have had the effect of replacing timber extraction with another type of forest exploitation, and in doing so enhanced the elite's grip on the country's forestland.

The social construction of the resource values ascribed to Cambodia's forests played a central role in this trend. I examine the mechanisms by which resources contained in Cambodia's forests have been redefined over time in a manner that gives impetus to their conversion to plantations. These mechanisms emerged out of the interaction between aid donors, Cambodia's political elite, business entities and social groups living in forest areas. A key contribution this chapter makes is to situate the process of resource definition that I term "appropriation" in the practice of state rule. I highlight the autonomy of local actors who, in combination with nascent business entities, used reforms for their own ends even if constrained in some ways. Contrary to often-held assumptions that external actors are the central agent of restraint in relation to logging, I show how the impetus for changes in resource values was at crucial intervals driven by local factors.

I use the plight of resin tappers to analyse this process of appropriation. Resin tapping entails a use of *Dipterocarps* financially competitive over a 30–50-year interval with logging of these same trees. My analysis of this practice shows how conceptions of the "resources" forest areas contained and the multitude of social, cultural and environmental values they represented came to be narrowed. Cambodia's forests were redefined as valuable primarily as a repository of timber, and in this sense appropriated. Then, on the pretext that timber-based values had degraded through logging, government subsequently promoted the enclosure of forests in plantation schemes. A range of business actors subsequently emerged to take advantage of this trend in government policy. As they have done so, their ties and relative importance *vis-à-vis* the Cambodian state have shifted, although the two remain inextricably linked.

To develop this argument concerning how forest areas came to be appropriated for their timber values, I make detailed use of Khmer-language sources, including the internal correspondence of government officials, letters written by community leaders to government and the reports of government and donor agencies. Much of the material is unpublished and was obtained during five years of research into the politics of forestry while based in Cambodia.

Appropriating forests for their timber values

Perceptions of the "resources" available for extraction from tropical forest landscapes are born out of social interaction with those landscapes. The notion of a forest as a repository of "resources", and the particular bio-output given this privileged standing, derive from variable frameworks of knowledge and practice.[1] This applies not only to Cambodia but much more broadly. Recall, for instance, Bernard Fernow's (1913) early-twentieth-century observation that tropical timbers, apart from a few select species, had little commercial value. As social constructions, the status of particular types of bio-output as a "resource" shifts over time. It also depends on the perspective from which one views a landscape.[2] A forested landscape as a domain overlaid by a complex of tenures, prohibitions, exclusion zones, spirits and burial sites that are meaningful to those who live in it (and engage in an almost endless variety of collection, cultivation and hunting practices) is a domain either invisible or of limited importance to adopting a perspective informed by the aspirations of scientific forestry, with its focus on maximizing yields of wood (Scott, 1998). Even proponents of "sustainable forest management", with their claim to have incorporated social issues in the forest management planning process, reify this socially textured landscape.[3] The management aspirations of such proponents continue to be anchored to the sweeping spatial categories of scientific forestry: production forests, protection forests and conversion forests.

Overlaying these spatial distinctions is the categorization of the "products" forests are claimed to contain. The central distinction of scientific forestry is between timber and an aggregation of residuals that has *inter alia* been termed "minor forest products", "non-timber forest products" and "non-wood forest products". From the perspective of scientific forestry, however valuable they may be as exotics, products other than timber are deemed to occur in too small quantities or inconsistent qualities to be considered of comparable aggregate value to timber. The notion of a "production forest" has almost always meant a forest directed predominantly, if not exclusively, to production of timber.

This binary between timber and some type of aggregation of the residuals (e.g. "non-timber") has no inherent standing, but it does have significant implications for how forests are used. Two definitions of appropriation are important in conveying the shifting nature of ideas concerning what constitutes a "resource". Appropriation can entail a process by which an object (such as a "forest") is assigned a special attribution or application (such as its status as a repository of timber). Further, appropriation can involve the taking of an object as one's own or for one's own purpose. In this regard, a provision in the 1993 constitution granted tenure over all forest areas to the Cambodian state. The forest was in a sense "appropriated" to serve a purported national development purpose via the industrial production of timber. Thus the "forest" was assigned attributes and areas of it annexed or deployed by holders of political, and in some cases economic, power for particular uses through enactment of the systems of knowledge and practice inscribed in the forestry discipline.

Appropriation constitutes a key influence on patterns of forest governance, and in Cambodia's case is intertwined with the activities of companies that converted forest areas into land development schemes. The rationality of appropriation frames both what is to be valued as forestland and the purposes for which forestland is managed. By denying or marginalizing other types of forest uses and alternative forest valuations, dominant timber-centred valuations have come, in the context of the extraction of timber via logging operations, to feed into justifications for enclosing forest areas in plantation schemes. In analysing how this occurred in Cambodia, particularly from the early 2000s onwards, I examine how social groups were typecast in studies undertaken as part of the formulation of the forestry reform agenda. This is a particularly significant period, being a time when Cambodia's forestry institutions were remade as part of this reform agenda. It is also a time of accelerating growth in East Asia and heightened demand for agro-industrial commodities. The issue of resin powerfully illustrates how the implementation of a set of policy reforms designed by aid donors and aimed at the promotion of "sustainable forest management" came to be confronted by the implicit political underpinnings of this typecast. As contestation over forest areas came to be increasingly apparent and claims as to the legitimacy of a reform agenda centred on the continued operation of a forest concession system subject to overt critique, aid donors withdrew from their engagement in the promotion of forestry reforms and the ruling elite's growing ties to business entities led to accelerated conversion of forest areas into plantations.

The contested nature of Cambodia's forest resources

Summarizing the findings of the "Cambodia Forest Policy Assessment" a decade after its completion, the World Bank noted that it:

> laid out the enormous economic, social and environmental potential of the forest resource and identified serious weaknesses in the Government's approach. Concessions stood out as a critical constraint to the emergence of sustainable, diverse and socially responsible forestry in Cambodia. Illegal logging was also seen as a serious threat to the sector. (World Bank, 2005b)

However, the assessment had at a fundamental level failed to acknowledge that the forest areas where concessions had been allocated were already occupied, cultivated, harvested and much modified. Some 3 million people were estimated to be residing in and on the fringes of forest areas, with more than 500,000 inside forest concession areas (World Food Programme, 2001: 6). Forests throughout the country provided substantial "economic", "social" and "environmental" benefits – although communities residing in and around forest areas would not have conceived of them in terms of those discrete disciplinary domains. What the Bank meant was that in relation to the conception of resources conveyed in the particular notion of the "appropriate" reform agenda that external actors had sought to carry forward, those resources were yet to be fully or efficiently utilized as part of the development process. This was certainly valid in terms of the rapacious exploitation of forests associated with the timber boom, but was more problematic in terms of what legitimately constituted the forest's potential.

Just as Cambodia's wartime inaccessibility prevented the type of intensive logging that destroyed the forests throughout much of Southeast Asia, it also shielded the state from socialization of its institutional and regulatory framework.[4] Rather than becoming institutionally isonomic, the Cambodian state retained institutional structures that continued to recognize the distinctive ways in which the population utilized the forested landscape. However, viewed from the perspective of consultants engaged by aid donors, the Cambodian state had yet to enact fully the institutional and regulatory framework that would promote practices of forest exploitation appropriate for "forest-rich countries".[5] Subsistence-centred economic practices and the imperatives of Cambodia's protracted economic isolation meant that rural communities retained systems of forest utilization that might have become significantly more marginal under the weight of outside influence had Cambodia not remained so closed during the last two decades of the Cold War;[6] and these systems continued to be reflected in Cambodian laws and regulations. An example of this is the "Guidelines on Official Fee Rates for Forest Products" issued by the Cambodian Ministry of Agriculture, Forestry and Fisheries in July 2000. This document lists fees for the transport of 71 types of forest products, ranging from tiger bone and skin to sambur antler, ivory, aloe-wood, bamboos, rattan and resin. In these guidelines, an anachronism when measured in terms of the norms of both wildlife conservation and "scientific forestry", a diversity of extractive forest practices is evident, with these still viewed by the state as of commercial importance.[7]

Studies commissioned by external actors as part of the reform process examined social aspects of forest use in remarkably limited detail and within a pre-constituted forest taxonomy. This was acknowledged by the "Cambodia Forest Policy Assessment" in noting that its focus was "on commercial and industrial forest uses ... [and] there remains a large agenda for further policy analysis and development related to agroforestry, wood energy production, biodiversity conservation and human resource development" (World Bank, UNDP and UN FAO, 1996: 1). The report pointed to the derivative nature of what were assumed to be non-"commercial and industrial forest uses". It noted that "These important topics will ultimately require detailed review and project preparation, but the recommendations offered here on an overall policy framework are suitable for extension into these areas" (ibid.).[8]

The limited studies on forests and livelihoods that were undertaken contained a sweeping division as to what were the important resources for those living in and around forest areas. The division mirrored that made by scientific forestry. For instance, a provincial workshop in Kratie (eastern Cambodia) held as part of the 1997–1998 Forest Policy Reform Project determined that the importance of forests for proximate populations mostly related to the extraction of timber-based products. Other biooutput was of secondary importance. The report of the workshop noted:

> The main forest products consumed daily by local people are: fuel wood, building material, processing wood for handicraft, leaves and thatch. Forest products of secondary important [sic] for subsistence and supplemental income include: vines (lianas), resin, rattan, wildlife, traditional medicine, honey, fruit, bamboo, bamboo shoots, and mushrooms ... (Associates in Rural Development, 1997: 5)

This type of finding concerning community forest use largely supported the precept that logging concessions were, with some modifications, an appropriate basis for "managing" Cambodia's forests. At a meeting of donor representatives and Cambodian government officials, consultants to the forest policy component of the broader Forest Policy Reform Project assured attendees: "The Forest Concession system of forest land allocation is the most appropriate for commercial development of forest resources in Cambodia but needs refinement to suit Cambodian conditions" (Associates in Rural Development, 1998a). Suiting Cambodian conditions was to involve the production of new management plans to govern logging operations, but with the continuation of timber extraction and the rationalization of systems to provide transparency in the granting of further forest concessions. The impact of these logging operations on social groups living in concessions areas received little attention.

One example of how this was manifested is the case of resin. In the limited studies of forests and livelihoods that were undertaken, resin (when included at all) was treated as a "supplement", with this defined as: "The kinds of wood and nonwood products which villagers harvest to improve their living standards and are not necessary" (Associates in Rural Development, 1998b). In contrast, the "essential" (ibid.) or "necessary" (Associates in Rural Development, 1997)[9] were defined as "The kinds of wood and non wood products which villagers harvest to use everyday and are a requirement" (Associates in Rural Development, 1998b). These were in most cases wood. The next section shows how this facet of the particular perspective on forest "resources" deployed in the formulation of the forest policy reform agenda came to be increasingly problematic from mid-2000 onwards as the issue of resin tree cutting came to strip the agenda of its technical façade.

The contesting of timber-based values: The case of resin

Forest policy reform associated with the promotion of "sustainable forest management" entailed assigning people living in forest areas to pre-constituted categories. The categories divided the forest both territorially and in terms of product types that anchored people to particular notions of "subsistence" and "local". The few attempts that were made as part of the formulation of the reform agenda to examine the importance of forests to rural dwellers were peculiarly ahistorical, mirroring the taxonomy of the forest generated out of scientific forestry. This resulted in conceptions of the social importance of forest resources that bore little relation to the scope, complexity and even the commercial value of forest product collection and trade in post-UNTAC Cambodia. This applies starkly to the collection and trade of oleoresin derived from the same *Dipterocarp* tree species targeted by loggers.

Dipterocarpus, a genus of trees of the family *Dipterocarpaceae*, dominates the forests of Cambodia. About 70 different species of this tree are found in South and Southeast Asia, and commonly form the bulk of the tree species targeted by loggers.[10] In addition to the timber, which was described by Burkill et al. (1966) as "an excellent cheap wood for general purposes",[11] oleoresin is collected from live trees. The word "resin" refers to fluids produced by trees to limit the risks of infection caused by breaks in wood tissue. Resins often contain volatile and non-volatile components, and may have various consistencies from solid to semi-liquid depending on the percentage of volatile compounds. If the percentage is high, the substance will be more liquid and is often labelled an "oleoresin" or "wood oil" (see de Beer and McDermott, 1996).

Many species of *Dipterocarp* can be tapped for the oleoresin, which is a sticky, oily substance often present in high enough quantities in freshly cut logs to exude and cover the exposed sap-wood at the ends of logs. Tapping holes in the base of the living tree to draw its resin has been an occupation of importance to many forest-dwelling groups, to the point where it was considered necessary in colonial Burma to distinguish between "wood oil" and "earth oil" to clarify the origin of the type of "oil" in question (Longmuir, 2001).[12] "The process of tapping" was, according to Burkill et al. (1966: 853), "so simple as to arise wherever the occurrence of trees made tapping possible; and the trade developed within geographic zones each with its own name for the resin".[13]

In the case of Cambodia, not only were large numbers of people involved in the collection of resin but it became increasingly lucrative as a commercial extractive practice from the 1990s onwards.[14] The collection of resin was also an activity subject to social regulation in many areas, in that it involved a tenure system recognized by forest-dwelling communities and was implicitly recognized in forest law in the People's Republic of Kampuchea (PRK) era.[15] This made it an extraction practice that competed with logging operations.

A customary system of tenure had long existed, with the first person to find and mark a resin tree considered the "owner" of the tree. In some areas where resin trees were located in well-defined groups (30–50 or more trees), the same person might find, mark and own all trees in the group. In other areas where resin trees were predominantly located along streams or scattered about the forest, ownership might be more dispersed. A tapping household commonly owned somewhere between 30 and 100 trees. Tenure exists in the sense that village members and neighbouring villagers would recognize resin trees as a particular person's or family's property. The transfer of ownership of trees was hence possible through inheritance or donation, or by the sale of rights to tap trees for a specified time.

The context within which resin rose to prominence in Cambodia was a long tradition of tapping *Dipterocarps* (particularly chhoe teal[16]) to supply local needs and a rapidly rising demand that prompted the creation or expansion of export routes into Viet Nam and Thailand.[17] Cambodia's forest laws, including laws formulated during the PRK regime, inscribed rights to resin tappers by restricting the cutting of resin trees. Under the 1988 Forestry Law, which remained Cambodia's basic forestry legislation until 2002, the logging of resin trees was prohibited. Item "chhor" (g) of Article 17 of the 1988 law stated that it "shall be forbidden ... to fell trees that people have tapped for resin" (Ministry of Agriculture, Forestry and Fisheries, 1988a). The Department of Forestry had issued instructions for interpretation of this provision in a manner that limited its application, defining resin trees as those within a limited size range and promoting the concept of negotiation between tappers and loggers.[18] "Negotiation", in practice, entailed loggers coercing villagers into "selling" their resin trees under the threat they would be cut either way.[19] But it was also an implicit recognition that villagers had rights of ownership (or at least a form of usufruct). In addition, it provided a legal basis to make claims and issue complaints against forest concessionaires. Conflicts between loggers and resin collectors were not new, but neither were they visible and tended only to be acknowledged in generic terms as a clash between commercial and traditional forest uses. However, as forest areas became increasingly accessible following the surrender of the final Khmer Rouge remnants at the end of 1998, a stream of complaints emerged concerning the cutting of resin trees.

From mid-2000 the logging of resin trees rose to prominence as advocacy networks were constructed through which to channel complaints from forest-dwelling communities into the public arena, including at the domestic and international levels. The first attempt to do this was a complaint letter to the Cambodian National Assembly and Prime Minister Hun Sen in May 2000. The letter, sent by villagers from Brome commune in the northern province of Preah Vihear, asserted that they had been threatened with violence by the Taiwanese-owned Cambodia Cherndar Plywood Company if they continued to tap resin from trees located in the company's forest concession.[20] According to the letter, the Preah Vihear governor had met with villagers in an attempt to resolve the dispute, and agreed that the company was not allowed to "touch any tree from which the villages collect oil" (O'Connell and Bou Saroeun, 2000). At a subsequent meeting not attended by provincial officials, a representative of the logging company told villagers that the governor did not know the rules under which concessionaires operated, and it had received authorization from the highest political levels. The villagers were warned that soldiers hired to guard the concession would be used against them if they came into the forest (ibid.). This was the first of a number of complaints filed by resin-tapping villagers during 2000 and 2001. For instance, complaints dated 10 January 2001 from four communes in Kampong Thom were sent to the National Assembly and a variety of state institutions.[21] President of the Senate Commission on Human Rights Kem Sokha wrote to the minister of agriculture, forestry and fisheries via Senate and CPP President Chea Sim, calling for him to "intervene and find justice" (Kem Sokha, 2001).[22] The large number of complaints, combined with media coverage of conflicts between loggers and resin tappers, raised the public profile of the resin tree issue. Due to the extent of external scrutiny of the government's forest policy reform initiatives, key officials rapidly responded.[23]

The response took the form of a restatement of prohibitions on the logging of resin trees as per the existing forest law and the issuance of new declarations calling on concessionaires to halt the cutting of resin trees. A "directive order" was issued by Hun Sen in April 2001 calling for the suspension of the cutting of resin trees.[24] It was followed a short time later by a letter sent from Ty Sokhun, director of the (then) Department of Forestry, to the forest concessionaires. The letter referred to the suspension of resin tree cutting as temporary and requested that concessionaires study the potential for alternative employment for tappers. It points to the distinctive way in which the ruling elite understood the issue and their relationship with resin-tapping communities. As a matter of justice, these groups should be able to tap some trees; enough so as to be able to subsist. This conception of justice was embedded in the regulatory compromise by which tappers had rights to collect from resin trees within a certain diameter range and were permitted to negotiate with loggers regarding the cutting of those trees. However, these provisions were designed to restrict the scope of their claims and not entirely impede logging.[25]

As knowledge of the level of disputation percolated up to senior government officials and awareness among external actors grew, a stop-gap measure was required that entailed suspension of cutting of all resin trees. Resin tapping would be protected from the operations of logging companies, but only until the government could initiate developmental alternatives that, in the opinion of senior officials, would improve the livelihoods of these rural groups. As Ty Sokhun wrote to forest concessionaires: "Permission to resume the cutting of resin trees can be discussed after you have finished and presented the results of the above study" (Ministry of Agriculture, Forestry and Fisheries, 2001).[26]

The rise of the resin issue occurred largely in the absence of direct pressure from external actors, with their in-house experts and the consultants they engaged largely ignorant as to what resin trees were, or to the prevalence of resin tapping. An indication of this is the way the provisions on resin were rewritten in a draft forest law prepared under the Asian Development Bank Sustainable Forest Management Project of 1999–2000. Provisions on *Dipterocarp* resin became, in Article 65 of the draft, "harvesting of pine trees and pine resin", with the article stating: "The felling of pine trees before the confirmation of the Forestry Administration that they produce no more resin shall be forbidden" (Asian Development Bank, 1999). In revisions incorporated into the Ministry of Agriculture "final" draft of 30 May 2000, the provisions on *Dipterocarp* resin were reinstated.[27]

As aid donors became aware of the scale of resin tapping, they sought to incorporate the resin tree issue into the reform agenda in ways that contrasted with how the issue was framed within Cambodia's institutional structures. Support was given for the rights of resin tappers to be taken into account in the context of the preparation of "strategic forest concession management plans". However, inventories of timber volumes undertaken to calculate the "sustainable yield" of particular concession areas continued to include resin trees.[28] Reference was made to the "current" ban of their cutting, implying that as new systems to govern forest concession management were enacted, this prohibition could be lifted. In a fundamental sense, the "sustainable forest management" reform agenda promoted by external actors failed to recognize the implications that the prohibition of the cutting of resin trees would have for logging operations.

Contrary to the widely held assumption that external actors were the key agent of restraint in relation to logging, the evolution of the treatment of the resin tree issue was not shaped, at least not decisively, by external pressures. Non-governmental organizations (NGOs) had tutored forest-dwelling communities to enable them to recognize the scope of their rights under Cambodia's forest laws.[29] NGOs also sought to distribute copies of the forestry law widely, helped organize meetings and assisted with the preparation and dissemination of complaint letters. But the impetus for change was largely internal to Cambodia. Resin tapping was an issue that reform-promoting external actors had not enquired into and generally neglected to give much weight within the context of their more abstract support for "sustainable forest management". The production of resin had never been part of the forestry reform agenda they envisaged, and had not been documented as a significant livelihood activity. Indeed, a UN Food and Agriculture Organization (FAO) project was undertaking an inventory of forest resources in Sandan district at the time a resin tapper was murdered for complaining to a Colexim concession subcontractor over the cutting of resin trees.[30] While FAO staff helped to fund the victim's funeral, neither the FAO nor the project's co-sponsor, the UN Development Programme (UNDP), pursued the killing with government counterparts nor sought to publicize the issue. A subsequent project report relating to an inventory of trees that must have entailed the authors viewing hundreds of resin-tapping holes included no mention of resin tapping, with the socio-economics section of the report blandly stating: "Nearly 75% of the population are engaged in farming and forestry for their livelihoods" (Royal Government of Cambodia, UN FAO and UNDP, 1998). This is surely an example of the technocratic mindset of the forester, *par excellence*. It highlights an exceedingly narrow focus on the "resources" to be inventoried.

Much of the political anæmia of the reform agenda related to how it sought to locate forest-dwelling social groups in relation to the business interests that shaped the forest concession system. External actors sought to modify – "to rationalize incentives motivating stakeholders" – the operations of concessionaries by developing new management systems (World Bank, UNDP and UN FAO, 1996: ii). The new planning systems that formed a central part of the shift towards "sustainable forest management" aimed to encourage the participation of forest dwellers. However, these social groups were not seen as significant resource competitors to logging businesses and were thus not given the opportunity to question the legitimacy of industrial logging.

The notion that rural dwellers, 80 per cent or more of the Cambodian population, might ultimately seek to expunge these businesses from the forest areas where they live and overturn the system of extraction was not countenanced. Rather, dialogue over "reform" was a duel-track process. One track involved closed-door meetings between senior government officials such as from the Ministry of Economy and Finance and the Ministry of Agriculture and representatives of aid agencies.[31] The other track entailed discussion, largely conducted in English, by foreign specialists working for multilateral or bilateral donors and NGOs.

But as the contested nature of forests assigned to logging concessions grew due to the rise to prominence of the resin issue, Cambodia's elite came to seek out other uses for forestlands.

"Degraded" forests into plantation businesses

What I earlier termed "appropriation" was, in essence, the process by which forest valuations were narrowed so as to reinforce the notion that timber is the main, and certainly the most important, resource available for extraction from forest areas. This section considers how this "appropriation" of the forested landscape intermeshes with the enclosure of forestlands into plantation schemes. At foundation this involves the practices and normative justifications for converting forest areas for "social benefit" when the timber values of these areas have been degraded. Resin tappers were key victims of this shift as new justifications came to be found for logging and clearing forests.

Plantations came to prominence from the early 2000s, although many schemes were based on contracts or approvals in principle that had been negotiated from the mid- to late 1990s. Even more than a decade later, much remains unknown in relation to areas of land granted and the nature of the business entities that obtained the "land" concessions, including the identity of their ultimate beneficiaries.

In accounting for the rise of plantation businesses, it is useful to highlight the important legal distinction that exists concerning the purpose of forest and land concessions. Under Cambodia's land law, forests, rivers, temples and so on are classified as "state public property". As such, the law mandates that these assets should be managed in a manner that promotes the public interest. In contrast, land concessions can only be granted on "state private property", which is state-owned land that is deemed to have lost its public interest value. Thus land concessions are recognized as primarily aimed at providing a commercial benefit to the business entity holding the concession right, whereas forest concessions are primarily aimed at promoting the public interest in the "sustainable management" of a state-owned asset. However, there are two twists to this. For land concessions to be (legally) granted in forest areas, the forest must be deemed to have lost its public interest value, which is the claim advanced by state officials in the case of many land concession grants. A second twist is that state-owned companies, such as Chup rubber plantation company (privatized in October 2008), could clear forestland still classified as state public property and claim that such a scheme amounted to a conversion of one type of public interest benefit (forest) to another (rubber plantation).

This set of legal distinctions between "state public" and "state private" property ties directly to the notion of "appropriation" outlined earlier. Integral to the forestry reform agenda was the building of the state's capacity to capture rents generated through logging operations. Justified as the necessary way in which the forest sector was "to be part of the Cambodian development process", the focus on forest concessions that this entailed contributed to a shift in domestic understandings of forest resources (World Bank, 1999: 6). This corroded the claims over trees and forested land, in relation to state institutions and the pre-reform regulatory regime, of forest-dwelling groups. A key effect of the reform agenda was to add legitimacy to patterns of forest resource utilization focused on the production of timber. However, the degrading of these (timber-related) forest values that the reform agenda had functioned to elevate gave the ruling elite a key opportunity to work with closely connected businesses to evade the restraints imposed on the forest concession system. The case of the Tum Ring rubber plantation shows how this occurred.

Forest concessions into plantations

Tum Ring commune is located in the north of the central province of Kampong Thom. It is situated inside a forest block known as Prey Lang in what remains one of the more heavily forested parts of Cambodia. This area was one of the few Cambodian landscapes that may not have been subject to periodic burning associated with a change in the ecological composition towards a more open, deciduous forest. In the early to mid-1990s five forest concessions were granted and roads were driven into the heart of the forest block. As a lucrative area for timber extraction, particularly well-connected companies received logging rights.[32]

Rubber came to Tum Ring as part of government attempts to make use of red soil areas that experience had shown to be suitable for its cultivation. In October 2000 Hun Sen authorized 4,000–5,000 hectares of red soil to be excised from forest concessions located in the Tum Ring commune and granted to the (then) state-owned rubber company Chup (Ministry of Agriculture, Forestry and Fisheries, 2001). Studies subsequently undertaken provided support for the decision to convert the forestland into a plantation development. One such study was undertaken in November 2000 by the Kampong Thom Provincial Department of Agriculture. In justifying the benefits of reassigning the forestland to Chup, the author claimed that the area was degraded to the point of having "no commercial value trees" (Aem Phean, 2000). Likewise, another Department of Agriculture study noted of the 5,000 hectares that "this area is mostly old farm ... and relatively rare evergreen forest growing along the stream" (Hie Dimoly, 2001). The planting of rubber was therefore encouraged:

> In order to enhance the people's living conditions through increase of the source of income derived from rubber plantation, poverty reduction of remote people and contribution to national economic growth it is necessary to plant rubber trees for the export that helps to protect the environment and reduce natural drought and heat and soil erosion. (Aem Phean, 2000)

In February 2001 the acting minister of agriculture, Chan Tong Yves, led a follow-up study in conjunction with officials from the para-statal Chup and the Provincial Departments of Agriculture and Forestry. The report on this one-day trip to the commune noted "some areas being mixed evergreen forest, some secondary forest, some low grade forest". It endorsed the development of the rubber plantation, noting that if the red soil areas were removed from the forest concessions and granted to Chup, the company would try to plant rubber on 100–200 ha in the first year, expanding in the following years. At the same time, the General Directorate of Rubber Plantations would "examine the actual possibility of raising awareness and motivating farmers to plant rubber on a family scale on their own small chamkar land" (Ministry of Agriculture, Forestry and Fisheries, 2001).[33] These "family-scale" plantations, supported by long-term loans, were to be promoted around the core industrial plantation. Hun Sen, in a handwritten annotation to this report, endorsed the scheme, urging Chan Tong Yves to "please continue this work, cutting the area of red soil out of the logging concession and giving it to Chup Rubber to plant rubber and motivate villagers there to plant family rubber trees".

Hun Sen subsequently visited the commune by helicopter to promote the plantation development and inaugurate the Hun Sen-Tum Ring primary school. During a speech in the commune he defined the population's "poverty" in terms of their swidden cultivation systems and resin collection, promising that the plantation development would improve living standards. The new plantation business, Hun Sen claimed, was critical for improving Chup's future economic efficiency and also important in "rehabilitating the ecological balance of the region, which was degraded to some extent by logging". The "project would also create jobs and generate revenue for the poor, thereby complementing the government's efforts to alleviate [the] poverty of our population" (Hun Sen, 2001: 1). Rubber would replace the "meager revenue" generated from rice, "slash-and-burn farming" and the collection of forest by-products such as vines, rattan and wood resin. Hun Sen claimed that in most cases "the revenue is not adequate to meet the living costs of our people" (ibid.: 2).

To reassure villagers, Hun Sen also made a number of comments related to the logging of resin trees. These comments, captured on video footage, were not included in the official version of the speech, excerpts of which were subsequently posted on the Cambodia New Vision website.[34] In these impromptu remarks, directed more to government officials than to the villagers present, Hun Sen noted: "Because we used to draw concession maps including provincial towns, including district towns, communes, villages of the people, included them in the concessions. Therefore I ask you to cut."[35] He reassured villagers concerning their resin trees:

> People in Tumring go into the forest, they aren't allowed to collect vines, they aren't allowed to collect rattan ... they don't let you go to collect liquid resin

or dry resin. So don't be too mean. If you are too mean, I will eliminate the forest concession. If we develop this way, it isn't any different than investment which leads to the loss of villagers' land. I cannot accept this kind of investment. So, go to work. But, friends, don't go cut trees. And I have ordered – whatever forest people are collecting resin, don't cut it. Ty Sokhun, right?[36] You know? The forest where people collect resin these days, don't yet give permission to cut. Because they can only cut if you give your seal. So, forestry officials, if you see forest where people are collecting resin, don't sign for them to cut. If you don't sign for them, they won't cut. And if they dare to cut, they are violating the law. We have to do this very clearly, make this point very clear. And if you stop your investment, no problem. The trees can be kept for 100 years and they won't go bad, don't go bad . . .[37]

Chup's most tangible and immediate impact on villagers residing in the vicinity of the plantation was on their land holdings and access to forest resources. Hun Sen's speech in Tum Ring emphasized their impoverished lives with "unstable incomes", and the benefits that would flow to them through their involvement in the production of an "industrial crop". In addition, swidden farming areas were not recognized as the property of villagers regardless of how long they had been cultivated. Because these areas did not meet government preconceptions of order and notions of efficient cultivation, they were to be replaced with the plantation. Kampong Thom governor Nou Phoeung explained the rationale for appropriating these areas and giving them to Chup: "They are doing slash and burn agriculture and have not much skill in improving their crops" (Bou Saroeun and Carmichael, 2002). Parcels of land were therefore to be exchanged to create a visual appearance of order – undermining the logic that farm areas be chosen at sites of optimal soil quality, water availability and so on, regardless of their proximity to villages.

The internal-external dynamics of this plantation development deserve emphasis. As noted, the elite understood resin tapping in a way that contrasted markedly with how it could be framed within the reform agenda. While for external actors resin was to be slotted into an overarching framework for "sustainable forest management", for the elite resin was to be nominally protected until a "better" alternative could be developed. That better alternative was to be land "development" such as via rubber plantation schemes. The Tum Ring plantation accorded with the leadership's notions of development and progress in creating "stable incomes". In practice it excused the wholesale clearance of the forest, including those resin trees that had earlier been protected from logging. Despite the moratorium on logging in concession areas, logs were available for extraction by the same business entities which formed part of the forest concession system.[38]

Conclusion

A key element of the Cambodian government's "strategies to enhance rural livelihood" is to "promote the expansion of agro-industrial crops such as rubber, cashew nuts, coffee, coconuts and palm oil and many others" (Hun Sen, 2003). An ambition of government officials from the mid-1980s, the impetus to convert forest areas was catalysed by the ideological certitude of the emphasis on poverty reduction in contemporary development agendas. The Tum Ring rubber plantation is an example of a trend in the creation of agro-industrial schemes that has driven an exceptionally high rate of deforestation over the past decade.

Plantations have emerged as one of the dominant agro-social forms of organization in modern Cambodia. Patterns of forest governance supported the enclosure of forestland, legitimated with reference to the denudation of timber supplies (the most important forest "resource") and the imperative that the "poverty" of forest-dwelling communities must be alleviated.[39] This agrarian development model continues to be broadly endorsed by external actors as Cambodia's appropriate economic niche.

This chapter seeks to show how aid donor interaction with the Cambodian elite shaped the shift in types of businesses seeking to harness forest areas. I show, using the example of resin, how conceptions of the "resources" the forest contained and the multitude of social, cultural and environmental values came to be narrowed. Cambodia's forest was redefined as valuable primarily as a repository of timber, and in this sense appropriated. Then, on the pretext that timber-based values had degraded, the ruling class subsequently promoted the conversion of forests into plantation schemes.

Integral to forest policy reform in Cambodia was the enhancement of the state's capacity to capture rents that logging operations generated. Justified as the necessary way in which the forest sector was "to be part of the Cambodian development process", both forest resource extraction and forest policy reform came to focus on logging concessions. This chapter examines the trajectory of forest governance engendered by the promotion of reforms. One element of the shift in patterns of governance related to the narrowing of forest resource valuations to accentuate the significance of timber. Patterns of forest resource utilization focused on production of timber were legitimated, while other types of forest use had their marginal status certified. This ultimately contributed to the undermining of the rights, in relation to state institutions and the pre-reform regulatory regime, of forest-dwelling groups. When the timber values of the forest were later claimed to have been degraded, a pretext was provided for accelerated creation of land "development" schemes.

Appropriation locked in a particular logic to extraction because it implied a devaluation of forest areas as their stocks of timber were exhausted. In Cambodia's case, this occurred in little more than a decade.

Notes

1. Scientific forestry is the dominant framework of knowledge and practice concerning the management of forested landscapes in the modern international system. For a description of the practice and its relation to state power see Scott (1998).
2. On perspectives as constitutive of our knowledge of landscapes, including forested ones, see Greenough and Tsing (2003). On social constructions see Berger and Luckmann (1967).
3. For a discussion of the normative underpinnings of "sustainable forest management" see Cock (2008).
4. On the concept of state socialization see Alderson (2001).
5. The term "forest-rich countries" is taken from World Bank, UNDP and UN FAO (1996: 16).
6. For comments on the implications of this see Duffield (2001: 121–125). Duffield notes that conflict has played a role not only in contributing to the breakdown of state structures and social groupings, but in tying people to landscapes that become *more than ordinarily* essential for their subsistence.
7. A translation is included as an appendix in Prom Tola and McKenney (2003).
8. The Inspection Panel estimated that 90 per cent of the studies undertaken had as their "major emphasis" concession logging (World Bank, 2006: 35).
9. Note that the two reports use these terms to convey the same meaning.
10. Frederick Foxworthy, forest research officer with the Malayan Forest Service, characterized them as follows: "The genus consists of very large trees with relatively small crowns and a high form factor. The buttresses are small, or absent. The total height is often more than 150 feet; trees as much as 180 feet high are not uncommon. Mature trees rise very often to more than 100 feet before the first branch. The average girth is about 7 feet, and the maximum recorded, about 20 feet. The crown is roughly flat, conical or irregular, open, and made up of a few large branches. Sap-wood is usually present in only small amount in large trees" (Burkill et al., 1966: 851).
11. In Cambodia the wood is rated as "second class". It can be used in construction in sheltered locations, but does not weather well unless treated and rapidly rots when placed in soil. Its main industrial use in Cambodia is in the manufacture of plywood. For a description of the dominant species in Cambodia, *Dipterocarpus alatus*, see Burkill et al. (1966: 852–853).
12. Longmuir (2001) notes that the term "earth oil" was used to distinguish it from the "wood oil" that abounded in Southeast Asia.
13. Names include "kĕrung oil" in Malaya, "garjan oil" in India, "kanyin oil" in Burma and "balau resin" in the Philippines.
14. The reasons for this include a rising demand for the essential oil and its use as a fixative in the manufacture of perfume. Alternatives, such as essential oil derived from *Dipterocarp* species found in other parts of Southeast Asia, were increasingly scarce.
15. The PRK is the Vietnamese-backed regime that ruled Cambodia from 1979 to 1989.
16. *Dipterocarpus alatus*.
17. Local needs related to the use of resin as a source of lighting and a sealant on wooden boats.

18. In its instructions on implementing Decree Law No. 35, 25 June 1988 (the Forestry Sector Law), the Ministry of Agriculture, Forestry and Fisheries (1988b) issued advice on resin trees. Chapter 2, section 3.3 stated:

> About cutting trees which villagers have tapped for resin. "Article 17 paragraph (g)." According to technical forestry guidelines, *chhoe teal* [*Dipterocarpus alatus*] must have a diameter of at least 0.47 m at a height of 1.00 meters from the ground in order for it to be permitted to be tapped for resin, when it has a diameter of 1.20 meters, it is to be considered a tree which is too old and must be exploited and removed. Therefore, giving permission to cut trees which villagers have tapped for resin is set as follows:
> 1. As for trees which reach the minimum size permitted to cut, but don't yet have a diameter of 1.20 meters, it is necessary to mediate with the villagers who tapped them and are collecting resin.
> 2. As for trees which have a diameter reaching 1.20 meters, permission can be given to cut without it being necessary to mediate.

19. For a report on this practice see Berelowitch and Reverchon (2004).
20. Details of the complaint are outlined in O'Connell and Bou Saroeun (2000).
21. This included a village in Tum Ring commune in which a resin tapper was killed for complaining over the cutting of resin trees in 1997.
22. On Kem Sokha's earlier role in questioning contracts the Cambodian government had signed with foreign companies see Lee (1995).
23. Articles documenting the rise in visibility of the resin-tree-cutting issue in this period include *Koh Santepheap* (2001), Devine and Van Roeun (2001) and Ham Samnang (2001).
24. Letter No. 33Tor/2001, 18 April 2001.
25. Wolf (1982: 80–81) notes of this type of relationship: "strong central rule often finds support among surplus-producing peasantries, since central rulers and peasants are linked by a common antagonism against power-holding and surplus-taking intermediaries".
26. The letter requested: "Please suspend temporarily the cutting of all trees from which people collect resin in the 2001 coupes of each forest concession or in the forest reserved for exploitation, even if you have negotiated and signed an agreement on suitable compensation for cutting resin trees."
27. See also the comments contained in World Bank (2005a: 48).
28. This is documented in World Bank (2005b: 4, 42 and 96).
29. Phnom Penh-based organizations collaborated with a host of provincial organizations in Cambodia's north. London-based NGO Global Witness, in the role of independent forest crimes monitor, devoted considerable effort to documenting the logging of resin trees.
30. A Global Witness "forest crimes report" of 30 July 2000 reports the killing (Global Witness, 2000). Publication of details of the killing first occurred in Global Witness (2001: 7).
31. A sampling of the World Bank's internal correspondence on these meetings can be found as an appendix to the Bank management response to the claim for a World Bank Inspection Panel investigation of the Forest Concession Management and Control Pilot Project (World Bank, 2005a).
32. The companies were Pheapimex, Colexim, GAT, Everbright and Mieng Ly Heng. They encompassed key regime supporters (Pheapimex), family members of senior leaders (Mieng Ly Heng), the military (GAT), China (Everbright) and Japan (Colexim).
33. *Chamkar* means swidden areas, and in some cases permanent gardens.
34. A website set up to improve Hun Sen's international profile. For background on these public relations efforts see Rosenberg (1998).

35. "Cut" in the sense of "reduction" or "excision" of areas of the forest concession.
36. Director of the Department of Forestry and Wildlife (Forest Administration) from 1999 to 2010. On Ty Sokhun's removal see Neou Vannarin (2010).
37. This quotation is from a partial transcript prepared from a video of Hun Sen's speech in Tum Ring. The transcription was undertaken by Peter Swift.
38. Numerous reports document removal of the timber from the plantation area. It was transported as "firewood" to the Kingwood forest concession factory in Kandal province near Phnom Penh. The factory was operated by Seng Kheang, the wife of Hun Sen's cousin (Hun Chhouch). Royalty rates for firewood of $1 per cubic metre were applied to this timber, as opposed to an average $54 per cubic metre for timber extracted under the guise of forest concessions. Details, including assertions of the family connections, are contained in Barron (2003). For detail on the family connections of the elite involved in logging see Global Witness (2007).
39. An example of this is October 2003 correspondence from a provincial politician to Hun Sen in support of a company requesting permission to construct a 400 km road to connect Mondulkiri to Ratanakiri along the Cambodian-Vietnamese border in exchange for "land concession ... 1 kilometer wide along the road sides (left and right) so that the company will plant rubber-acacia-Chan Kreusna trees and various plants for the company's ... source of income". To allay concerns about any potential damage to the forest it was noted that "the forest in this region suffered completely destruction" (Hibou, 2004, cited in World Bank, 2006: 103).

REFERENCES

Aem Phean (2000) "Request in Principle for the Development of Family Scale Rubber Plantation for 5,000 ha in Tum Ring Commune, Sandan District, Kampong Thom", 27 November, Provincial Department of Agriculture, Kampong Thom.

Alderson, Kai (2001) "Making Sense of State Socialization", *Review of International Studies* 27(3), pp. 415–433.

Asian Development Bank (1999) "Technical Assistance to the Kingdom of Cambodia for the Sustainable Forest Management Project TA 3152-CAM", first draft submitted to Minister of Agriculture, Forestry and Fisheries Chhea Song, Phnom Penh, 27 August.

Associates in Rural Development (1997) "Public Discussion on Forest Land Allocation Issues, Kampong Thom and Kratie Provinces", provincial workshop report, 4 and 16 December, ARD and Cambodian Department of Forestry and Wildlife, Phnom Penh.

—— (1998a) "Proceeds of Meeting to Brief the International Community and Senior Officials of the Royal Government of Cambodia on Forest Policy Reform", FORTECH presentation, ARD, Phnom Penh.

—— (1998b) "The Study of Effects of Forests on Rural Livelihoods in Kampong Thom Province, Cambodia", ARD and Cambodian Department of Forestry and Wildlife, Phnom Penh.

Barron, Porter (2003) "Borders Unclear at K Thom Rubber Plantation", *Cambodia Daily*, 2 September, pp. 1, 13.

Berelowitch, Irene and Antoine Reverchon (2004) "The Stripping of Cambodia: Legal Loopholes Allow Plunder of Country's Precious Timber Resources", *Guardian Weekly*, 25 June–1 July, p. 27.

Berger, Peter L. and Thomas Luckmann (1967) *The Social Construction of Reality: A Treatise in the Sociology of Knowledge*, London: Penguin.

Bou Saroeun and Robert Carmichael (2002) "Farmers Appeal against Rubber Baron", *Phnom Penh Post*, 1–14 March, p. 6.

Burkill, I. H., William Birtwistle, Frederick W. Foxworthy, J. B. Scrivenor and J. G. Watson (1966) *A Dictionary of the Economic Products of the Malay Peninsula*, 2nd edn, Kuala Lumpur: Ministry of Agriculture and Co-operatives.

Cock, Andrew Robert (2008) "Tropical Forests in the Global States System", *International Affairs* 84(2), pp. 315–333.

de Beer, Jenne H. and Melanie J. McDermott (1996) *The Economic Value of Non-Timber Forest Products in Southeast Asia*, 2nd edn, Amsterdam: Netherlands Committee for IUCN.

Devine, Alex and Van Roeun (2001) "Villagers Decry Loss of Forests for Timber", *Cambodia Daily*, 18 May, p. 12.

Duffield, Mark (2001) *Global Governance and the New Wars: The Merging of Development and Security*, London: Zed Books.

Fernow, Bernard Edward (1913) *Brief History of Forestry in Europe, the United States and Other Countries*, 3rd edn, Toronto, ON: University Press.

Global Witness (2000) "Forest Crime Report, Sandan District, Kampong Thom", 30 July, Global Witness, Phnom Penh.

—— (2001) "The Credibility Gap – And the Need to Bridge It: Increasing the Pace of Forestry Reform", briefing document, May, Global Witness, London.

—— (2007) *Cambodia's Family Trees: Illegal Logging and the Stripping of Public Assets by Cambodia's Elite*, London: Global Witness.

Greenough, Paul R. and Anna Lowenhaupt Tsing (2003) *Nature in the Global South: Environmental Projects in South and Southeast Asia*, Durham, NC: Duke University Press.

Ham Samnang (2001) "Villagers Say Loggers Are Illegally Cutting Down Resin Trees", *Cambodia Daily*, 18 January, p. 10.

Hibou, Béatrice (2004) "Quel Modèle Concessionnaire?", in Jean-François Bayart, Romain Bertrand, Béatrice Hibou, Roland Marchal and Françoise Mengin (eds) *Le royaume concessionnaire: libéralisation économique et violence politique au Cambodge*, FASOPO, December, available at www.fasopo.org/publications/cambodge_bh_1204.pdf.

Hie Dimoly (2001) "Study Group on the Red Land in Tum Ring Commune, Sandan District, Kampong Thom Province", 21 February, Department of Agriculture, Kampong Thom.

Hun Sen (2001) "Address to the Inauguration of Hun Sen-Tumring Primary School and the Launch of a Rubber Seed Plantation in Kampong Thom Province", Cambodia New Vision, 29 August, available at http://cnv.org.kh/en/.

—— (2003) "The Economic Government and Strategies to Enhance Rural Livelihood", keynote address at Cambodia Development Research Institute seminar for provincial and municipal leaders, Phnom Penh, 12 May.

Kem Sokha (2001) "Attention to Excellency Minister of Agriculture, Forestry and Fisheries Regarding to Colexim, Mien Ly Heng, GAT, and Pheapimex Company that Are Violating the Resin Trees of People, Number 022 K.Sor.B.P.", 31 January, Phnom Penh.

Koh Santepheap (2001) "Forest Concession Companies Impact on People in Mountain Areas", *Koh Santepheap*, 8 May.

Lee, Matthew (1995) "Divided We Fall: Party Leadership Coup Weakens Coalition Member", *Far Eastern Economic Review*, 27 July, p. 31.

Longmuir, Marilyn V. (2001) *Oil in Burma: The Extraction of "Earth Oil" to 1914*, Bangkok: White Lotus.

Malcolm, Teresa (1998) "Villagers Losing Land", *National Catholic Reporter* 34(27), 8 May, p. 9.

Ministry of Agriculture, Forestry and Fisheries (1988a) "Forestry Sector Law, *kret chbab* Number 35", 25 June, Department of Forestry and Wildlife, Phnom Penh.

—— (1988b) "Instructions on Implementing the *kret chbab* on the Management of the Forestry Sector, Number 1446, ror.prar.kar.ror", 8 November, Department of Forestry and Wildlife, Phnom Penh.

—— (2001) "Report on the Results of a Visit to Study the Area of Red Soil Which Could Be Planted in Rubber in Kampong Thom", Royal Government of Cambodia, Phnom Penh.

Neou Vannarin (2010) "PM Removes Forestry Chief, Citing Failures", *Cambodia Daily*, 7 April.

O'Connell, Stephen and Bou Saroeun (2000) "Ethnic Oiltappers Feel Logging Company Heat", *Phnom Penh Post*, 12–25 May.

Prom Tola and Bruce McKenney (2003) *Trading Forest Products in Cambodia: Challenges, Threats, and Opportunities for Resin*, Phnom Penh: Cambodia Development Resource Institute.

Rosenberg, Tina (1998) "Hun Sen Stages an Election", *New York Times*, 30 August, p. 26.

Royal Government of Cambodia, UN FAO and UNDP (1998) "Report on Establishment of a Forest Resources Inventory Process in Cambodia", Project CMB/95/002, FAO, Phnom Penh.

Scott, James C. (1998) *Seeing Like a State: How Certain Schemes to Improve the Human Condition Have Failed*, New Haven, CT: Yale University Press.

Wolf, Eric R. (1982) *Europe and the People without History*, Berkeley, CA: University of California Press.

World Bank (1999) "Cambodia: A Vision for Forestry Sector Development", background note, 1 February, World Bank, Washington, DC.

—— (2005a) "Bank Management Response to Request for Inspection Panel Review of the Cambodia Forest Concession Management and Control Pilot Project (Credit No. 3365-KH)", 8 March, World Bank, Washington, DC.

—— (2005b) "Report and Recommendation. Cambodia: Forest Concession Management and Control Pilot Project (Credit No. 3365-KH and Trust Fund 26419-JPN)", Inspection Panel, 30 March, World Bank, Washington, DC.

—— (2006) "Investigation Report. Cambodia: Forest Concession Management and Control Pilot Project (Credit No. 3365-KH and Trust Fund 26419-JPN)", Inspection Panel Report No. 35556, 30 March, World Bank, Washington, DC.

World Bank, UNDP and UN FAO (1996) "Cambodia Forest Policy Assessment", Report No. 15777-KH, 14 August, World Bank, Washington, DC.

World Food Programme (2001) "Forestry and Food Security: A First Attempt at Nation-wide Analysis", Vulnerability Analysis and Mapping, WFP Cambodia, Phnom Penh.

5

Incomplete mechanisms for conflict resolution: The case of Mt Pulag National Park, Philippines

Masahide Horita and Doreen Allasiw

Introduction

Resources are polymorphic. The same set of physical constituents can be defined as different kinds of resources, according to the ways in which human beings see their potential functions and uses. Thus there is inherent plurality in the definition of natural resources, which corresponds to the multiple possibilities of utilizing them. The plurality of natural resources leads to multiple systems of governance, and different governance systems could themselves produce a conflict through overlapping or ambiguous jurisdictional boundaries.

This plurality sometimes causes conflict between different uses of the same natural resources. Rivers often become sources of conflict over different usages, such as water use and flood control. On one hand, those who are responsible for operating upstream dams, with a duty to serve the population with sufficient water, may have their primary interest in storing as much water as possible in reservoirs for fear of possible scarcity. On the other hand, all the land might be put under excessive flood risk unless these operators decide to open the water gates and release enough water downstream at a sufficiently early stage. Resources are not just polymorphic and socially constructed, but also inherently conflictual; ever-changing definitions and social meanings of a certain physical being as resources can all be a cause of potential conflict with other definitions and social priorities.

Governance of natural resources: Uncovering the social purpose of materials in nature, Sato (ed.), United Nations University Press, 2013, ISBN 978-92-808-1228-2

The objective of this chapter is to consider what is the nature of such conflicts and how they are coped with. An attempt is made to shed light on a rather complex and ambiguous structure of resource conflict and resolution schemes. The point to be made here is that the plurality of natural resources leads to their conflicting uses, which in turn tend to make their governance systems inevitably incomplete as all logical possibilities of such conflicts are not describable *ex ante*. The chapter also introduces some examples of consequences that arise from the incompleteness of governance systems. A case is drawn from indigenous dispute resolution in the mountainous region of the north Philippines, where a series of land disputes filed over a long period has seen significant changes in the relevant legal and administrative frameworks. The case is illustrative of what we see as a web of polymorphism in governance of forest resources, each striving for priority in its definition, privilege and control over the resources.

In this chapter, three significant theoretical issues surrounding dispute resolution mechanisms in resource management are discussed: meta-level conflict resolution; complete and incomplete mechanisms; and multiple and overlapping legal frameworks. The next section introduces the fundamental debate that surrounds this theoretical issue – that of meta-level conflict resolution. The following sections delve into detail about how this fundamental debate manifests itself in dispute resolution systems, and provide examples of how these issues have been explored using a case study from a real resource conflict: the governing of Mt Pulag in the Philippines. Before discussing these issues in detail, the chapter provides an explanation of the background and an overview of the case discussed, as well as a description of the methodology employed to generate the discussion.

Resource conflicts in Mt Pulag – An overview

Mt Pulag is the second-highest mountain in the Philippines at 2,922 metres above sea level. It was proclaimed a national park in 1987. Recently, this mountain attracted attention when its control was feared to be fragmented, ironically by those responsible for its protection. According to Pinel (2009), the mountain is historically perceived to have been governed by no single ethnic or tribal group, but rather considered as shared resources. This does not simply mean that the whole mountain is divided into subsections of jurisdiction; the layers of jurisdiction, such as ethnicity, administration and ancestral domains, are not clearly separable and their boundaries are also ambiguous. The resulting complexity has become the cause of various conflicts between different groups over control of the mountain.

At one level there are conflicts among indigenous tribal groups. The Kabayan and the Kalanguya Tribal Organization (KTO), for example, have sought entitlement as ancestral domain holders. Their attempts first had their basis in the authority of the Department of Environment and Natural Resources (DENR), the government agency in charge of managing protected areas such as national parks. However, different laws implemented thereafter, such as the Indigenous Peoples Rights Act (IPRA), blurred the remit of each legal or governmental institution and produced a chaos of legitimacy. This section briefly overviews how each stakeholder responds to this situation and its consequences.

Legal, ethnographic and historical context

According to Pinel's (ibid.) historical review of land resource management in the Philippines, land without legitimate legal titles was traditionally considered to belong to the state, and communal property right was not formally recognized. Rooted in the Regalian doctrine in the Spanish era, this remained unchanged after independence. Contrary to the doctrine, communities around Mt Pulag regarded the lands which they have occupied since time immemorial as their ancestral domain. According to Prill-Brett (1988: 1), the concept of ancestral domain:

> includes (a) the indigenous people's right to avail of direct benefits from the exploitation of resources within its territories; and (b) the right to directly decide how land, water and other resources will be allocated, used or managed ... Ownership of land refers to the possession of a right or rights in respect to that land, and ultimately the legal or customary power to exclude other persons from exercising such rights.

Mt Pulag supplies irrigation to the main rice-producing provinces of the country. The national park covers an area of 11,500 hectares encompassing three provinces: Benguet, Ifugao and Nueva Vizcaya. It was later included as an "initial component" of the Philippine protected area system defined by the 1992 National Integrated Protected Area Systems Act (NIPAS). Around this time the European Union funded the National Integrated Protected Area Programme (NIPAP, locally known as "the programme") with €12.7 million (US$10.7 million) for establishing eight of the initial component parks of NIPAS (Figure 5.1). Mt Pulag was one of the parks included, with an approximate share of US$330,000–350,000.

Mt Pulag (also called "the park") is inhabited by different indigenous groups which define their ethnicity according to their first language.

Figure 5.1 Eight NIPAP sites
Source: National Integrated Protected Area Programme 1996–2001
(www.iapad.org/pa/about_nipap.htm).

Among these groups, the Ibaloi and Kalanguya tribes have the largest population in the park. According to the National Statistics Office, the 14 barangays/villages surrounding and extending across the park had a total population of 13,600 in 2010. One notable feature of this cordillera region is that it is largely governed by indigenous groups, which have held a substantial proportion of governing positions since the early twentieth century (Scott, 1982). The indigenous ethnic groups are not just minorities here.

Following an invitation from the DENR to map out their ancestral domains, in 1996 Kabayan ancestral domain, which covers 80 per cent of Mt Pulag, became the first such domain in the country. Unexpectedly, another law, IPRA, changed perceived power relations when it was implemented in 1997. Initial protected area regulations had not anticipated IPRA, which added to the ambiguous state of park ownership. Pinel (2009: 65) claims these laws "represent only a few of the multitude of laws affecting natural resource management". Further, in the case of Mt Pulag the boundary of the protected area crosses the borders of different indigenous groups as well as local governments. The mountain "represents a particularly complex problem of stakeholder representation and overlapping land tenure and planning authorities" (ibid.). Kabayan ancestral domain, which covers almost the entire park, was awarded to the municipality of Kabayan in 1996. However, following implementation of

IPRA, several other municipalities such as Tinoc, Bokod, Buguias and Kayapa also applied for their own ancestral domains.

This is rather confusing, as IPRA law stipulates that ancestral domains should be awarded to indigenous groups. Mt Pulag, however, presents a unique case because the indigenous groups themselves are the government officials. Due to the political history of the area, where the natives were made self-governing during the American occupation, there is a se-mantic overlap between local governance and indigenous systems. As Pinel (ibid.: 154) argues, "political interest overlapped with cultural interest, and the application for ancestral domain title became a strategy of polit-ical boundary demarcation". Consequently a number of conflicts arose from overlapping domains that are claimed by different municipalities.

Methodology

This chapter employs Ostrom's (1999) institutional analysis and develop-ment framework, in which a primary focus is placed "on how rules, physi-cal and material conditions and community attributes shape action arenas and incentives faced by individuals and hence, how these conditions com-bine to determine outcomes" (ibid.: 1). In the present study, a continuous flow of systemic changes with little inter-institutional coordination is noteworthy, thus how different stakeholders react to such perplexing sequences could enlighten the relationship between their incentives to engage in collective actions and resource governance regimes.

Data were gathered by participatory methods, including focus groups and key informant interviews. Secondary data analysis reviewed rele-vant government policies and programmes. Initial data gathering was conducted in August 2009, with a second visit in March 2010. The 2009 fieldwork was primarily exploratory in nature, with key informants interviewed about the protected area status of Mt Pulag. Purposeful and snowball sampling was used to select informants ranging from govern-ment officials to members of the Protected Area Management Board (PAMB). Interviews included queries on the benefits or disadvantages of Mt Pulag being a protected area and local management of resources.

Other field methods included participant observation during barangay meetings, review of official documents provided by park staff and local government offices and attending a municipal meeting where Mt Pulag representation and management concerns were discussed. During the second visit 30 semi-structured interviews with local residents, govern-ment officials and PAMB members were conducted. The park super-intendent and representatives from the DENR and the National Commission on Indigenous Peoples (NCIP) were also interviewed to contrast the viewpoints of these agencies.

Theoretical framework: Conflict, complexity and incompleteness in natural resources governance

The literature abounds with both theoretical and practical examinations of conflict resolution over natural resource use. There have been extensive reviews of various mechanisms and legal/policy frameworks within specific fields (e.g. Humphreys, 2005; Balliet, 2010). What distinguishes this chapter from these prior contributions is the viewpoint that conflict resolution mechanisms could and do themselves conflict with each other, and this calls for a meta-decision question of how to resolve such conflicts over resolution schemes. More concretely, when a conflict arises from mutually inconsistent claims to the use of certain common resources (e.g. a section of a forest), how does each party attempt to resolve it? And, more importantly, when they fail to agree on how to resolve the conflict, how do they react to that situation?

When, for example, two parties both conceive they are claiming for mutually exclusive use of the same section of a forest, each party may propose a resolution scheme that could potentially favour one over another. As a result they may fail to agree on any proposal, including those from a possible third party. They may then be obliged to defend their proposals by suggesting which principle should be employed in distinguishing one proposal from the others. Or the two parties may each propose a different set of principles, and now face a question of which principle is to be employed based on what principle. The resulting infinite spiral is notoriously prevalent in real-world disputes over the use of natural resources. It is hence our primary interest to highlight this meta-decision issue in the current problem and discuss how this analytical perspective could help to understand the complexity regarding the real face of multifaceted, polymorphic natural resources.

Meta-level conflict resolution

Attempts have been made to tackle the meta-decision problems over choice of resolution schemes in resource governance. The natural temptation is to write a new, more inclusive and exhaustive scheme that can deal with a meta-decision problem at a level one step higher than existing schemes.

An example can be drawn from river basin management. When a river flows through the territories of multiple sovereign states, a conflict could arise from water resource development in the upper riparian countries, as their actions can cause possible scarcity of water in downstream countries. The construction of a barrage by a downstream country at its border with the upstream country could cause transboundary inundation. There are thus a number of international treaties (e.g. the Indus Water Treaty and the Nile Waters Treaty) and co-riparian organizations established for building trust and collective decision-making. Similar examples can be found at a smaller geographical scale (Chapter 6 in this volume introduces Japan's recent attempt to establish a regional committee for coordinating riparian interests at the national level). In these settings member countries (or units of governance) agree a set of procedures or norms on each country's actions that could affect the state of the river or its basin, which are expected to act as an institutional device for preventing destructive confrontation.

These institutions are designed to provide an arena where all stakeholders can share their collective interests and identify the potential value of cooperation. Their primary function is to remove ambiguity as to what action is to be allowed and which claim by each disputant is considered legitimate over its counterclaims. However, history shows that any such institution cannot exhaustively cover, let alone resolve, all possible claims made by the concerned parties. As soon as one formalizes a procedure that can respond to a certain course of actions, others find an element of ambiguity that makes the procedure inconclusive in its ruling. The lack of a formal procedure concerning transboundary environmental impact assessment in the Mekong River basin, for example, has evoked the need for an alternative arena among the riparian countries (Matsumoto and Nakayama, 2010). As a consequence, additional clauses may be added to the original procedure, or an additional body of judgement may be created to eliminate the ambiguity. There is always a possibility, however, that the revised scheme again reveals yet another element of ambiguity, and thus the situation continues to proliferate.

Similar trends can be seen in environmental and social safeguard policies regarding large-scale development projects. Currently, most major development agencies have their own operating policies and/or guidelines that set out procedures for monitoring possible adverse effects of development projects (cf. World Bank, 2011; Asian Development Bank, 2009). The development of a dam or a highway necessitates exclusive use of land resources, which often interferes with current entitlement to the use of land, rivers, forest and so on. At times grievances are put forward by those affected by these projects, and historically there have been a number of cases where there were criticisms for not handling such grievances appropriately – see, for example, the case of Jamuna Bridge in Bangladesh (World Bank, 1996).

Thus the tendency is to develop a system of conflict resolution within an existing legal framework as part of a project package. Such a system is expected to ensure the interests of the affected people are not underrepresented and all possible problems are handled in compliance with the normative principles of both the relevant country and the international community. A typical method is to establish a grievance redress committee, usually set up in each affected community, with procedures for selecting members, organizing hearings from disputants and delivering a resolution.

It has thus been observed that there are an increasing number of development projects with complex, multilayered and detailed dispute resolution schemes to cover any possible situation in a dispute (e.g. Asian Development Bank, 2010). The orientation of such an approach is towards completeness of the resolution system, such that any new problem can be handled within the system as it foresees all the logical combinations of possible situations exhaustively.

Whether such exhaustivity is ever possible, or even practically sensible, is the central question this chapter attempts to address. Surely there are merits to having a complete system where theoretically or practically possible. One might argue that even if complete systems are not realistically possible, attempts towards completeness should still be desirable or imperative. However, such an attempt may possibly produce overly inefficient systems, as it may be prohibitively costly to maintain a higher-level conflict resolution scheme when the probability of using such institutions is significantly small. Those who argue for completeness might still claim that lack of finer and more complete systems could leave some potential disputant in a disadvantageous or oppressed state. It is therefore mandatory to examine carefully what problem might occur from abandoning an attempt (possibly everlasting) towards complete resolution schemes if we decide to leave some part of the system deliberately incomplete. The next section explores the merits and demerits of having such incomplete systems.

Complete and incomplete dispute resolution mechanisms

As argued by Grimble and Chan (1995: 117), "many natural resources are not owned or managed privately but are rather common or public resources ... typically there are multiple users acting competitively and numerous stakeholders". Most often, resource governance cuts across social, economic and political jurisdictions. This cross-cutting sometimes causes ambiguity as to which jurisdictive system is to be followed; and different interpretations create multiple possibilities for schemes for conflict resolution. Due to the logical infiniteness in questioning a set of principles to justify any level of schemes for conflict resolution, one is never able to write a scheme that fully resolves the typical meta-decision problem. Nevertheless, in reality the goal is to write a scheme with which all the parties involved can agree. Their agreement with a particular scheme by no means implies they have agreed on all the principles as to how challenges against that scheme at any higher level should be resolved. In that sense these schemes are incomplete, as they have not exhaustively explored all the logical combinations of deontic claims and counterclaims. Yet the parties involved still choose to make such an incomplete agreement and manage many possible conflicts through the agreed scheme.

Questions to be posed here are when and why people do or do not agree on an incomplete scheme. A number of attempts have been made to explore the merits and demerits of having an incomplete agreement, as well as what it means. Among these, the schools of law and economics have extensively tackled the issue of incomplete mechanisms from the viewpoint of contract theory. In general, the concept of incompleteness in any system or mechanism is based on the general assumption that it is difficult to specify future actions, schedules and contingencies precisely in advance; thus discussions on the foundations of incompleteness are often based on the constraints or costs associated with uncertainty, unverifiability, unforeseeable contingencies, indescribability and bounded rationality.

Studies on the inevitability of incompleteness often make reference to Williamson's (1979) arguments on the trade-offs between completeness and incompleteness in economic governance structures. Using the notion of transaction cost, Williamson argues that it is possible to characterize the main governance structures using transaction costs. In this argument, "governance structures" are referred to as the framework within which transactions are decided. A central idea is that "ideal" transaction or structural completeness entails the specification of "all relevant future contingencies pertaining to [the transaction] with respect to both likelihood and futurity" (ibid.: 236). However, Williamson (ibid.: 237) notes that completeness is apt to be prohibitively costly, if not impossible:

> First, not all future contingencies for which adaptations are required can be anticipated at the outset. Second, the appropriate adaptations will not be evident for many contingencies until the circumstances materialize. Third, except as changes in states of the world are unambiguous, hard contracting between autonomous parties may well give rise to veridical disputes when state-contingent claims are made.

Hart and Moore (1999) support the view that incompleteness is a common aspect of reality. Even when all obligations are specified in advance, a contract is considered incomplete if the parties wish to add contingent clauses but are prevented from doing so by the fact that the state of nature cannot be verified (or because states are too expensive to describe *ex ante*) (Maskin, 2002).

Case example: The Protected Area Management Board

Incomplete systems of resource governance were observed in Mt Pulag in the presence of the PAMB. The PAMB is a body expected to address structural aspects, such as the adjudication of disputes that arise from the interpretation of the rules of resource governance. Multiple actors within and outside may have divergent interests and strategic choices among and within both customary and state institutions. Perceived alternatives to agreement may expand, especially within the Philippines and Mt Pulag's general management plan, where a complex and contradictory system of American land titles, agricultural land reform certificates, national forests and changing ancestral domain and land property rights underlie the shared sacred landscape (Prill-Brett, 1994, 2003).

As noted in Pinel (2009), "the programme" assumed that the conflict of interest among local and indigenous communities would be overcome by a shared interest in managing a nationally defined critical resource. The final progress report to NIPAP cited municipal boundary disputes as a main reason for stalemate on park boundaries. It said that key actors organized conflicting interests into opposing proposals, and did not represent the local communities' true sentiments – a perception shared by some but not all PAMB members. Healey (1997, 1999) suggested that the PAMB may have provided a setting to forge shared interests and plans to be implemented by partnering jurisdictions, if the perceived rights and alternatives had remained clear and stable. At the time when mediation of these interests was most critical, some parties saw a new opportunity to meet the interests through IPRA combined with local political authority in the Local Government Code. PAMB members who initially advocated people's participation in co-management switched perspectives at public hearings when they contrasted IPRA to NIPAS.

As is also partially observed in Pinel (2009), there are three important differences for indigenous PAMB members between rights under IPRA and the previous DENR-issued Certificate of Ancestral Domain Claim. First the DENR no longer administers ancestral domains; rather, the NCIP administers them. Second, with the issuance of a title, the status of an indigenous community changes from stakeholder to landowner. Landowners have primary authority to manage protected areas in accordance with their own ancestral domain plans, stipulated under the Ancestral Domain Sustainable Development Protection Plan. NCIP implementing regulations (which have the force of law) specify that existing ancestral domain claims and lands will be converted to title after verification (NCIP-Cordillera Administrative Region, Gallerdo and Pekas, 2003). Thus land tenure will change so that private and communal lands can receive title, possibly fragmenting control of the protected area. Thirdly,

NCIP regulations state that councils of elders evaluate protected areas within their domains, and then decide if and how to protect them using their indigenous knowledge systems and practices. Domain holders may choose to contract with the DENR, or other government agencies, rather than be consulted as a stakeholder. Regulations oblige national agencies to provide technical assistance and transfer funding to the indigenous community, reversing power relations.

The DENR, as the government body tasked to manage national forests and parks, is bounded by its mandate to respect ancestral rights and culture in its management of protected areas, but not to turn over exclusive control. On the other hand, the NCIP with IPRA gives ancestral domain holders the control and responsibility to incorporate protected area goals into their own plans. Thus by 2000 Kabayan leaders could envisage the possibility of finally "owning" Mt Pulag and controlling the park and its surrounding areas, rather than sharing jurisdiction with the DENR. At the same time, the KTO leaders saw a new opportunity within both NIPAS and IPRA to change the balance of power and wrest some control away from the Kabayan.

Thus when the KTO produced a recommendation to manage the park as a Kalanguya domain, Kabayan leaders hardened their position to partner with the government. When the DENR would not recognize/adopt the classification of "ancestral park", Kabayan and Kalanguya leaders turned to IPRA. These two major stakeholders would not agree on how to manage the park and its benefits, when in fact the real issue was who would control these. However, because the outcome of this alternative for each stakeholder remained uncertain, they continued to participate beyond 2001 and "negotiate to avoid agreement" in order to protect their interests and options (Pinel, 2007; Wallihan, 1998).

These observations reveal how opportunity structures provided by overlapping legal and customary institutions affected outcomes of the resolution of conflict between the Kabayan and the KTO. The PAMB, where all stakeholders are ideally represented, embodies collaboration and is expected to have the power to manage conflicting agendas and interests of the members. Nevertheless, members acted in direct contradiction with the PAMB plan and sought other legal alternatives in their claim on the resource. Strategies of some partners included using IPRA, the Local Government Code, international funds, politicians and the co-management institution itself to pursue their interests for resource control.

After 2001, when it became evident that neither the Kabayan nor the KTO could gain control of Mt Pulag as an ancestral domain, both stakeholders shifted competition to outside the PAMB jurisdiction, and turned to the Local Government Code to pursue municipal boundaries as another strategy to claim ownership. Hence the boundary dispute became a dispute between the municipalities of Kabayan and Tinoc.

At present, the PAMB continues to meet and manage the park based on the 2001 general management plan; its varied members include representatives from the Ibaloi and Kalanguya tribes, as well as local government representatives from the municipalities of Tinoc and Kabayan. This suggests that the incompleteness of the PAMB allows flexibility for members to seek the best option on how to manage their resources. In addition, although stakeholders are more intent on their own plans in obtaining ancestral domain titles or the more recent municipal jurisdiction over the park area, they cannot afford to abandon the PAMB but nor can they afford to invest in it with all their authority.

Case example: Traditional dispute resolution – Tongtong

The implementation of several laws that delineate park boundaries opened up dispute over park control. IPRA fostered competition over land ownership and the share of the landscape. Although Mt Pulag probably had environmental and spiritual importance to the majority of stakeholders and leaders who invested in the environmental management programme, the laws called for the landscape to be divided. This inevitably created winners and losers.

In the case of private property disputes among individuals, claimants can choose different justifications and legal claims over the resources. They also have a choice between different institutions for conflict resolution. One has the option to rely on the customary dispute settlement through the council of elders, Tongtong, or to use an official court such as the barangay. Ordinarily, land disputes are first settled through the customary Tongtong dispute resolution by the council of elders before they are brought to official courts. Tongtong is endorsed by the national government to save money on courts and minimize court docket congestion.

Nowadays, Tongtong is integrated with the barangay court. Cases involving members of the same barangays are settled by the village head, assisted by a group of elderly men. Cases which involve parties from different barangays invite a judge or judges from neutral barangays to settle the matter. The settlement is usually accomplished by reconciliation or arbitration. When a dispute is brought to the village head for judgment, his first course of action is to convince the disputants to settle their dispute based on their own satisfaction. If conciliation fails, a formal hearing is held; at the beginning, the disputants are made to swear to the council (village head and elders) to abide by the decision. Witnesses from both parties are presented, and a verdict is delivered immediately if it is not contested by all parties.

However, in the case of Tongtong, should the parties refuse to settle the council requires the disputants to perform a ritual, which usually includes butchering a chicken or a pig to please the spirits and guide them to make the best decision. After the ritual the settlement process is resumed; according to interviews with elders, disputes are always settled amicably whenever the ritual is performed. Tongtong relies on the involvement of the community for the efficient resolution of disputes, because betrayal of public trust is a major offence in the community; one is thus expected to be most honest when disputes are tried in public. Strong communal networks make incomplete social contracts feasible and even effective.

Yet this also becomes a weakness of the system, as was observed in other cases surveyed. Several respondents refused to appear before the council of elders and the community. A person can only be held accountable to the council or the community if he/she appears before them at least once, regardless of whether the person is a respondent or a complainant. Not all disputes among community members are solved through Tongtong. When an agreement is reached by all parties, the problem is settled. But if any disputant refuses to agree and rejects the Tongtong decision, the case may remain unsolved or be appealed at higher courts.

Conflict over land in Mt Pulag has increased after the enactment of decentralization policies. Land titling as a consequence of those policies generates the commoditization and alienation of land. People outside the community are now able to acquire land holdings. As the value of land increases, and as we see further increase in migration and diminution in authority of Tongtong, the way in which conflicts are resolved may be rapidly changing.

Apparently, even in earlier periods, not all cases were resolved through Tongtong, as disputants do not always comply with its decision. Tongtong also has a problem of compliance enforceability. Although the system is authorized by the state to give physical sanctions in terms of fines and imprisonment, such authority has seldom, if at all, been exercised as it contradicts the fundamental principle of bridging a divide in the community. The success of Tongtong thus seems to rely on community trust and cohesion. It has worked in communities with strong group cohesion in which all disputing parties belong to the same community. It has been observed that as heterogeneity in the community increases, the authority and appreciation of such indigenous mechanisms may be decreasing.

Both the PAMB and Tongtong are examples of incomplete dispute resolution systems that are flexible in responding to the complexity of resource issues. As societies and institutions create incomplete mechanisms to deal with unforeseeable resource conflicts, one begins to see the development of overlapping mechanisms, and stakeholders often find themselves with the option of choosing between several methods of dispute resolution.

Multiple and overlapping legal frameworks

The way in which the issue of proliferation is tackled has been extensively studied in the international law community, where proliferation of dispute settlement mechanisms is prevalent. In the context of international dispute settlement, the existence of multiple bodies or mechanisms has been a source of intense discussion. As Oellers-Frahm (2001) observes, this multiplicity has both positive and negative effects. It is positive because people can have more choices of settlement bodies and are thus more likely to find one that all parties can agree with. Furthermore, a greater number of dispute settlement bodies can promote more exhaustive systems for ensuring and monitoring compliance. It is negative because the multiplicity could cause conflicting jurisprudence. The more mechanisms we have, the greater the risks associated with possible contradictions among these mechanisms. The situation surrounding the international law community mirrors that of resource governance, where the fragmentation and decentralization of mechanisms are inherent: some indigenous rules are binding only upon those concerned, and these rules are already reflective of that fact. In Hafner's (2004: 850) views on the current fragmentation of international law systems, one may find curious symmetry with that of resource governance:

> [International law] consists of erratic blocks and elements; different partial systems; and universal, regional, or even bilateral subsystems and sub-subsystems of different levels of legal integration. All these parts interacting with one another create what may paradoxically be called an "unorganized system," full of intra-systematic tensions, contradictions and frictions.

The theory of legal pluralism, which contributes to many of these concepts, has wide-ranging implications for resource governance. Recent studies on such governance have increasingly focused on the coexistence and interaction between multiple legal orders, both state and customary, all of which provide bases for claiming property rights that determine the extent to which individuals gain access to natural resources (e.g. Peluso and Vandergeest, 2001; Benjamin, 2008). Legal pluralism is generally defined as "a situation in which two or more legal systems coexist in the same social field" (Pospisil, 1971, cited in Merry, 1988). This makes it possible for individuals strategically to choose a certain legal framework in defence of their claims for a resource use, a process which is informally referred to as forum shopping. From the viewpoint of meta-decision problems, this situation is interpreted as having no normative agreement as to which legal procedures are to be collectively employed, making the whole system incomplete at the level of determining a forum for resolution.

In situations of legal pluralism, individuals have options of laws to advance their claims: depending on which they choose, the legitimacy of the claims may be affected. The choice of a legal framework may be strategic or self-motivated, being "a matter of expediency, of local knowledge, perceived contexts of interaction, and power relations" (Spiertz, 2000: 191). In one of the earliest works on forum shopping in resource governance, von Benda-Beckmann (1981) reports on an example where an indigenous group, formerly exercising only their local rules, gradually turned to more formal legal forums under statutory law and government enforcement as their contacts with outside communities increased.

Case example: Ambiguous partnerships and overlapping legal frameworks in the Philippines

A look into Philippine laws reveals how different mechanisms of formal and informal dispute settlement coexist, compete against and/or complement each other. The Philippines adopted international conventions for decentralization, indigenous rights and co-management of protected areas through the 1991 Local Government Code, the 1997 IPRA and the 1992 NIPAS. This decentralized park planning to multistakeholder boards comprising local governments and indigenous communities. Thus the PAMB system is defined as co-management because the DENR shares authority for planning and management agreements between representatives from different indigenous groups and local government units (Pinel, 2007). Hence instead of representing transfer of powers and accountability to either the PAMB or its members, co-management in the Philippines remained ambiguous even to its participants.

Larson and Ribot (2004) define this as incomplete decentralization in which the transfer of environmental authority is highly restricted while minimum environment standards are weakly implemented, mainly because they are unclear. Interviews with local residents reveal that they are confused by the division of authority between the NCIP, DENR and even their municipalities and barangays. For example, when illegal loggers are caught, they can reason that there is no barangay ordinance banning logging, hence they think it is not illegal. When the DENR catches illegal poachers, it turns them over to the council of elders for punishment. However, the problem comes with poachers residing outside the community. The residents claim these kinds of situations weaken implementation of laws because it is unclear whose authority can be applied to certain situations. The DENR retained final decision-making power and revenue but without the financial or political resources (and future land ownership) to deliver on the promises of NIPAS. The seeming unwillingness of the national government to share authority over "national" natural resources with local governments conflicted with the Local Government Code. Hence it provided for decentralization of power and decision-making to the local government, and the provisions of IPRA. This conflict of laws unexpectedly reversed power relations. With the implementation of IPRA, the DENR struggled to retain its voice in management decisions, while the NCIP proceeded to issue titles and approve ancestral domains as if the park was not there (Pinel, 2007). As a result, resource governance was challenged by the changes in institutional power relations. Table 5.1 provides a brief description of the three main laws that the different stakeholders use to assert their claims to Mt Pulag.

Table 5.1 Overlapping laws and jurisdictions in the Philippines

Law and year of implementation	Implementing agency	Mandate
National Integrated Protected Areas Systems Act, 1992 (NIPAS)	Department of Environment and Natural Resources, Protected Areas and Wildlife Bureau Regional Office	Propose and designate park boundaries and buffer zones Facilitate crafting and implementation of protected area general management plan Serve as steering committee for Protected Area Management Board
Indigenous Peoples Rights Act, 1997 (IPRA)	National Commission on Indigenous Peoples	Surveying, validation and awarding of certificates of ancestral domain claim Facilitate crafting and implementation of Ancestral Domain Sustainable Development Protection Plan
Local Government Code, 1991	Local government units: national, provincial, municipal, barangay	Decentralization of power, resources and responsibilities to local government units Facilitate crafting and implementation of local government resource management plans

Source: Based on Pinel (2007).

The series of events that ultimately led to the stalemate between the Kabayan and the KTO on the reproclamation and boundary decision of Mt Pulag – as narrated by the park superintendent and verified in interviews with PAMB members – is chronologically arranged as follows. First is the organization of the management board by the DENR, where initial meetings were primarily about park restriction laws. During this time the DENR documented the resources for protection. The entry of NIPAP, which aims to establish eight protected areas in the Philippines including Mt Pulag, marks the second important event. This is also the time that boundary finalization was discussed for the reproclamation of Mt Pulag as a national park. Unexpectedly, the implementation of IPRA changed the stakeholders' agenda from co-management to competition for control of the park and the PAMB, which represents the third stage. At this time several PAMB members left during a meeting and never came back, giving the board no other choice but to look for replacements. With the new members, the PAMB tried to start again to work together but was unable to resolve the problems. Meanwhile the NIPAP funds from the European Union ended in 2001, and local politicians and stakeholders strategically shifted their competition for control to other arenas and laws while continuing to adopt policies on the PAMB.

Ironically, the apparent mutual interest in reproclaiming the park for co-management ruptured into cross-cutting conflicts and stalemate between the DENR and NIPAP, the municipality of Kabayan and the Kalanguya domain advocates. Although many factors converged, Pinel (2007) highlights two underlying conflicts that stand out from the stalemate. First was the perceived conflict between park designation and potential future private property rights, a conflict only temporarily suppressed by the promise of projects to be funded by NIPAP. Second, there were conflicts between Kabayan politicians and the KTO to represent people's interests, control programme resources and control the landscape within and around the park.

Sometime in early December 1999 the KTO conducted a public hearing on the redesignation of Mt Pulag for co-management under NIPAS, where NIPAP staff underscored the aspiration to create a Kalanguya ancestral domain as a framework for controlling and protecting resources for the Kalanguya people. With the objective of gaining the support of the Kalanguya without necessarily abandoning the Ibaloi, the mayor suggested Mt Pulag be managed not as a national park but as an ancestral domain park, and the name changed to Mt Pulag Ancestral Domain Plan. He rationalized that this name will include everyone, regardless of tribal affiliation.

A scheduled Ibaloi meeting was moved due to lack of attendance. However, before the new date, the PAMB decided to hold an interim meeting to decide on a general management planning committee and process. During this meeting, the PAMB Executive Committee with NIPAP staff members reviewed the results of the Kalanguya hearing and concluded that people did not trust the DENR and were confused by the many overlapping and frequently changing laws. In spite of this, the European Union and NIPAP directors pushed for the creation of a general management plan that would leave the question of control undecided. It becomes evident that NIPAP staff wanted to succeed in their mission and timeframe; but major actors were unwilling to make a plan without deciding the question of control.

Kabayan politicians were informed of these developments and decided to hold their own consultation meeting on the control of Mt Pulag, even before the scheduled Ibaloi public hearing and PAMB general meeting held in the same month. During the meeting the former vice-mayor of Kabayan, who also chaired the committee to obtain the 1996 Certificate of Ancestral Domain Claim for Kabayan and served as lawyer-representative of the NCIP, emphasized the power of IPRA to deliver ownership of ancestral domains and land. He asserted that the Kabayan had the largest portion in Mt Pulag and Kabayan includes the Kalanguya domain, not the other way round. The discussion revolved around whether the park should be managed under NIPAS and the management board, or be locally managed. After intense discussions, a position paper was drafted to declare Mt Pulag not a national park but an ancestral domain park. This was later presented at a public rally. The resulting public outcry and community conflicts quickly escalated to concerns about who would control the park, the resources and the PAMB – would it be the KTO, the municipality of Kabayan or the DENR?

During the PAMB general management workshop a NIPAP staff member tried to resolve the conflict between the KTO and the Kabayan municipality by explaining that both can benefit from the general management plan. He encouraged the representatives present to cooperate in crafting its content. However, both parties objected, and disputed the legitimacy of the management plan since major stakeholders did not yet agree on the designation as a park.

These and many other examples show that multiple legal frameworks are a product of incomplete mechanisms, which in turn are attempts to create schemes to deal with complex resource conflicts; all of which begin from the need to address meta-level questions of conflict resolution, as yet showing no sign of convergence. Climbing up a ladder of meta-level conflict resolution may have no end. As legal pluralism and resulting forum shopping are inevitable reality here, this complexity and ambiguity could perhaps only be tackled by exploring what discursive forum can be self-sustained in the face of disputed institutions and procedures.

Towards logical pluralists' turn in resource governance

This chapter illustrates how incompleteness, ambiguity and polymorphism play a role in conflict resolution over natural resource use from both theoretical and practical perspectives. The issues presented here, including indeterminability of jurisdictional boundaries, availability of multiple legal frameworks, need for meta-level conflict resolution and resulting strategic behaviours, all constitute familiar parts of everyday life surrounding resource use in many communities. Most are arguably rooted in the polymorphic nature of natural resources: multiplicity in their definition and continuous transformation in reaction to their interconnected subsystems.

An empirical examination into the case of Mt Pulag provides a clue in the question as to when the multiplicity of dispute settlement mechanisms in resource governance produces desirable or undesirable outcomes. It is also an issue of project design concerning how disputes that might arise from conflicting resource use should be coped with. Solutions often proposed are additional schemes for conflict resolution, but the discussion in this chapter provides a ground to argue that such an intervention may not always be effective. It could merely add yet another layer of fragmentation to existing governance systems with no recognition by the involved parties. Rather, a traditional mechanism once disregarded by the modern systems might prove to play a better role as a result of careful analysis of what resolution scheme the people truly need.

Acknowledgement

The authors acknowledge assistance from Lisa Yagasaki, Ali Muhyidin and Anthony Odoemena at the University of Tokyo in completing this chapter.

REFERENCES

Asian Development Bank (2009) "Safeguard Policy Statement", Asian Development Bank, available at www.adb.org/documents/safeguard-policy-statement.
—— (2010) "Involuntary Resettlement Assessment and Measures: BAN: Padma Bridge Project", Asian Development Bank, available at www2.adb.org/Documents/Resettlement_Plans/BAN/35049/35049-01-ban-rp-02.pdf.
Balliet, D. (2010) "Communication and Cooperation in Social Dilemmas: A Meta-Analytic Review", *Journal of Conflict Resolution* 54(1), pp. 39–57.
Benjamin, C. E. (2008) "Legal Pluralism and Decentralization: Natural Resource Management in Mali", *World Development* 36(11), pp. 2255–2276.

Grimble, Robin and Man-Kwun Chan (1995) "Stakeholder Analysis for Natural Resource Management in Developing Countries", *Natural Resource Forum* 19(2), pp. 113–124.

Hafner, G. (2004) "Pros and Cons Ensuing from Fragmentation of International Law", *Michigan Journal of International Law* 25, pp. 849–863.

Hart, O. and J. Moore (1999) "Foundations of Incomplete Contracts", *Review of Economic Studies* 66, pp. 115–138.

Healey, P. (1997) *Collaborative Planning: Shaping Places in Fragmented Societies*, 2nd edn, Vancouver, BC: University of British Columbia Press.

—— (1999) "Institutional Analysis, Communicative Planning and Shaping Places", *Journal of Planning Education and Research* 19, pp. 111–121.

Humphreys, M. (2005) "Natural Resources, Conflict, and Conflict Resolution: Uncovering the Mechanisms", *Journal of Conflict Resolution* 49(4), pp. 508–537.

Larson, A. M. and Ribot, J. (2004) "Democratic Decentralization Through a Natural Resource Lens: An Introduction", *European Journal of Development Research* 16(1), pp. 1–25.

Maskin, E. (2002) "On Indescribable Contingencies and Incomplete Contracts", *European Economic Review* 16(4/5), pp. 725–733.

Matsumoto, K. and M. Nakayama (2010) "Issues of Elaborating Transboundary Environmental Impact Assessment Modalities: Case of the Mekong River", *Asian Journal of Environment and Disaster Management* 2(3), pp. 351–360.

Merry, S. E. (1988) "Legal Pluralism", *Law and Society Review* 22(5), pp. 869–896.

NCIP-Cordillera Administrative Region, L. Gallerdo and G. Pekas (2003) *IPRA Implementing Rules and Regulations*, La Trinidad, Benguet: NCIP-CAR.

Oellers-Frahm, K. (2001) "Multiplication of International Courts and Tribunals and Conflicting Jurisdiction – Problems and Possible Solutions", in J. A. Frowein and R. Wolfrum (eds) *Max Planck Yearbook of United Nations Law* 5, pp. 67–104.

Ostrom, E. (1999) "Institutional Rational Choice – An Assessment of the Institutional Analysis and Development Framework", in Paul A. Sabatier (ed.) *Theories of the Policy Process*, Boulder, CO: Westview Press.

Peluso, N. L. and Peter Vandergeest (2001) "Genealogies of the Political Forest and Customary Rights in Indonesia, Malaysia, and Thailand", *Journal of Asian Studies* 60(3), pp. 761–812.

Pinel, S. Lee (2007) "Co-Management of Cultural Landscapes: Collaborating to Compete at Mt. Pulag National Park, the Philippines", doctoral dissertation, University of Wisconsin – Madison, unpublished, available at http://search.proquest.com/docview/304770349/13B883C692D6995C773/1?accountid=14357.

—— (2009) "Collaborating to Compete – The Governance Implications of Stakeholder Agendas at Mount Pulag National Park, the Philippines", *Planning Theory and Practice* 10(1), pp. 105–129.

Pospisil, L. (1971) *The Anthropology of Law: A Comparative Theory of Law*, New York: Harper & Row.

Prill-Brett, J. (1988) "Preliminary Perspectives on Local Territorial Boundaries and Resource Control", Cordillera Studies Center Working Paper 6, University of the Philippines College, Baguio City.

—— (1994) "Indigenous Land Rights and Legal Pluralism among Philippine Highlanders", *Law and Society Review* 28(3), pp. 687–698.

—— (2003) "Changes in Indigenous Common Property Regimes and Development Policies in Northern Philippines", available at http://dlc.dlib.indiana.edu/archive/00001109/.

Scott, W. H. (1982) *Cracks in the Parchment Curtain and Other Essays in Philippine History*, Quezon City: New Day Publishers.

Spiertz, H. L. Joep (2000) "Water Rights and Legal Pluralism: Some Basics of a Legal Anthropological Approach", in Bryan R. Bruns and Ruth S. Meinzen-Dick (eds) *Negotiating Water Rights*, London: Intermediate Technology Publications.

von Benda-Beckmann, K. (1981) "Forum Shopping and Shopping Forums: Dispute Processing in a Minangkabau Village in West Sumatra", *Legal Pluralism and Unofficial Law* 19, pp. 117–159.

Wallihan, J. (1998) "Negotiating to Avoid Agreement", *Negotiation Journal* 14(3), pp. 257–268.

Williamson, O. E. (1979) "Transaction-Cost Economics: The Governance of Contractual Relations", *Journal of Law and Economics* 22(2), pp. 233–261.

World Bank (1996) "The Inspection Panel: Bangladesh: Jamuna Multipurpose Bridge Project", World Bank, available at http://web.worldbank.org/WBSITE/EXTERNAL/EXTINSPECTIONPANEL/0,,contentMDK:22520379~pagePK:64129751~piPK:64128378~theSitePK:380794,00.html.

—— (2011) "OP 4.12 – Involuntary Resettlement", World Bank, available at http://web.worldbank.org/WBSITE/EXTERNAL/PROJECTS/EXTPOLICIES/EXTOPMANUAL/0,,contentMDK:20064610~menuPK:64701637~pagePK:64709096~piPK:64709108~theSitePK:502184,00.html.

6

Participation and diluted stakes in river management in Japan: The challenge of alternative constructions of resource governance

Naruhiko Takesada

Introduction

Whose victory?

At the end of March 2009 newspapers reported the suspension of construction of the Daidogawa Dam, begun 40 years previously, in Shiga prefecture, Japan (*Asahi Shimbun*, 2009). After many years citizens concerned with the region's natural environment and the river system's sustainability won the fight to halt construction of the dam by the central government authority. The victory was attributed to what had been termed an advanced, democratic process of participatory resource governance, the Yodo River Committee. Most taxpayers in the region approved the decision and environmentalists celebrated.

However, the victory left some people feeling betrayed and helpless; some residents reported that their lives had been rendered meaningless. Ten years previously these people had been displaced from their original village to a newly developed resettlement site as part of the construction plan. They had been contesting the dam since the plan was officially announced in 1968. After a long, painful fight and bitter negotiations, they finally accepted displacement and resettlement in 1994, and were moved to the new village in 1998. Today, they seem to be the only remaining party supporting construction of the dam.

How did this situation come about? Resettled local residents, who once fought fiercely against dam construction, now wish to see its construction.

Governance of natural resources: Uncovering the social purpose of materials in nature, Sato (ed.), United Nations University Press, 2013, ISBN 978-92-808-1228-2

Had they lost their stakes once they received compensation money and accepted the resettlement programme? What was discussed in the participatory and deliberative process of the Yodo River Committee? Examining this case as a process of resource governance in light of the definition of "resources" in the Introduction of this volume reveals an important aspect of "participatory" resource governance that usually goes unnoticed.

As background to the discussion, a brief overview of Japan's water resource management is helpful. In Japan the governance of water resources has historically involved two issues: the dynamism of the relationship between people and rivers, and the displacement of people by dam construction.

Dynamism of the relationship between people and rivers

Before modernization in Japan – that is, before the Meiji era (1868–1912) – the people enjoyed a close relationship with water, especially rivers. Rivers not only provided essential resources but were also a part of nature: the source of Japanese people's lives and culture. They were used for agricultural production and boat transportation routes. In the past, logs from the mountains were transported downstream bound together as rafts. The close relationship between people and rivers included some of the negative characteristics of rivers as well, such as floods. Owing to Japan's topographical conditions, rivers are relatively steep. Concentrated seasonal precipitation or typhoons have occasionally resulted in floods, damaging property and endangering lives. In short, rivers have been both a benefit and a burden to the Japanese people.

During the Meiji era the relationship between people and rivers underwent a transformation with the philosophy of river management (Toyama, 1974). Before the Meiji era, it was very important for local landlords to manage rivers using diversion and other traditional civil engineering technologies, but they could not tame the rivers completely and people sometimes had to endure their negative effects in order to utilize their water on a daily basis. Early management technologies such as *kasumi tei* (levees) were not intended to restrain rivers and streams completely.

After the beginning of the Meiji era (after 1876), modern technology was introduced with assistance from foreign experts. The River Law and two related acts – the Forest Law and Sabo (debris control) Law – were enacted around 1896. The existing comprehensive watershed management practices were divided into different administrative responsibilities and activities among several central government ministries.

With regard to rivers, modern management became possible with the introduction of civil engineering technologies such as levees and dams. This enabled the Japanese to obtain the maximum benefit from surface water resources while lessening the risk of flooding. Modern water resource management consequently deprived people of their close ties with rivers, and they gradually became distanced from waterways because they were surrounded by solid levees; furthermore, lifestyle changes increased the distancing effect of modernization.

The topographical and meteorological conditions in Japan make dams a very efficient means of water resource management (Takahasi, 2004), and nationwide there are more than 2,700 dams (barriers higher than 15 metres, according to the Japanese definition). The post-war period saw particularly massive development of dams as Japan hastened to reconstruct its war-torn economy and revive the livelihood of its people. Dam development had various benefits (such as the increased availability of water and electricity), and made Japan's rapid economic growth possible. At the same time, dams were accused of irreversibly transforming the environment and damaging people's lives.

Since the 1990s movements to reverse the trend of distancing people from rivers have emerged. The environment has become a major issue in Japanese society and anti-dam sentiment can be an important factor in local elections. Anti-dam and anti-public-works movements have been successful in Japanese society, resulting in major changes in river management and the revision of the River Law in 1997.

A participatory development process was officially introduced in river basin management in the 1997 revision of the River Law. When developing management plans, river authorities must consult with experts as well as representatives of the general public and civil society. This new system gathers various opinions and expertise that would not otherwise be included in the planning of water resource management.

Dams and displacement

The construction of dams and reservoirs often requires the displacement of people who inhabit areas that will be submerged as a result of the project; these people have to resettle in other places and rebuild their livelihoods. Displacement implies the loss of not only houses but also agricultural land, forests and access to other natural resources that the local residents have enjoyed for generations.

The compensation and reconstruction of disturbed livelihoods are a complicated issue and no easy task. Displaced people face many difficulties; for example, farmers need to acquire sufficient productive land, while others need to change jobs, find adequate education for their children and maintain social relationships with their displaced community members. Dr Michael Cernea, former senior sociologist of the World Bank, analysed the process of resettlement and livelihood reconstruction and advised the governments of many developing countries attempting to formulate resettlement policies. He described these difficulties as "impoverishment risks", one or more of which can trigger the impoverishment process among displaced or resettled people (Cernea, 2000).

Japan is no exception in facing difficulties caused by displacement and resettlement. In the course of its rapid economic growth, it experienced a number of cases of displacement of communities induced by dam construction. If one examines the scale of displacement caused by dams in Japan, it might seem relatively small. On average, 97 households have been displaced per dam, and these families have received government subsidies for livelihood reconstruction (Takesada, 2009). The largest instance of displacement occurred before the Second World War and involved fewer than 1,000 households. In a sense, the situation in Japan is very different from that in developing countries, where people have been displaced on a much larger scale (in thousands or tens of thousands). However, the different scales of resettlement are mainly the concern of government administrations, because the affected households and individuals are not worried about the scale of the resettlement, but rather the hardship they must endure in their loss and reconstruction of their livelihoods.

Before the Second World War virtually no compensation was given for dam-induced displacement in Japan. The government authorities were not usually concerned with resistance from or negotiation with the local population (Hanayama, 1969). For some time after the war there were no guidelines for the compensation owed in public works projects, including dam construction, even though the necessity of "just compensation" was stipulated in the new constitution. Different ministries and local governments used different standards for compensation. At the same time, there was tremendous pressure towards accelerating development of water resources for hydroelectric power generation to aid the country's reconstruction. During these years of turmoil, people were often displaced without proper compensation and resistance gradually increased under the new democratic constitution.

Consequently, in 1962 the central government introduced "Guidelines for Compensation for Losses in Acquisition of Land for Public Use". These guidelines (it should be noted they were not part of an act) stated that compensation should be in cash and based on the market price for any appropriated property. In-kind compensation was not allowed; furthermore, it was not mandated for project owners to bear responsibility for the reconstruction of livelihoods because monetary compensation for lost assets was thought to be "just compensation" in accordance with the new constitution. Naturally, social disputes related to displacement and compensation prevailed. The necessary preparation and/or negotiation period before dam construction became remarkably prolonged, in some cases up to 10–30 years.

Among the struggles related to dam displacement in Japan, one intense and prolonged conflict resulted in improvements to the government's compensation policy. In the 1960s a major landowner in Oita prefecture in Kyushu region resisted the construction of the Shimouke Dam through a number of lawsuits against the government and physical resistance via a barricade-like fort in his own cedar forest. The famous *Hachinosu-jou Tousou* (Beehive Castle dispute) drew attention to the insufficient compensation policy, and the government thereafter supplemented the existing guidelines by implementing new laws (Takahasi, 2004).

The Act on Special Measures for Reservoir Areas Development was introduced in 1972. This law established a mechanism to develop public infrastructure in reservoir areas according to a specific development plan. Another system was introduced to establish a fund for the purpose of resettlement assistance through monetary contributions from downstream local municipalities that could be supposed to obtain major benefits from a dam.

Even with these compensation policy improvements, many problems continue to prevail during resettlement negotiations. The Kawabe-gawa Dam (Kumamoto prefecture) and Yamba Dam (Gunma prefecture) are frequently mentioned as cases where prolonged negotiations and changes in economic and political environments have brought turmoil to the lives of the affected local residents.

Aside from concern for the natural environment, which could be irreversibly affected by dam construction, the issue of displacement has become a major topic for the anti-dam movement in Japan. In several cases, people who had been fighting against displacement for over 20 years suddenly gained support from international environmentally concerned groups who wished to stop dam construction. Some people have expressed embarrassment regarding this change in public sentiment, asking, "Why now?" If resettlement could be avoided, such a change would probably be welcomed, but in the case of Daidogawa Dam the support arrived too late.

Is democratic resource governance sufficient?

The changes in public attitudes and water management, including dam construction, have produced a new democratic mechanism for water resource governance. However, in the case of the Daidogawa Dam this new mechanism, which achieved a historic victory for environmentalists, has left those affected by resettlement bewildered, disappointed and angry. Even though one would think these people would be strong proponents

of the fight against the dam's construction, the newly instituted democratic resource governance mechanism did not work for them, so they
remain among the dam's few supporters. What brought about this turn of
events? Does this case highlight the limitations of democratic resource
governance in Japan and elsewhere? To answer these questions, the theoretical issues surrounding "participation" and "democracy" in resource
governance are reviewed in the next section.

Theoretical background

Participatory resource governance and participatory development

Participatory resource governance can be seen as a practice aimed at re-
covering democratic control of resource management. As noted, in the
case of water in Japan, resource management was gradually monopolized
by central government and people became detached from nearby resources and rivers. Even local governments lost their control over major
river systems. In other words, participatory resource governance is an
attempt to maintain democratic control over the central government's
decisions regarding water resource management.

Studies on communal resource governance, or "commons", flourished
after Garrett Hardin's famous "Tragedy of the Commons" (Matsushita,
2007), and have attempted to determine the conditions or institutions
that enable long-term and sustainable resource management (Ostrom,
1990). However, one of the limitations of such studies lies in the scale
and boundary of the commons. To determine the conditions for sustainable use of common pool resources, research has tended to concentrate on
small-scale communities with closed boundaries. Further research is required to determine the external factors that affect the commons. Inoue
and Miyauchi (2001) and Inoue (2004) introduce the concept of "collaborative governance" to bridge the gap between the commons and broader
resource governance.

In North America the concept of "adaptive co-management" has been
introduced in the field of sustainable resource use. This concept combines
"adaptive management" and "co-management". Adaptive management is
a strategy characterized by experiments and learning in the face of uncertainty, and is derived from the field of ecology. Co-management, or "collaborative management", shares authority and responsibilities between
the government and the people.

Armitage, Berkes and Doubleday (2007) describe the potential benefits of co-management as being "more appropriate, more efficient, and
more equitable governance, and the improvement of a number of pro-

cesses and functions of management". In addition, co-management is referred to as being a mechanism for reducing conflict through participatory democracy. However, the illustrations in that volume do not show this democratic function of co-management clearly. In other words, conflict resolution is assumed to occur once such a management vehicle is installed.

This tendency is broadly shared by studies and participatory development practices in the field of international development. Participatory development was introduced as a concept to counter the top-down development practices of the past (Saito, 2002). The concept entails the empowerment of people or participants in the development process. Critics of participatory development point out that its research and practice do not pay enough attention to existing social and power structures, agencies and politics (Hicky and Mohan, 2004). Participation is sometimes treated as a technical issue in the process of project planning and implementation, as if empowerment and democracy would be attained automatically if people attended meetings and other activities.

Political aspects of participatory resource governance or participatory development are treated rather well in discussions of deliberative democracy.

Democracy as problem solving or politics

If participation in either resource governance or development is broadened, it tends to result in conflicts of interest among diverse stakeholders. In this sense, participatory resource governance or participatory development might be seen as an inherently political process.

Usually, in the practice of participatory resource governance and participatory development, "participation" is seen as being an objective, and the discussion process is reduced to procedural steps. Deliberation or consensus building through deliberation tends to be seen as a technique or art (e.g. Susskind and Cruikshank, 2006). This practice is backed by the belief that deliberation will bring about rational and reasonable agreement. This idea, which has its origins in Habermas, has been criticized as being too optimistic and placing too much confidence in the potential of rational deliberation (Shinohara, 2004; Tamura, 2008). The conditions for bringing about meaningful deliberation or consensus building, such as information disclosure, fair opportunity and the ability to talk and communicate, are difficult to fulfil in reality. Similarly, participation is also seen as an objective in development practice, as if empowerment could be automatically realized once participation occurs.

Another criticism of deliberative democracy is that it underestimates or ignores existing differences or antagonisms among diverse parties in the social arena. From this viewpoint, in social life such differences or antagonisms do not facilitate compromise. Democracy should not suppress this difference into one rational and reasonable agreement; rather, it should be perceived as a continuous process of changing antagonism to "agonism" (Mouffe, 2000).

It is not the purpose here to evaluate different theories or concepts of democracy. If a forum for participatory resource governance or participatory development is required, it usually means that there is an issue to be solved. If the issue is related to a particular policy or a particular project, it should be treated in a limited timeframe. Therefore, this study focuses on determining how solutions or agreements are reached through a "democratic" process.

Relevance in the context of developing countries

The basic premise of this study is that focusing on resources will allow us to determine a comprehensive approach to the issue in terms of both development and environment. A resource becomes such when people touch it and try to explore it. In this sense, the governance of resources is inevitably related to the governance of people's activities (Sato, 2008).

In developing countries, participatory resource governance will occur more frequently in the near future. As seen in Japan, the recent trend towards participatory resource governance can be perceived as a recovery of the democratic control of resources. Furthermore, this is said to result in resource use that is more sustainable than under a government monopoly. Thus governments and/or civil society in developed countries will try to introduce participatory resource governance in developing countries with financial and/or technical assistance as participatory development programmes.

At the same time, the introduction of participatory resource governance might benefit developing countries' governments in two ways. First, it might overlap with or provide governance for people's activities, especially in terms of resource use. If the purpose of participatory resource governance is to establish sustainable resource use, governments may find in it a convenient excuse to exercise their power over people's resource use. Second, a government might be able to reduce or avoid its cost and responsibility when negotiating with each stakeholder if part of an upcoming negotiation – for example, with potential resettlers in dam construction – becomes a multistakeholder dialogue as part of the deliberative democratic process.

It is thus useful to review the process of participatory resource governance in Japan by focusing on participation and democracy, even though it might be premature to introduce this governance in developing countries.

The Yodo River Committee and resettlers' struggle in the case of the Daidogawa Dam

The Yodo River and Yodo River Committee

The Yodo is a major river in Japan, located in the Kinki region (Figure 6.1). The length of the main channel is 75 km and the total catchment

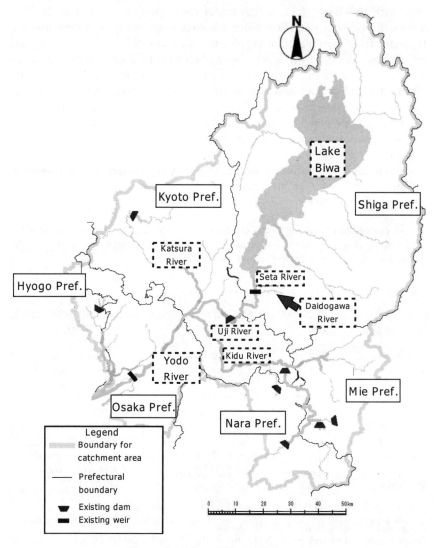

Figure 6.1 Map of Yodo River area

area is 8,240 km², including Lake Biwa, the biggest lake in Japan. The lake and river combined have more than 900 tributaries in six prefectures (Osaka, Hyogo, Kyoto, Shiga, Mie and Nara); the river runs through Lake Biwa to Osaka Bay. The riparian population includes more than 10 million people and multiple kinds of water use support the region's life and economic activities; for example, the river supplies drinking water for 17 million people (Yodogawa River Office, 2009).

The Yodo River Committee (YRC) was established in 2001 in accordance with the River Law, which underwent a major revision in 1997 to reflect the present needs of water resource management. As mentioned, Japanese river management began with flood control. In 1939 water utilization was added as the next major objective. In recent years concerns over the environment, sustainability and citizen participation have come into focus, and the revised law clearly states that "maintaining and conserving the fluvial environment" is one of its objectives (Figure 6.2).

To reflect civic participation in river management, the revised law states the necessary procedures in Article 16-2, sections 3–5:

3 When river administrators intend to draft a river improvement plan, they shall *consider opinions from persons with experience or an academic background when necessary.*

4 In connection with the previous paragraph (Paragraph 3), river administrators shall *take necessary measures, such as public hearings, etc., to reflect the opinion of the people concerned whenever necessary.*

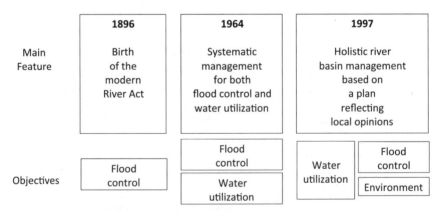

Figure 6.2 Development of the River Act
Source: Translated and modified by the author from Ministry of Land, Infrastructure, Transportation and Tourism Kinki Regional Development Bureau website.

5 When river administrators intend to establish a river improvement plan, they shall *consider opinions from concerned prefectural governors and mayors in advance* as provided in the Government Ordinance.

A "river improvement plan" is one that stipulates the concrete measures used to manage a river in accordance with the fundamental management policy that has been established for each major river system. Thus concrete activities or items related to river management such as the purpose, type, location and function of river works should be set forth in the improvement plan (Figure 6.3).

The YRC is a new concept for the government and civil society. It is different to an ordinary council consisting of designated members or experts who answer enquiries from government administration. The characteristics of the YRC are summarized below.

- *Thorough deliberation.* The YRC initiated discussions for creating an original draft of the river improvement plan. A conventional council can only provide input to a draft that has already been prepared by the ministry. The results of the YRC's initial discussions formed the basis of the ministry's draft.

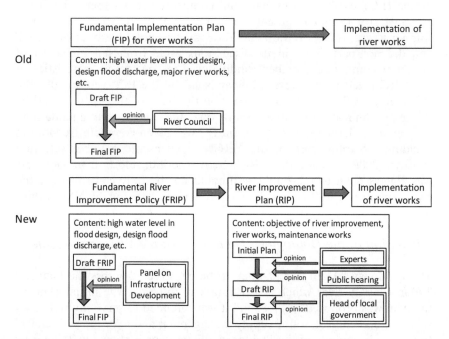

Figure 6.3 New process of river management
Source: Translated and modified by the author from Ministry of Land, Infrastructure, Transportation and Tourism Kinki Regional Development Bureau website.

- *Information disclosure and transparency*. All documents and materials viewed in the YRC, as well as the record of its discussions, are made public on the YRC website. Meetings are open to the public. Multiple hearings and occasions for disseminating information were scheduled.
- *Emphasis on public opinion*. The YRC tried to gather and listen to all available input from the public and stakeholders (for example, field surveys and special interview sessions were held).
- *Reports and recommendations prepared by members*. Each report and recommendation derived from the discussions was written by a committee member.
- *Independent operation*. YRC operation is independent of the ministry that gathers opinions and recommendations from the YRC. The schedule and agenda are set by the YRC, and the YRC secretariat commissioned its administrative arrangements from a third party.

The YRC prides itself on these characteristics and considers itself to be a "model of new public works decision making" (Yodo River Committee, 2001).

Another important aspect of the YRC is its member selection process. The initial YRC members were selected by the YRC Preparation Committee (PC), established in 2000 and comprising four experts. The river administrator (Kinki Regional Development Bureau, Ministry of Land, Infrastructure, Transportation and Tourism) was not a member of the PC and did not participate in its discussions aside from sending a list of potential committee member candidates. The specific characteristics of the YRC listed above were all established by the PC. Additionally, the PC selected YRC members not only on the basis of the list provided by the river administrator but also on its own and others' recommendations. One member later reported that the PC was given complete freedom in deciding the framework of the YRC as well as the member selection (Furuya, 2009). During the YRC's active period, selection of members was always open to the public and could not be fully controlled by the river administrator; this was changed in August 2007 for the YRC's third term.

Discussion of the Daidogawa Dam between the YRC and resettlers

The Daidogawa Dam was planned to be constructed across the Daido, a 39 km Class A river which is a tributary of the Seta. The initial plan for the dam was proposed in 1968, and it was intended to serve multiple uses such as flood control, water supply management and hydropower generation. The chronology of the Daidogawa Dam issue is shown in Table 6.1.

In all, 55 households were displaced by the planned construction of the Daidogawa Dam. They fought against the dam from the beginning until

Table 6.1 Chronology of Daidogawa Dam issue

1968	Initial preparatory survey began.
1986	Resettlement site was selected for Ohtorii area residents.
1994	Agreement reached on the standard of compensation between the resettlers and the ministry.
1998	Resettlers moved to the resettlement site.
2001	The Yodo River Committee was established.
2003	"Recommendation" by the YRC ("In principle, dam construction will not be employed").
2006	Anti-dam governor elected in Shiga prefecture.
2007	MLIT published "Fundamental River Management Policy for the Yodogawa River". According to the policy, the construction of the Daidogawa Dam would be implemented as planned.
2008	The YRC published its opinion paper (no. 18), concluding that the YRC could not approve inclusion of the Daidogawa Dam construction in the river improvement plan.
2008	Governors in Shiga, Kyoto, Osaka and Mie prefectures expressed their common opinion against construction of the Daidogawa Dam.
2009	Shiga Prefectural Assembly endorsed the governor's opinion against the dam to be submitted to the central ministry.
2009	MLIT published the river improvement plan for the Yodogawa River and the Daidogawa Dam plan was suspended again.
Present	The YRC is in recess.

Source: YRC website (www.yodoriver.org/).

1994, when, after persuasion by the ministry and a former governor of Shiga prefecture, they accepted displacement and agreed to a standard of compensation. After completion of the new resettlement site, 53 households moved and resettled about 6 km away from their original village. At the time, they never imagined that the dam plan would be suspended.

After its establishment in 2001, the YRC was expected to provide input to the original draft of the river improvement plan and make necessary comments and recommendations for a revised draft which would be prepared by the river administrator on the basis of the original. While the fundamental river management policy was being formulated in the central ministry, the YRC published its recommendations for the upcoming draft plan, stating, "In principle dam construction will not be employed." From this point on, five planned dams, including Daidogawa Dam, became major issues in YRC discussions, and conflicts between the ministry and the YRC began to surface. (Up to then, the YRC's counterpart in the ministry, the head of the Kinki Regional Development Bureau river department, had been the leading force behind reform in river administration and assisted the YRC fully. However, after the recommendations were published, this person was removed from post and returned to

Tokyo.) I will not go into detail about the process of the debate over the five dams, mainly because it was primarily a technical discussion on the effects of flood mitigation.

As a result of the debate, the YRC concluded that the five dams might not be properly justified in the revised river improvement plan. The river administrator ignored the YRC's conclusion and prepared the improvement plan including the dams. This created severe friction between the YRC and the river administrator. In the meantime an anti-dam, anti-public-works candidate was elected governor in Shiga prefecture, thus the river administrator's attempts to reduce the involvement and influence of the YRC were in vain. The YRC voluntarily began work on an opinion paper and proposed suspending construction of the five dams in a major comment on the ministry's river improvement plan. The governors of four riparian prefectures, including Shiga, expressed their unwillingness to support dam construction or share the financial burden. Finally, the ministry proposed a river improvement plan that included suspension of construction of the five dams.

The resettlers did not hide their disappointment with this result. They showed dissatisfaction by saying "We were just outnumbered" and "Our feelings and wishes were never heard nor understood." It is possible that they felt this decision was an affront to their struggle to prevent resettlement, the hardship they endured owing to the decision to resettle and their feelings of rejection after resettlement. They have accepted neither the governor's apology nor an appointment to discuss the issue.

As mentioned, the YRC is considered to be the new model for public works decision-making. If this is the case, how were resettlers perceived and given a voice in this participatory resource governance practice? How did their position in the YRC process affect the conclusion of the conflict and the resulting situation? Thanks to publicly available resources, the following points are known:

- the resettlers were not represented on the committee
- the debate over the five-dam plan concentrated on the flood mitigation effects on the basis of scientific rationality, and rarely touched on social issues such as displacement
- two special sessions were held to hear resettlers' opinions.

The resettlers were not represented on the committee

It is unclear why a representative from the resettlers' community was not appointed as a committee member. It seems they were not listed in the initial candidate list prepared by the river administrator. During the process of establishing the YRC, there seemed to be no consideration of making a representative of the resettlers a member. There may have been an opportunity for them to apply for public recruitment, but if this was so they did not take it.

Although the process of the YRC seemed democratic compared to a conventional council, its composition appeared biased in several ways and failed to maintain sufficient diversity. According to the member list of the first-term YRC (Table 6.2), the main group consisted of people from the scientific or academic community. Out of 52 members, 25 were university professors (including emeritus professors) and four others were from research institutes (both public and private). All 14 members from NGOs, the second-biggest group on the YRC, were engaged in environmental conservation activities. Another category, "Members with knowledge of local characteristics", was added on top of the 17 categories (or kinds of expertise) prepared by the river authority in the PC process to accommodate local and/or lay people's opinions. From the record of YRC discussions, it can be safely said that all 14 members of this category represented the environmentally conscious group in the riparian community rather than the beneficiaries of flood control. In other words, YRC member selection was biased in two ways: towards scientific expertise; and towards persons interested in environmental conservation.

This situation may provide a probable answer to the question of whether the result would have been different if the resettlers had been represented on the committee. Even if they had been members, the result of the discussion might not have changed.

The debate concentrated on the flood mitigation effects of the dams

Although the plan including the Daidogawa Dam was a major issue in the YRC process, discussion and debate on dams marginalized the resettlers on two levels. First, the debate focused on the whole river basin, and therefore the stakes surrounding one dam and its potential resettlers were inevitably diluted in the process. If the debate came down to a confrontation in terms of population, the downstream community had the advantage over the upstream community. Second, the discussions were held in accordance with the rules of scientific rationality. As seen, the composition of the YRC itself was biased toward scientific expertise, and the main discussion focused on the effect of the dams to reduce flood damage in scientific terms. There was an abundance of data and simulations in the debate. That is, scientific data were the basis of discussion, and there was no room for the sentiment of the resettlers.

Two special sessions were held to hear resettlers' opinions

In November 2004 and August 2005 special hearing sessions were held. The latter was specifically related to the Daidogawa Dam. In the two-hour

Table 6.2 Composition of initial YRC membership (February 2001–January 2005)

No.	Designation	Expertise/field
1 (chair)	Professor emeritus	General river environment
2	Local government nature conservation instructor	Plants
3	University professor	Hydrology, engineering
4*	Private organization	Recreational activities
5	Professor emeritus	Flood control, river engineering
6	University professor	Channel morphology
7	Professor emeritus	*Sabo* (debris control)
8	University professor	Agricultural water utilization
9	University professor	Environmental sociology, community development
10*	NGO	Environmental conservation, civic activity
11	Professor emeritus	Ecology
12	University professor	Ecology
13	High school teacher	Animals
14	Professor emeritus	Agriculture/forestry/fishery
15*	NGO, medical doctor	Environmental conservation, civic activity
16	Professor emeritus	Plant sociology
17	University professor	Water quality
18*	NGO, priest	Environmental ethics
19	University professor	Fishery
20	University professor	River ecology, insect phylogenetics
21	University professor	Administrative law
22*	NGO	Environmental conservation, social networking
23*	NGO	Environmental conservation
24	Lawyer	Environmental conservation/law
25	University professor	Environmental economics and policy
26	Public research institute	Environmental policy, environmental engineering
27	Public research institute	Freshwater biology
28	University professor	Economics
29	University professor	Agriculture
30	University professor	Plant ecology
31	University professor	Fishery
32	University professor	Media studies
33*	NGO	Environmental education
34*	NGO	Environmental conservation, consumer cooperative
35*	NGO	Environmental conservation
36*	NGO	Environmental conservation/ education
37	University professor, NGO	Community development, cultural landscape

Table 6.2 (cont.)

No.	Designation	Expertise/field
38*	NGO (organized by business community)	Local economy and environment
39*	Fishermen's cooperative	Fishery
40*	NGO	Environmental conservation/ education
41	University professor	*Sabo* (debris control)
42	University professor	Environmental education
43*	NGO	Bird ecology, Ramsar Convention
44	Research institute	Freshwater biology
45	Municipal waterworks	Water quality
46	Lawyer	Administrative/environmental law
47*	Residents in riparian areas	Not specified
48	NGO	Environmental conservation, ecology
49	University professor	Cultural studies on water
50	University professor	Plant ecology, conservation biology
51	Research institute	Isotope ecology
52	Ex-fishermen's cooperative	Fishery, environment

Source: Modified from member list on YRC website (www.yodoriver.org/about/iin_list.html).
Note:
* Categorized as "Members with knowledge of local characteristics".

session, two representatives each of a pro-dam group and an anti-dam group expressed their opinions. Six YRC members held discussions with them and other participants to put forward the YRC's views. Environmentally conscious representatives expressed their objections to the plan, citing reasons including environmental considerations, government financial deficits (which would be worsened by further public works expenditure) and the insufficient flood mitigation effects of the planned dam. Against these claims, representatives of the resettlers expressed their concern in terms of a "promise with the ancestors who had protected their land" and would be disappointed if the resettlers gave up the land, and their "trust in the government's decision after 30 years' struggle". One representative said, "We cannot understand the decision [to abandon the dam plan] while our feelings were hurt and no one seems to consider our difficult and bitter decision [to leave ancestral land]." Their claims were based on passion and emotion rather than reason.

The presence of special sessions for resettlers to express concerns might suggest they were better represented than other stakeholders, but the fact is that there were more than 300 meetings throughout the process. Aside from these two special sessions, resettlers were limited to expressing their opinions at the end of each meeting as members of the general audience. Their position in the YRC process was too weak to result in any meaningful communication.

In summary, the circumstances surrounding the YRC diluted the resettlers' stakes and consequently marginalized them, although it was not the intention of the YRC to do so.

Conclusion: The challenge of participatory resource governance

What lessons can be learned from reviewing the YRC process and its effect on the resettled people? Does it reveal the limitations of participatory resource governance or deliberative democracy?

If one wishes to evaluate participatory resource governance, one should not dismiss the achieved result. In this sense, the YRC process can be evaluated as having been successful: it suspended dam construction and helped environmental concerns prevail. But whether a result is appreciated might depend on the time and place. For example, in the 1960s Tomoyuki Murohara fought fiercely against the Matsubara and Shimouke Dam plan, and his efforts had a great influence on future dam disputes in Japan. However, if a participatory resource governance mechanism had existed at that time, Murohara's resistance might not have lasted as long as it did. When he finally ceased, a representative from the downstream area visited him. Contrary to Murohara's expectations, the person strongly criticized him for his reckless resistance to the dam plan, saying this had put thousands of lives at risk of flood danger. As this anecdote shows, desirable resource use might differ according to the social and historical context, so the evaluation of participatory resource governance might be more complicated than has been imagined.

Accordingly, we must also examine the "process" of participatory resource governance. In this regard, the case of the Daidogawa Dam allows us to make two observations. First, as reviewed in the YRC, there is a risk of marginalizing specific stakeholders even in well-intentioned governance processes. Conventionally, marginalization occurs under more authoritarian processes because of the asymmetry of power. However, in relatively democratic (or broad-based) participatory governance, marginalization may occur owing to diluted stakes, especially if the process is implemented in a top-down fashion or introduced as a foreign-assisted project in a developing country.

Second, when diverse stakeholders are involved, participatory resource governance inevitably involves conflicts of interest and creates opportunities for antagonism. The YRC process seemed to indicate the relevance of agonistic democracy over and above deliberative democracy. However, this does not imply that the ideal of deliberative democracy should be abandoned. The deliberative process has its own benefits in transforming the values and opinions of participants. In the YRC process there were a number of cases of shifts in individual values and positions during the discussions and debates (Furuya, 2009). Such a transformation increases the opportunities for rational and satisfactory agreements among diverse participants.

Regarding disagreements or dissatisfaction among members of the participatory resource governance process, another important point can be observed from the YRC: the overlap of the stakeholders' lives and the governance process. One must consider the meaning of life, as suggested by the fact that the Daidogawa Dam resettlers felt their lives had become meaningless after the decision of the YRC. For most stakeholders and government officials, participatory resource governance is a part of the governmental/administrative process. On the other hand, some stakeholders' lives might overlap with the process of resource governance. For example, for the resettlers in the Daidogawa Dam process, the whole 30 years of their struggle had been a process of resource governance, and the YRC was supposed to be part of or a continuation of this. However, the YRC process did not give them a proper standing and they felt the whole process of resource governance "for them" had been abandoned. If stakeholders of this kind are marginalized (or feel marginalized) in the process, they could easily think their lives hold little or no meaning.

As mentioned, participatory resource management cannot totally avoid dissatisfaction or loss. As this process is different from an ideal deliberative democracy, it is usually necessary to decide to take some kind of action, because it is impossible to continue deliberations forever. If it is not possible to avoid marginalizing some stakeholders in the process, one must find ways to make deliberative democracy or participatory resource governance more fruitful.

To that end, there have been many studies on the institutional settings of deliberative democracy (Smith, 2009; Goodin, 2008), and it is likely that these include clues for improving the process of deliberative democracy. However, in the context of the focus of this study (namely resources), I would like to suggest another way to construct participatory resource governance. If one sees a resource as the "bundle of possibilities" associated with a given set of objects, resource governance in one place does not necessarily mean governing one single object and one single possibility. For example, the YRC handled the Yodo River basin, and the Yodo River is perceived as a water resource according to the conventional understanding of the term; the YRC's discussions thus naturally focused on water as the main resource and issue. On the other hand, the unsatisfied resettlers' stake was not in or on the water, but on the land adjacent to the river on which their livelihoods depended. What is more, if the people participating in the YRC could have seen the different possibilities of the Yodo River, those differences could have been connected with the intensity or depth of the respective stakes, and thus their decision-making power. It is true that different people view resources differently: some see water as a life-sustaining resource (such as drinking water) and others see it in terms of amenities or recreational resources (such as nature or riverside parks). An examination of the functional differences in these possibilities could reveal the differentiated stakes in the deliberations. In other words, the YRC practice bundled many diverse views of the resources surrounding the Yodo River into one single term: water resources. Using a broader concept of resources, participatory resource governance can be constructed to create better-scrutinized and differentiated stakeholder deliberations that cover diverse objects and possibilities. This alternative interpretation of participatory resource governance might diminish the risk of diluted or outnumbered stakes, resulting in less loss of meaning in the participants' lives.

REFERENCES

Armitage, D., F. Berkes and N. Doubleday (eds) (2007) *Adaptive Co-Management: Collaboration, Learning, and Multi-Level Governance*, Vancouver, BC: UBC Press.

Asahi Shimbun (2009) "Daidogawa Dam Plan Suspended", *Asahi Shimbun*, 31 March.

Cernea, M. (2000) "Risks, Safeguards, and Reconstruction: A Model for Population Displacement and Resettlement", in M. Cernea and C. McDowell (eds) *Risks and Reconstruction: Experiences of Resettlers and Refugees*, Washington, DC: World Bank, pp. 11–55.

Furuya, K. (2009) *Why Do You Insist upon Dam Construction?*, Tokyo: Iwanami Shoten (in Japanese).

Goodin, R. E. (2008) *Innovating Democracy: Democratic Theory and Practice after the Deliberative Turn*, Oxford: Oxford University Press.

Hanayama, Y. (1969) *The Theory and Practice of Compensation*, Tokyo: Keiso Shobo (in Japanese).

Hicky, S. and G. Mohan (eds) (2004) *Participation: From Tyranny to Transformation*, London: Zed Books.

Inoue, M. (2004) *Searching for the Theory of Commons*, Tokyo: Iwanami Shoten (in Japanese).

Inoue, M. and T. Miyauchi (eds) (2001) *The Sociology of Commons*, Tokyo: Shinyosha (in Japanese).

Matsushita, K. (ed.) (2007) *Theory of Environmental Governance*, Kyoto: University of Kyoto Press (in Japanese).

Mouffe, C. (2000) *The Democratic Paradox*, London: Verso.

Ostrom, E. (1990) *Governing the Commons*, Cambridge: Cambridge University Press.

Saito, F. (2002) *Participatory Development*, Tokyo: Nihon Hyoronsha (in Japanese).

Sato, J. (ed.) (2008) *A Viewpoint for Resources*, Tokyo: Toshindo Publishing (in Japanese).

Shinohara, H. (2004) *Citizen Politics: What is Deliberative Democracy?*, Tokyo: Iwanami Shoten (in Japanese).

Smith, G. (2009) *Democratic Innovations: Designing Institutions for Citizen Participation*, Cambridge: Cambridge University Press.

Susskind, L. and J. Cruikshank (2006) *Breaking Robert's Rules: The New Way to Run Your Meeting, Build Consensus, and Get Results*, Oxford: Oxford University Press.

Takahasi, Y. (2004) "Dams, Environment and Regional Development in Japan", *International Journal of Water Resources Development* 20(1), pp. 35–45.

Takesada, N. (2009) "A Research on Compensation and Resettlement Policy for Dam-Induced Displacement", doctoral dissertation, Department of International Studies, University of Tokyo (in Japanese).

Tamura, T. (2008) *Reasons for Deliberation: Democratic Theory in Reflexive and Divided Societies*, Tokyo: Keiso Shobo.

Toyama, K. (1974) *Water, Forest, and Land*, Tokyo: Chuokouronsha (in Japanese).

Yodo River Committee (2001) "About the Yodo River Committee", available at www.yodoriver.org/about/toha.html#tokuchou (web page in Japanese).

Yodogawa River Office (2009) "Yodogawa River Water Use", Ministry of Land, Infrastructure, Transportation and Tourism, March, available at www.yodogawa. kkr.mlit.go.jp/know/data/use/index.html (web page in Japanese).

7

Distribution of mineral resources in Zambia: A longitudinal analysis of the mining community

Michiko Ishisone

Introduction

Over the last few decades a deepening sense of crisis has arisen among those concerned with African resource abundance. Issues regarding abundance of natural resources – particularly oil and minerals – are not unique to Africa, nor are the factors inhibiting economic development confined to that continent. However, among oil- and mineral-rich developing countries worldwide, apart from Botswana, it is the African countries which have experienced the most severe "resource curse" conditions. Since the 1990s researchers have actively examined the difficulties surrounding economic growth and good governance in resource-rich countries. They have pointed to political and economic factors related to resource abundance, and isolated social and historical impediments. A consensus has emerged that the socio-economic development failures are due to economic, political and institutional factors (Basedau and Mehler, 2005).

Economists and political scientists who study the problems of resource abundance in developing countries usually observe how ownership arrangements, taxation policies and investment programmes are determined (Humphreys, Sachs and Stiglitz, 2007), rather than mining development employment and domestic distribution. The reasons for this emphasis are rooted in the widely accepted preference for maximizing the growth of national product. Meanwhile, despite the fact that the GDP (gross domestic product) of resource-rich countries has increased in recent years

Governance of natural resources: Uncovering the social purpose of materials in nature, Sato (ed.), United Nations University Press, 2013, ISBN 978-92-808-1228-2

due to higher prices, it has been noted that social conflicts and grievances have also grown in resource-producing communities (Fraser and Lungu, 2007). Why and how have the conflicts come about? How are they related to distribution issues? This study may answer these questions better than conventional explanations have thus far, by focusing on the distributional consequences in resource-producing communities and the reasons behind social conflict. The chapter seeks to go beyond the conventional studies on natural resource abundance by examining the historical process of resource governance, as elements of this process may be the source of the distribution problems.

Interventions in resource control and management – resource governance – have a large influence on communities in resource-rich areas. For example, as Scott (1998) showed, mapping, gridding and other standardizing techniques were implemented to calculate revenue and sustainable yield for the commercial timber industry, and this eventually increased the society's visibility for the state. When a particular natural resource needs to be governed, laws and institutions are implemented to regulate the resource and determine who has access to benefits and who does not. In other words, natural resource management can be a trigger to manipulate society. Even if the original purpose for implementing resource laws, regulations and institutions is to manage a particular natural resource, the new system fundamentally functions as an apparatus for both protection of the stakeholder's interests and management of the people.

Thus it is not surprising that social conflict emerges over the evolution of resource governance. Given the notion of resource governance, this chapter raises two questions. What social conflicts emerge in the distributional structure created over the evolution of a resource governance system? Further, how do social conflicts change over different resource development periods? In answering these questions, I analyse how resource governance has shaped the relationships between central governments, mining companies and local communities with mineral resources.

In searching for an explanation behind social conflict created by resource governance, the most useful case is one in which the country has a relatively long history of resource development and has experienced neither violent nor ethnic conflict. Such an example can show the historical sequence of resource governance, and identify more directly the ways in which it connects with social conflict. Zambia, which is dependent upon its copper export industry, matches these criteria best among the oil- and mineral-abundant countries in Africa.

Formerly known as Northern Rhodesia, Zambia gained its independence in 1964 after 74 years of colonial rule in various forms. At that time Zambia was one of the best examples of successful macro-economic development in sub-Saharan Africa. In terms of GDP per capita it was more advanced than some Asian countries, such as Malaysia and Indonesia. Yet in the last 30 years Zambia has become one of the poorest countries. The main reason behind its significant economic decline is its over-reliance on copper.

Zambia's economic structure was established during the colonial period, and when it achieved independence the economy was already highly monocultural. In 1965 the mining industry's contributions to GDP, export totals and revenue were 40 per cent, 92 per cent and 71 per cent, respectively[1] (Copper Industry Service Bureau, 1973). Despite the declining dependence on mining since then, 70 per cent of Zambia's exports and 10 per cent of its GDP still come from the mineral sector. Although Zambia enjoyed a resource boom from 2003 until the world financial crisis of 2008, when the price of copper fell, it again faced macro-economic stagnation and living standard deterioration. Rather than just look at a snapshot of the Zambian copper economy, as other studies have done (Auty, 1991; Bates and Collier, 1995), this chapter takes a historical approach to Zambian mining development. It addresses the timeframe from 1890 to 2008, including the colonial period during which extractive development began (1890–1964); the post-independence period (1964–1990s), during which the mining industry was nationalized by the Zambian government; and the period following Zambia's severe economic decline, during which the mines were privatized as a part of the structural adjustment programmes (SAPs) urged upon Zambia by the International Monetary Fund (IMF) and the World Bank. The focus is on social conflicts in the Copperbelt region, where most of the copper mining in the country takes place.

Methods and theoretical framework

The data presented in this case come from both archival work and fieldwork. The historical data were collected from archives in Britain in 2008 and Zambia in 2009. For fieldwork, I visited Copperbelt in 2006, 2007 and 2009. The fieldwork data were gathered through about 200 interviews – both structured and informal – with local people in five districts of Copperbelt, central and local government officials, mine officials and mining company officials in Copperbelt and Lusaka. Of the five districts, three were mine townships (Kitwe, Chingola and Luanshya) and two were rural areas (Masaiti and Lufwanyama).

In Copperbelt households depend either directly or indirectly on copper mining for their livelihoods. Urban households in Kitwe, Chingola and Luanshya are more directly connected to mining development through both employment and local businesses. Rural households are indirectly affected by the mines in that the buyers of their produce are mainly miners and other urban dwellers.

To give a theoretical explanation for my analysis, I am taking the idea of legibility from the work of James Scott. Scott maintains that "legibility" implies an expansive way of thinking about governance and rule in relation to the exercise of standardization by the state.[2] For Scott (1998: 183), legibility referred to the "condition of manipulation", essentially a calculated and rational set of methods used both to shape society and to secure rule:

> Any substantial state intervention in society – to vaccinate a population, produce goods, mobilize labor, tax people and their property, conduct literacy campaigns, conscript soldiers, enforce sanitation standards, catch criminals, start universal schooling – requires the invention of units that are visible.

Describing functions of maps and statistics, language, surnames and so on, Scott (ibid.: 2) argued how a state can attempt to "make a society legible, to arrange the population in ways that simplified the classic state functions of taxation, conscription, and presentation of rebellion".

Legibility, the unitization of objects which authorities want to visualize, can be assessed through analysis of the methods of intervention – in other words, analysis of the processes by which the authorities govern a particular public sphere. With natural resources, for instance, Scott (ibid.: 15) observed that German scientific forestry methods work as "standardizing techniques" that lead towards the highest and most sustainable revenue. Cadastral maps, property registration and standardized measures are invaluable for the authorities to be able to use valuable natural resources better and collect taxes more efficiently.

By applying this theoretical concept to Zambia, relevant maps and regulations were created for the administration of mineral resources, and statistics were taken to determine tax revenue and supply of labour as the British authorities sought to harvest minerals and confirm the potential extent of any sources they found. Put simply, the British intervened in mineral resources governance in an attempt to force legibility on the copper-producing area. Given this perspective, I explore how legibility has changed as different systems of resource governance were implemented with each change in political regime.

The historical background of copper mining in Zambia

The origins of modern copper mining in Zambia go back to the British colonial administration of the late nineteenth century. The British government had limited knowledge about Central Africa, and the extension of its African empire was considered difficult and costly at that time. To pursue its goal of expanding its colonial power across Africa, the British government let private companies take the lead in administrating the land by conferring charters. The British South Africa Company (BSAC), founded by Cecil Rhodes, was granted a charter over the territory of Northern Rhodesia (now Zambia).

Although the BSAC's power was transferred back to the Colonial Office in 1924, the company did not relinquish the extractive concessions until the eve of Zambia's independence in 1964. In the late 1920s large-scale mining development was begun by two foreign companies, namely the Rhodesian Selection Trust (RST) and the Anglo American Corporation (AAC). For the next 40 years the control of the Zambian mining sector remained under the BSAC and those two mining companies.

Until the 1920s the economy of Northern Rhodesia was relatively backward, but less than a decade after mining exploration began it had become attractive to not only the British but also other Europeans – the European population increased more than threefold from 3,634 in 1921 to 13,846 in 1931 (Great Britain Colonial Office, 1936). By the late 1930s Northern Rhodesia had emerged as one of the biggest copper producers in the world, and mining exploration brought significant economic development to Copperbelt. Urbanization was one of the most striking symptoms of this: it encouraged labour migrations, large-scale farms and the development of a rail system. Copperbelt mines also attracted the interest of commercial enterprises, and secondary industries began to develop in association with the mines.

With this basic ownership and operational structure in place, the Rhodesian economy was deeply dependent on the mining sector. It was truly the Europeans – specifically BSAC, AAC and RST, the Commonwealth and European miners – who formed this monoculture economy, and profited most from mining development. The extent of the country's reliance on mining was even greater under the government of the Federation of Rhodesia and Nyasaland (1953–1964) because the profits from copper mining were used for the development of Southern Rhodesia. Little thought was given to the economic diversification and social development of Northern Rhodesia, and it lost about £7 million per year to Southern Rhodesia (Sklar, 1975). At independence Zambia was faced with a highly distorted economy and a severe shortage of human capital. At the time, 40–50 per cent of its GDP was dependent on the mining industry, and over 90 per cent of its exports were related to the industry (Copper Industry Service Bureau, 1973). Zambia inherited a huge mining industry that was poorly integrated with the national economy as a whole. In addition, the total number of native Zambians who had completed secondary school was only just over 1,200, and only 109 had university certificates (Sklar, 1975).

After the Second World War, the most powerful influence on social and political change in Africa was the growth of nationalism and the creation of new nation-states. With the leadership of Kenneth Kaunda, of the United National Independence Party, the colony of Northern Rhodesia became the independent nation of Zambia in 1964. For a newly independent country, one of its first priorities was the establishment of its own economic controls in order to obtain economic independence as well.

The Zambian government thus took its first steps towards state ownership of the mining sector. In 1968 President Kaunda announced the "Mulungushi" reforms, which called for an economic nationalization programme under which the state would acquire a 51 per cent interest in 25 leading private companies in Zambia. Then, in 1969, he issued the "Matero" declaration, which announced the government's takeover of mine rights and ownership. After negotiations between the governments of Zambia and Great Britain and the two mining companies, the companies were reorganized into Nchanga Consolidated Copper Mines (NCCM) and Roan Consolidated Mines (RCM). In 1982 NCCM and RCM merged and became Zambia Consolidated Copper Mines (ZCCM).

With copper prices high and steady during the 1960s and early 1970s, the Zambian economy was also relatively stable. However, in the mid-1970s the world copper price began a long decline, geological conditions began to deteriorate and the geopolitical environment of Southern Africa began to limit landlocked Zambia's engagement with the world economy severely.[3]

Zambia's economy started to decline. Treating the temporary positive shock as if it were permanent and the negative shock as it were temporary, the government failed to save during the boom. In addition, through extensive external borrowing, it sustained spending levels during the long slump. As the mining sector became inefficient, costly and unprofitable, privatization became inevitable.

By the early 1990s, as multiparty movements were gaining popularity worldwide, the one-party government of President Kaunda was defeated by the Movement for Multiparty Democracy led by Frederic Chiluba. After the failure of the economic measures undertaken by Kaunda's government,[4] Chiluba took the initiative as Zambia's second president to liberalize the economy – including ZCCM, the largest state enterprise. The privatization of ZCCM was largely due to pressures from the IMF and World Bank. It was a condition for several loans from donor institutions, and a precondition for Zambia to qualify for debt relief through the Highly Indebted Poor Countries initiative (ACTSA, Christian Aid and SCIAF, 2007). In 1995 the government revised the Mines and Minerals Act to improve the investment climate and promote foreign investment. Rights to mines managed by ZCCM were sold to seven foreign mining companies, and mines are currently owned by the government and operated by foreign companies.

Conflicts and resource governance

The beginnings of resource governance: Colonial period

The BSAC played an important role in paving the way towards colonial administration. In the late nineteenth century Cecil Rhodes's company took its first steps in exploring the potential mineral resources in what it considered to be the far north,[5] and sent a representative named Frank Lochner north of the Zambezi River to a region called Barotseland. Lochner began negotiations with Lewanika, the paramount chief of Barotseland, and in 1890 the BSAC obtained commercial mining concessions for the land. The Barotse feared the raids of the Matabele tribe of Southern Rhodesia and Zimbabwe, and desired British protection (Gann, 1958). In exchange for protection of the British Crown, a yearly subsidy payment of £850 and the creation of social facilities, the BSAC acquired the prospecting and mining rights for the territory. In fact, this treaty was discussed even before the company discovered the region's mineral reserves.

Historical materials such as pictures and documents can be seen in a chronological exhibit at the National Museum in Lusaka. The first part of the exhibit displays documents of ordinances and rules created by the BSAC and the British Colonial Office.

To govern a permanent European settlement in the region, it was necessary to implement a system of law and order (ibid.). The BSAC brought various rules and laws to Northern Rhodesia, such as a taxation system, education guidelines and municipal corporation ordinances. In the early years the BSAC's most urgent task was to exploit every possible stream of revenue, because it had not only to govern a vast area, but also to show its shareholders a profit. In fact the BSAC operated at a heavy loss until 1924, when administration of the region was handed over to the Colonial Office (ibid.). The shareholders had never received a dividend.

The BSAC had to minimize administrative costs and maintain an economically profitable environment, which could only be achieved through the establishment of a peaceful and collaborative society. A peaceful society can prevent outbreaks of social unrest, and negates the need for unnecessary expenditure on a standing military force. The BSAC also had to create a society in which Africans would be willing to pay hut taxes. The question was how to impose taxes in the region. As Scott (1998) indicated, the society needed legibility in order for the BSAC to collect taxes.

The first census was taken in 1911, and by the 1920s an annual report was being published. Many types of map were created, showing vegetation, ethnic distribution, topography and other information. More importantly in terms of mining development, in 1912 the first Mineral Act was passed, maintaining that all mining activity rights belonged to the BSAC. Scott (ibid.: 39) noted:

> As long as common property was abundant and had essentially no fiscal value, the illegibility of its tenure was no problem. But the moment it became scarce (when "nature" became "natural resources"), it became the subject of property rights in law, whether of the state or of the citizens.

Thus the BSAC found potential value in the public space, and that space became subject to property rights. It was no longer just a space; it was a resource. The Mineral Act, which established property rights for prospecting mining space, was enacted before any profitable ore was discovered, which means the BSAC knew how important it was for it to regulate property rights in order to be an owner of the rights. Indeed, even after administrative power was transferred to the British government in 1924, the BSAC was still deemed to be owner of the mineral rights. Until the independence of Northern Rhodesia, the company maintained an administrative position for the purpose of dictating mineral prospecting and mining rights (Great Britain Colonial Office, 1951).

Although a railway connecting Livingstone and Katanga was in operation from 1904 and both lead and zinc were being mined in Kabwe from 1902, real urbanization and modernization did not occur until after 1925 when economically workable copper ores were discovered (Ohadike, 1969) – more than 20 years after the BSAC had first undertaken prospecting.

Once large-scale exploitation of copper began in the late 1920s, Copperbelt attracted a large number of workers from South Africa, Europe and neighbouring countries, plus commercial enterprises and related secondary industries. It became the second most urbanized area in Africa, next to parts of South Africa. Amenities which were previously completely non-existent began to appear: big hotels and public buildings; comfortable tin-roofed bungalows with pleasant gardens; and turf lawns and flowerbeds. Wide, tar-sealed roads carried an endless stream of the latest cars, shops were stocked with every necessity and luxury article imaginable, and beauty parlours, hairdressers, manicurists, swimming baths and cinemas lined the roads of mine townships in Copperbelt (Brown, 1941).

The commercial exploitation of huge deposits of copper encouraged labour migration, mainly composed of two culturally and economically different and disparate groups: a small number of skilled and semi-skilled, highly paid migrant Europeans, and a large number of unskilled and largely illiterate low-paid indigenous Africans. The big advantage of Copperbelt for mining companies was that it served as a reservoir of cheap labour (ibid.). In South Africa a "colour bar" system had been implemented to prioritize white employees, but the Colonial Office in Northern Rhodesia was against the introduction of the system as it would displace native employees with Europeans.[6] However, it was inevitable that in the early stages of copper development all the skilled and semi-skilled jobs would be filled by Europeans. Stratification by race and by industrial skill coincided, and authority engendered a set of superior minds and attitudes among Europeans.

By the time of the mine township ordinance enacted in the 1920s, people were beginning to condemn the practice of mining companies providing all services for mine townships. Board members selected by these companies were responsible for the provision and maintenance of lighting, water supplies, drains, public health, streets and any other necessary services.[7] The mine compounds for Africans were not very roomy, but well enough built, and trees were planted in the better compounds. Furthermore, each mine had a well-equipped and well-run hospital and other social centres for African miners. In addition to accommodation, the mine companies provided the miners with a balanced diet and paid attention to their health (ibid.).

However, wages were somewhat low compared to the high average wage paid to European miners and considering the steadily rising cost of living. And although the African miners were relatively well treated and in a much better position than other African labourers, their standard of living was nothing compared to that of the Europeans.

As can be seen in the riots and strikes among African miners, everything was not well. Before 1949 African miners had no labour unions to stand up for their needs and air their grievances. Following a successful strike among European miners for increased pay, African miners began to protest and strike themselves (Northern Rhodesia, 1941). Although wages for Africans were lower than those for Europeans, African miners were taxed far more heavily in proportion to their earnings. The average wage of a white miner in the late 1930s was £42 per month, almost 40 times greater than that of an African miner (Brown, 1941). In addition, a married European with one child was exempt from paying income tax on income up to about £700. These facts caused great indignation among African miners, who accordingly began protesting for African advancement under the slogan "equal pay for equal work and responsibility" (Guillebaud, 1954).

As Brown (1941) pointed out, "it is not enough that the African worker be well housed, fed and doctored; that is little more than would be conceded to draught animals or an expensive piece of machinery". However, it was neither the colonial government nor the mining companies that prevented Africans from being promoted. Unlike in South Africa, the management of human resources in Northern Rhodesia was more on an economic, rather than a racial, basis.

The mining companies recognized that African advancement was a "necessity" (*Birmingham Post*, 1954). They were prepared to provide generously for their African employees since the companies' main concern was to obtain cheap labour, and the Africans would take over the positions of higher-paid European employees. The government held the view that the problem should be solved by the industry itself, and in fact supported a policy of encouraging the formation of African labour unions (Great Britain Colonial Office, 1954–1956).

The main obstacle to African advancement was the opposition of the European trade union. Europeans employed in the mines enjoyed a high standard of living, and their interests were protected by the powerful Northern Rhodesia European Mineworkers Union. The union had succeeded in inserting a clause in its labour agreement with the companies that all work being done by Europeans at the date of the agreement would be exclusively reserved for Europeans (Northern Rhodesia, 1953). In consequence, even some jobs which could be satisfactorily performed by Africans continued to be done by Europeans.

The taking of resource ownership: Nationalization period

When Zambia gained its independence in 1964, its economy depended overwhelmingly upon the copper industry. Its urban communities had been shaped by the industry's requirements and the growth of its labour. In a sort of copper industry trickle-down effect, urban areas were mainly populated by employees of the mines, railways and other enterprises.

Despite having successfully attained independence, the government was dissatisfied. Its economy was still controlled by non-Zambian interests which, instead of reinvesting in the mining industry, remitted a large amount of money overseas.[8] The government sought economic independence, and wanted to put control of the nation into Zambian hands. The massive copper industry was Zambia's only source of wealth, and Zambians hoped this wealth would be used to develop the country as a whole.

For a newly independent nation in such a situation, obtaining ownership was the only way to take control of domestic economic resources at that time.[9] The only question was how the government should nationalize the mines.

In 1969 President Kaunda announced that his government would acquire a 51 per cent interest in the existing mines as a means to control the conditions, influences and profits of mine production. In the same year new mining and mineral rights were introduced that dealt with material ownership rights, receipt of royalties and prospecting and mining rights. According to Bostock and Harvey (1972), a 51 per cent ownership was actually the cheapest way of acquiring nominal control because some of the advantages of private enterprise, such as better management techniques, had to be retained.

In addition to economic independence, another issue remained to be solved: racial inequality. President Kaunda espoused a policy of "humanism", which was a commitment to equality of opportunity for all Zambians. After independence the employment of foreigners was drastically reduced while that of native Zambians was increased. The majority of junior supervisors became Zambian, but above that level there were only nine native Zambians as senior supervisors while the foreign total was 714 (Sklar, 1975). So the government sought to replace those foreign employees with Zambians, in a process known as "Zambianization". The Committee on Zambianization was established in 1966.

Zambianization was defined as "the improved access of Zambians to posts carrying increased pay and responsibility" (Daniel, 1979: 104). A large number of foreign African labourers held semi-skilled jobs at the time, and like the European labourers they became targets of the Zambianization programme, to be phased out and blocked from promotion opportunities. In the first step of the programme, the mining industry replaced the previous contracts of foreign workers with "expatriate" contracts with three-year terms. Correspondingly, emphasis was placed on training skilled Zambian workers, through both an expanded Zambian education system and the industry's own training system.

However, the consequences of the programme were not always those intended. Zambianization, which was designed to free the country of foreign influence, did not end the mining industry's reliance on foreign labour. Although the programme was successful in giving Zambians access to more skilled and highly paid jobs, there was only a limited reduction in the size of the foreign workforce. In addition, there was an inevitable lag between the implementation of education and training programmes and the actual employment of people who benefited from those programmes, which also resulted in continued reliance on foreign workers (Cobbe, 1979). There was an increasing need for skilled foreign workers to

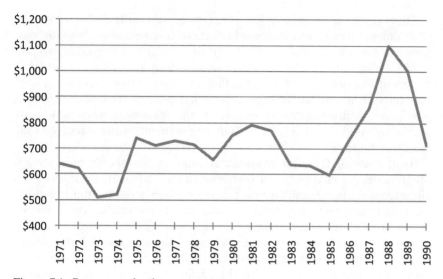

Figure 7.1 Copper production cost per tonne
Source: NCCM, RCM and ZCCM annual reports.
Note: Production cost per tonne is calculated by dividing the total cost of goods sold by the amount of copper production in the entire mining industry.

perform training and supervisory tasks, as well as specialized technical work, so they were given new positions. Thus newly promoted Zambians, and the foreign workers displaced by those Zambians, essentially did the same jobs as before (Burawoy, 1972). Only their salaries and job titles changed.

Furthermore, Zambianization was not wholly compatible with maximization of economic objectives. As Figure 7.1 shows, the cost of copper production gradually increased, except for a few years after the merger of RCM and NCCM in 1982. The reason for the drop in labour efficiency seems to be the colonial legacy: almost nothing had been done to develop the human capital of Zambia. Plus, the original profitability of mining in Zambia was a result of the comparatively low cost of African labourers, but this changed when salaries were increased. When copper prices were high, as they were in the 1960s, the industry could afford the cost of the Zambianization programme, but as prices dropped in the late 1970s it became evident that the strategy was not sustainable in the long run.

How did the distributional structure change through the Zambianization programme? Did it solve the previous colonial issue? Prior to independence, the dual economy was rooted in racial discrimination and, as mentioned, although there was a significant gap between European and African workers, Zambian miners were relatively privileged when compared to other Zambian labourers, earning higher-than-average wages.

Salary levels in the mining industry rose continuously and substantially after independence, and mineworkers came to constitute a "labour aristocracy" comprising only about an eighth of total industrial employment (ibid.). Indeed, in an interview with some elderly people who worked as miners at Copperbelt in the 1980s, they mentioned that they "longed for the fruits of mining activities in this period such as secured high wages, job security, opportunities of education and training, houses and foods, and other good social services". Thus employment in the mines was the most sought after.

By introducing the mine nationalization policy and the Zambianization programme, the inequality between foreign and indigenous workers actually narrowed, but Zambianization created a new stratification which became an underlying class structure. Sometimes described as the "national bourgeoisie", a new elite emerged, made up of political figures and executives of state-owned companies. Many of that "national bourgeoisie" acted like the colonial European rulers had, and their attitudes were sometimes worse, complete with the prejudice and arrogance typical of many a ruling class.

Additionally, there was a much higher level of direct government involvement during the period after independence. The organizational reform brought a pervasive programme of state participation in the ownership and management of the mining industry. For instance, the Mineworkers Union of Zambia (MUZ) won substantial wage increases for its members and gained financial as well as political power during the independence movement, but lost considerable clout as a labour union in the post-independence period.

Because the MUZ had been perceived by the Zambian government as a threat to the prosperity of the country, the government put pressure upon the union by regulating labour policy and forming the Zambia Congress of Trade Unions. The official union policy was to condemn strike action, absenteeism, etc., and encourage greater productivity among its membership. The government restricted both the union and its members in their pursuit of greater economic independence. Thus the MUZ faced problems more complicated than those that had arisen from deals the European labour union had made with the mining companies during the colonial period. Although the reforms were not as successful as the government initially intended, to some extent power and control of the mining industry came to be held by the national government.

During this period, management and control of the government increased drastically, particularly in the mining sector. To obtain ownership of the mines from foreign companies, and with the objective of economic independence, the government intervened conclusively in the economy, particularly in the copper industry and the labour resources connected to it. Although everything did not always go as intended, the government's legibility increased significantly and, through its interventions, the state gained the capacity to dominate society better. However, the copper industry gradually became a burden to the country, and almost paradoxically the Zambian policy of greater economic independence caused greater economic imbalance.

The fall of resource governance: Liberalization period

Zambia's second president, Frederic Chiluba, defeated Kaunda in the 1991 election and implemented a number of structural adjustments in co-operation with the World Bank, the IMF and other donor organizations. By the 1980s the country had drifted into a severe debt crisis and was showing no signs of economic recovery. It was obvious that Zambia would not be able to recover on its own. The new government was under great pressure from donor organizations, so implementation of the SAP was unavoidable. Although the previous government had aroused unrest with the introduction of its own SAP, in its deal with the World Bank/IMF the Chiluba administration had to accept it all – foreign exchange market liberalization, streamlining of the government sector, deregulation, economic liberalization and privatization of state-owned enterprises. Subsequent economic liberalization was remarkable, but the privatization of state-owned enterprises, which had accounted for 80 per cent of the formal economy, was recognized as one of the most difficult reforms – particularly the privatization of the giant mining company ZCCM.

Throughout the economic liberalization, the government was pushed by donors to create a favourable investment environment for foreign capital. The Investment Act and the Mines and Minerals Act were enacted in 1995 to provide incentives for mining investors. Incentives were also given through "development agreements" – contracts made between the government and specific mining companies.

Even though the Mines and Minerals Act stated that a mineral royalty rate of 3 per cent would be charged for large-scale mining licences, the royalties were set at 0.6 per cent in the development agreements so companies could avoid paying high fees. In addition, companies were exempted from customs and excise duties, and import taxes on machinery and equipment brought into the country. Moreover, the development agreements not only covered tax regulation, but also prescribed rules on the environment and on provision of social services, increasing the advantages enjoyed by the mining companies.

By 2000 ZCCM had been sold to seven foreign-based companies under these agreements. With the increase of copper prices, the privatization scheme seems to have succeeded in that previously closed mines have been reopened, copper production has increased and the economy has recovered. Indeed, GDP increased by 6.4 per cent, 6.2 per cent and 5.7 per cent in 2006, 2007 and 2008 respectively (World Bank, 2010).

However, in my fieldwork at Copperbelt 76 per cent of interviewees expressed their belief that life has become worse since the ZCCM years, due to low job security, low wages, a high unemployment rate and no community maintenance. Since privatization the number of casual workers has increased significantly and full-time employment has decreased. Unlike before, most new investors tend to hire fixed-term-contract miners directly or through contracting firms; they offer neither job security nor pensions, and sometimes do not even recompense those injured on the job. Labour costs for these contracted workers are generally lower than for permanent workers, and contracted workers do not always have the privilege of joining a labour union. Thus neither their pay nor their positions are as secure as those of permanent workers.

Furthermore, many respondents (63 per cent) emphasized that the mining company had provided more community benefits in the ZCCM period, indicating how ZCCM used to maintain the communities and its involvement in their development. In fact, most interviewees (97 per cent) mentioned their belief that mining companies should be involved in community development. Similar views were expressed by other interviewees. For instance, an officer of Kitwe City Council said:

> The local authority enjoyed a better and easier work relationship with ZCCM before privatization in that ZCCM used to provide all the social services to its mining areas and townships, such as houses, road maintenance, street-lights, refuse collection, water, sanitation, sports and recreation facilities, schools, hospitals, etc. These services are non-existent now since new investors concentrate only on the core mining business. Local authorities like Kitwe City Council carry a greater burden now, providing services which were provided by ZCCM in the past.

He also made a remark about tax revenue:

> The local authority used to easily collect property tax from the ZCCM head office for all mine properties, including [miners'] houses. After privatization, the mines were sold in shares which were bought by different investors, thereby making collection of property tax costly because the local authority must produce separate bills for each unit and receive payment from different head offices. Worse still, all housing units were sold to individual occupants, which meant that the Council staff must individually bill each house, and follow the individual occupants for payments of property tax. In short, the local authority gets less net revenue compared to during the ZCCM era, because the cost of collecting revenue has increased.

From these remarks by both the local authority and the people in Copperbelt, it is obvious they are not satisfied with the way the mining companies currently do business. However, from the viewpoint of the companies, issues regarding social services and community development were settled with the central government in the development agreements, and social services have been made the government's responsibility.

Access to jobs and social services is vital to maintaining a good standard of living in mining communities. The unequal distribution of benefits from mining development has resulted in social conflict in mining areas.

Discussion: Resource governance and legibility

The entire history of copper resource governance in Zambia shows that the government has always intervened in pursuit of its goals, sometimes causing conflict (see Table 7.1). Initial interventions were meant to gain control of the natural resources in colonial Zambia – the first time that any sort of resource governance had been implemented in the area. Mining development brought with it construction of vast mining towns and the far-reaching social investment necessary to attract hundreds of thousands of European and African workers. Mining towns during the colonial era were classic examples of corporate paternalism: companies provided not only housing, schools and hospitals, but also recreational amenities such as cinemas and sports clubs, and domestic education programmes for workers' wives. Even though mines were operated by private companies, the business of mining, unlike in the current business model, was undoubtedly a broader social project in those days. Such industrial and social investments helped create a national infrastructure, and particularly in urban areas created a legible society in which it was easier to collect taxes, administer rules and prevent social unrest.

Following independence in 1964, the mines were nationalized in 1969 under Kaunda's mildly socialist reforms. The state politically and economically depended on urban areas and could not ignore the powerful MUZ. Zambianization was one important response to the crucial problem facing Zambia after independence: could the national objectives of equitable economic and social development be achieved through ending racial discrimination and foreign domination in the mining industry? Removing the economic disparity between Europeans and Zambians was definitely a pressing task for the state, so the government tried to take away the privileges enjoyed by European workers and empower the Zambian workers. During the period in which resources were nationalized, it was not the government but the state-owned mining companies which provided social services like road maintenance, sanitation, education,

Table 7.1 Evolution of resource governance, conflict and state legibility in Zambia: 1890 to modern day

Period	Resource governance	Technologies of intervention	Issues/conflicts	Legibility
1890–1964 **Colonial period**	**Colonization** "Control of natural resources and labour/ development of mine townships"	Creating mining rights, laws/ regulations, institutions, census, statistics, taxation	Disparity between Africans and Europeans → **African miners versus European labour union**	Legible
1964–1990 **African socialism**	**Nationalization** "Retrieve control of national resources and improve access/benefits for Zambians"	Nationalized mining company Implementation of new mining and tax act "Zambianization" labour policy	Economic independence Expulsion of Europeans Hiring more Zambians → **Government versus state-owned mining company**	Very legible
1990s–now **Neoliberalism**	**Privatization** "Macro-economic recovery/minimization of state intervention – cutting budgets"	Privatized mining companies Revised mining and investment acts Introduction of development agreements	Foreign direct investment and production up Lower taxation capacity Low living standards Low mining company transparency → **Locals versus government versus foreign companies**	Illegible

Source: Author.

medical care, security and community development. The companies played a large role in the local government in Copperbelt, and through the efforts of the state-owned mining company, the mining communities of Copperbelt became more visible to the government.

In contrast to the situation during the colonial and post-independence periods, under the neoliberal regime of Chiluba the mining communities in Copperbelt became illegible. Privatization and neoliberal reform were meant to address the issues surrounding inefficient industries and government, and the goal was a more democratic and more efficient government. Instead, state capacity deteriorated rapidly, with the central government failing to collect sufficient tax income from the foreign mining companies and local governments failing to collect tax accurately from households. Neither the state nor the mining companies provide basic social services such as sanitary management, road maintenance and garbage collection. Maps have not been updated since the 1980s.

The state has lost its capacity to maintain and control communities. It has lost its legibility.

As indicated in Table 7.1, mineral resource governance intervention methods during the colonial and nationalization periods made Copperbelt a well-administrated area. In those days mine developers served as the local government, providing social infrastructure and services. Since privatization, Copperbelt has become disorganized and illegible, as neither the mining companies nor the local government maintain any community development. While operating revenue has increased, both the national and local governments have less capacity to manage the mineral resources and mining communities.

Conclusion and policy implications

Mineral resources have always been the basic source of Zambian macro-economic development, as well as the driving force behind community development in Copperbelt. In examining this mineral-rich country, the chapter attempts to show how resource governance has changed the distributional structure of mining communities and legibility of the government over time, and how the change of distributional structure has triggered social conflict. I also hope to persuade the reader that mining communities are dynamic entities, and the whole picture can hardly be captured in a single temporal snapshot.

Based on these objectives, the chapter reaches two conclusions. First, as conventional economic studies explain, the fluctuation of copper prices does influence livelihoods, yet resource governance can have a greater influence. Resource governance – the methods used to intervene in resource management – can determine the extent of access to benefits derived from resource development. It can improve (or reduce) the standard of living of people in mining communities, and trigger social conflict even when workers are relatively well off. As mentioned, resource governance is a multilateral process. To understand mining communities requires an examination of how methods of intervention have functioned in the past. Second, in contrast to Scott's (1998) implication, state legibility is not always abhorrent to the people. In fact, to some extent legibility is necessary for the state to provide relevant social services.

In terms of social services and community development, the role of mining companies has changed worldwide. Even private companies used to be a part of the community, to have more involvement in community development and play the role of the state. However, this notion has become outmoded, with mining companies failing to support communities the way they used to. They do some community development, but only as corporate social responsibility projects, and are unable to take on state responsibilities. As shown above, Copperbelt's case of privatization and neoliberal reform ended up causing the government, particularly local government, to take on more responsibilities than before.

In conclusion, whether the expectations in question are optimistic or pessimistic, the historical context of extractive activities needs more attention, as this could make for better analyses in the future. At the same time we should strive to understand what kind of government interventions should be undertaken to manage natural resources, and what impacts those interventions will have on both the resources and society. This understanding could improve the prospects for less-developed, resource-rich and opportunity-poor regions.

Notes

1. Zambia's mineral dependency was remarkably high even compared with Latin American mineral exporters. For instance, in the early 1970s Chile's mining sector made up 65 per cent of its exports, and Peru's 18 per cent (Lanning and Mueller, 1979).
2. For the theoretical framework I took a hint from Ferguson (2005), who briefly mentions Zambian copper mining.
3. Due to civil wars in Angola and Mozambique and economic sanctions after Rhodesia's unilateral declaration of independence, major transport routes to harbours were cut.
4. It is thought that Chiluba's government was the more corrupt, and after leaving office Chiluba became one target of the anti-corruption campaign undertaken by Zambia's third president, Levy Muwanawasa.
5. Until the late nineteenth century most Central and Southern African regions were unknown to Europeans, partly due to the uncertainties of tropical climate, disease and distance, but more importantly because the regions were simply not seen as very attractive to the Europeans (Gann, 1958).

6. A statement can be found dating as far back as 1921, when the British government stood in opposition to the colour bar system (Burawoy, 1972).
7. Available in the Lusaka National Museum collection.
8. From the companies' point of view, a new tax system enforced by the government had made new investments unattractive (Cobbe, 1979).
9. This development strategy is not unique to Africa. The Japanese government also enacted new mining rights to nationalize mines and prevent an influx of foreign concerns after the Meiji restoration.

REFERENCES

ACTSA (Action for Southern Africa), Christian Aid and SCIAF (Scottish Catholic International Aid Fund) (2007) "Undermining Development? Copper Mining in Zambia", available at www.actsa.org/Pictures/UpImages/pdf/Undermining%20development%20report.pdf.

Auty, Richard M. (1991) "Mismanaged Mineral Dependence: Zambia 1970–90", *Resources Policy* 17, pp. 170–183.

Basedau, Matthias and Andreas Mehler (2005) *Resource Politics in Sub-Saharan Africa*, Hamburg: Institute of African Affairs.

Bates, Robert H. and Paul Collier (1995) "The Politics and Economics of Policy Reform in Zambia", *Journal of African Economies* 4, pp. 115–143.

Birmingham Post (1954) "Equal Pay Claim by Black and White", *Birmingham Post*, 28 May.

Bostock, Mark and Charles Harvey (1972) *Economic Independence and Zambian Copper: A Case Study of Foreign Investment*, New York: Praeger.

Brown, T. Cocker (1941) *Copper in Africa*, London: Livingstone Press.

Burawoy, Michael (1972) *The Colour of Class on the Copper Mines, from African Advancement to Zambianization*, Manchester: Manchester University Press for Institute for African Studies, University of Zambia.

Cobbe, James H. (1979) *Governments and Mining Companies in Developing Countries*, Boulder, CO: Westview Press.

Copper Industry Service Bureau (1973) *Zambia Mining Year Book 1973*, Kitwe: Copper Industry Service Bureau.

Daniel, Philip (1979) *Africanisation, Nationalisation, and Inequality: Mining Labour and the Copperbelt in Zambian Development*, Cambridge and New York: Cambridge University Press.

Ferguson, James (2005) "Seeing Like an Oil Company: Space, Security, and Global Capital in Neoliberal Africa", *American Anthropologist* 107, pp. 377–382.

Fraser, Alastair and John Lungu (2007) *For Whom the Windfalls? Winners and Losers in the Privatisation of Zambia's Copper Mines*, Lusaka: Civil Society Trade Network of Zambia/Catholic Centre for Justice, Development and Peace.

Gann, Lewis Henry (1958) *The Birth of a Plural Society. The Development of Northern Rhodesia under the British South Africa Company, 1894–1914*, Manchester: Manchester University Press for Rhodes-Livingstone Institute.

Great Britain Colonial Office (1936) *Annual Report on Northern Rhodesia 1935*, London: HMSO.

—— (1951) "Mineral Rights in Northern Rhodesia", Doc. CO795/169/3, National Archives, London.

—— (1954–1956) "Labour Conditions in the Copper Companies of Northern Rhodesia", in *Labour Conditions in Northern Rhodesia Copper Mines*, Doc. CO1015/935, National Archives, London.

Guillebaud, C. W. (1954) "African Miners' Fight for Advancement: A Major Rhodesian Problem", *Birmingham Post*, 20 May.

Humphreys, Macartan, Jeffrey Sachs and Joseph E. Stiglitz (2007) *Escaping the Resource Curse*, New York: Columbia University Press.

Lanning, Greg and Marti Mueller (1979) *Africa Undermined: Mining Companies and the Underdevelopment of Africa*, Harmondsworth and New York: Penguin.

Northern Rhodesia (1941) "Report of the Commission Appointed to Inquire into the Disturbances in the Copperbelt, Northern Rhodesia", statement by government of Northern Rhodesia on recommendations of report of the Copperbelt Commission, 1940, Government Printer, Lusaka.

—— (1953) "Labour and Mines Department Annual Report for the Year 1952", UK National Archives, Lusaka.

Ohadike, Patrick O. (1969) *Development of and Factors in the Employment of African Migrants in the Copper Mines of Zambia, 1940–66*, Manchester: Manchester University Press for University of Zambia Institute for Social Research.

Scott, James C. (1998) *Seeing Like a State: How Certain Schemes to Improve the Human Condition Have Failed*, New Haven, CT, and London: Yale University Press.

Sklar, Richard L. (1975) *Corporate Power in an African State: The Political Impact of Multinational Mining Companies in Zambia*, Berkeley, CA: University of California Press.

World Bank (2010) "World Databank – World Development Indicators", available at http://databank.worldbank.org.

8

Post-growth community development and rediscovery of resources: A case of rural regeneration in a Japanese mountain village

Naofumi Suzuki

Introduction

Japanese rural communities are faced with the challenge of tackling problems of ageing and depopulation. While population ageing is a problem recognized worldwide (East-West Center, 2002; Chinese Academy of Social Sciences et al., 2010), it is arguably most pressing in Japan, which has the highest proportion in the world of people aged 65 years or older (CIA, 2009) – they constituted nearly a quarter of the population in 2011 (Cabinet Office, 2012). Moreover, population ageing is more severely felt in rural areas, as young adults tend to move to urban areas for better employment opportunities and accessible schools for their children. Indeed, a number of villages in Japan are now on the verge of extinction due to extreme ageing and depopulation (Ohno, 2005, 2008). The term *genkai-shuraku*[1] has been popular in Japanese media lately. It means a rural settlement that has lost its population, with the age distribution of the remaining inhabitants skewed disproportionately towards the elders, and is thus unlikely to be able to sustain itself in the near future. More specifically, Ohno (ibid.), who was quick to identify this problem in the early 1990s, defines it as a settlement where those aged 65 and over constitute 50 per cent or more of the population, making it incapable of conducting a range of traditional community activities.

This degeneration experienced by rural communities in Japan might be considered the inevitable side-effect of the economic prosperity the country has enjoyed for a long time. This growth would have never been

Governance of natural resources: Uncovering the social purpose of materials in nature, Sato (ed.),
United Nations University Press, 2013, ISBN 978-92-808-1228-2

possible without urbanization, and low mortality and fertility are the signs of a successful, modern, developed society. Thus Japan might have been destined for today's suffering when it set its sights on growth and development. Nonetheless, it still seeks GDP (gross domestic product) growth. Post-development thinkers are critical of the conventional belief that growth is the solution to the contemporary problems faced by global society. For Latouche (1993), development may never be achieved by the South, in part because the nations of the South have nowhere else to exploit, as did the North, and in part for cultural reasons. He uses the term "degrowth" to point out that growth itself may be the problem (Latouche, 2004). Although it would be unrealistic to discard the idea of development and growth altogether (Pieterse, 1998, 2000), the case of Japan's rural villages might provide valuable insights into what the consequence of "growth" could eventually look like and whether and how we might manage to survive the "post-growth" era without sacrificing the rural.

Whether or not we commit to growth, resources are essential for survival. The built environment surrounding us now may represent our effort to make the most of the resources at a given time and place. Once built, however, it is difficult to alter physical structures, while social structures are often more easily shifted from one form to another. Thus we might be required to negotiate this mismatch and discover innovative uses of our given built environment. The case presented here could be seen as an example of such a struggle for survival.

This chapter aims to explore the process through which people discover (and rediscover) the value of community resources and organize themselves to maintain them. In so doing, it reconsiders the relationship between resources and communities. The next section critically examines the current discourse on rural regeneration in Japan to provide the context of research. The case study, conducted in a remote mountain village in Kochi prefecture, seems to provide an alternative approach to the regeneration of an ageing, depopulated rural village. The final sections discuss the implications of the study for the need to rethink the relationship between resource governance and community development.

Resource governance and regeneration of Japanese rural villages

The degeneration of rural communities in Japan is of considerable relevance to resource governance, since the loss of community activities in these settlements would mean that the wealth of natural resources they used to provide would also be lost due to the lack of proper management (Ohno, 2005). This would result in the abandonment of agricultural fields and cessation of the maintenance of planted forests, causing increased risk of landslides, increased bird and animal damage and the loss of traditional lifestyles and beautiful scenery (Miyazaki, 2000; Chusankan Chiiki Forum, 2010). Thus the regeneration of these rural villages and the restoration of the surrounding natural and ecological environments are supposedly of considerable importance.

However, from the perspective of resource governance, it becomes unclear in what sense and for whom these elements of rural environment are "resources". To the individuals who have opted to abandon their fields and/or forests, these lands are clearly no longer "resources" required for livelihood; they have found more productive resources in what they are doing elsewhere. Some have left their villages to take up jobs in other sectors, usually in cities, and others have become too old for work in the fields but can get by on their pensions. Even for those who still farm, this is often not their primary source of income. Furthermore, the fewer people engaging in agriculture, the more costs are imposed on the remaining farmers for the maintenance of their farming practice. Thus the process of abandonment might be accelerating.

Hence the abandonment of agricultural fields and forests may be an inevitable consequence of the fact that these lands are no longer viable resources for private landowners. In the meantime, however, it is often claimed that the rural environment has to be preserved for the good of the wider public:

> Rural areas are where we Japanese can feel at home and enjoy the scenery of our childhood memories, as they preserve ecological diversity, beautiful scenery and traditional culture. Agricultural and mountain villages do not only produce food, but also have multifaceted public values in terms of the natural environment and national land conservation. (Chusankan Chiiki Forum, 2010, author's translation)

Miyazaki (2000: 200–201) argues that abandoned terraced rice fields in particular must be restored, since they constitute an "important natural resource" because of the biodiversity they accommodate, the rare species inhabiting them and the valuable traditional Japanese farming scenery they provide. Presumably, preservation of these "natural resources" is in the national interest.

Here, the question arises as to who should bear the cost of restoration. If fields and forests must be properly managed in the interests of the general public, then perhaps the state should bear it. However, the costs could easily be shifted to the local community. In arguing for the need to regenerate the ageing, depopulating mountain villages, Ohno (2005: 78) maintains that as the impoverishment of nature and people goes hand in hand, the "mountains" are faced with the loss of their capability to manage local resources, which in turn damages the national interest in both social and environmental terms, ranging from water resource conservation to the preservation of ecological systems. He goes on to argue that restoration of the capability of resource management is needed at the local level. It sounds as though local communities are to be maintained in order to serve the public good, although the "local resources" are not productive enough for the communities themselves. Such self-sacrifice would be unlikely. Local resources must serve local people directly for the community to want to manage them. The case below may in part illustrate this.

About the case study

The study was conducted in a remote rural mountain village, Choja, one of the villages within the jurisdiction of Niyodogawa-cho, located about 60 km west of Kochi city. Niyodogawa-cho was formed in 2005 through the merger of three municipalities, Agawa-mura, Niyodo-mura and Ikegawa-cho; the latter two were among Ohno's (2005, 2008) original case study areas. Choja is one of the largest villages within the old Niyodo-mura area. Its population was around 800, comprising 300 households, in 2009 (Nishimoto, Nagai and Suzuki, 2010).

While most of the other villages of old Niyodo-mura have already passed the threshold of *genkai-shuraku*, Choja has been fortunate enough to keep the proportion of those aged 65 and over to around 40 per cent, mainly because it has been the base of a limestone mining company for years and thus accommodates a significant working population. One of the two remaining primary schools within the old Niyodo-mura area is located in Choja as well, despite the recent closure of many others.

That said, the shrinking and ageing of the population seem inevitable there, too. Choja consists of 13 subsettlements spread across several kilometres, and each has maintained its unity as a community. Of these settlements, however, those on the peripheries that do not accommodate the employees of the mining company are indeed *genkai-shuraku*, and some are on a course of total abandonment. For example, only three households remain in the smallest of the subsettlements, which reportedly had around 16 households at its peak.

In response to this situation, local inhabitants have started revitalizing the village and three local festivals have been launched within the last five years: the Iris Festival in June, the Tanabata Festival in August and the Choja de Candle Night in December. These are now said to attract thousands of people. In running these events voluntarily, local people have started to organize themselves into a network of people joining forces to regenerate the community.

The study was conducted from December 2008 to date, including 10 field visits (a total of 46 days), participant observations in each of the three locally organized annual festivals, semi-/unstructured interviews with over 60 people, two workshops, communication network question-naires for workshop participants and a social network survey of the whole population. The main interest has been the process by which the endogenous effort to regenerate an ageing, depopulating village develops itself and gains momentum. Thus the central subject of the research is a voluntary community-based organization called the Dan-dan club, a name inspired by the once-abandoned terraced rice fields it has been at-tempting to restore and by the local dialectal greeting, which means "goodbye", "thank you" or "take it easy". The club voluntarily maintains the terraced rice fields situated in the centre of the village, which are also the venue for the aforementioned three events. The club was founded by a few people who, after retirement, started volunteering to mow and weed the fields and plant flowers to beautify them. It now has over 80 members.

Another community-based group, the Hoshigakubo-kai, is in charge of maintaining an open space at the top of the mountain looking down over the main settlement cluster of Choja. The site is called Hoshigakubo, or the "hollow of the star", named after the pond in the middle of this space, mythically believed to be the result of a meteorite impact. The Hoshigakubo-kai, with 15 or so members, was launched a few years ago to take over maintenance of the place from the forest owners' cooperative when pub-lic funding to outsource the work was halved. The local educational com-mittee has held an annual hiking event here for many years, which the Hoshigakubo-kai nonetheless regards as its own annual festival. These two groups, in partnership with Kochi University and Niyodogawa-cho, formed a community council engaged in starting up sustainable commu-nity regeneration projects endogenously. This study was designed to ex-amine their early efforts at driving the community towards that goal.

Choja's history and community resources

This section sketches a brief history of the community of Choja and the resources the inhabitants have been dependent upon in the post-war period. It is worth noting that rice cropping has never been the main in-dustry there. Until the 1960s paper mulberry provided monetary income, while rice cropping was primarily for private consumption. The 1960s and 1970s saw a rapid decline in the primary industry, along with a population outflow. Paper mulberry fields became unproductive and were rapidly turned into planted forests with generous state subsidization, promising a handsome return from the future lumber trade within a few decades. Forestry, though, is now virtually non-existent, as it could not compete against foreign lumber, leaving the forests unmaintained. The main industries in Niyodo have been mining and construction since the 1960s and 1970s. Mount Torigata was opened as Japan's largest limestone mine in the late 1960s, and related construction work boomed. Choja in particular provided one of the company dormitories, while one of its major contractors was also based in Choja (Niyodo-sonshi Henshu Iinkai, 2005). Hence, one can argue that Choja was first a community of paper mulberry and then became one of limestone.

Terraced rice fields, community organizations and the growth of regeneration activities

Choja's regeneration activities started in 2005, when local resident Akiyoshi[2] spoke to an amateur photographer taking pictures of the terraced rice fields. Having been on the cover of a book of selected terraced rice fields in Japan (Nakajima, 1999), Choja's stone walls were popular with photographers. On that day, though, the photographer told Akiyoshi that the deterioration of the stone walls due to the abandonment of the fields disappointed him. Akiyoshi and a few others started a volunteer group to mow and weed some of the fields that had been abandoned because landowners had either been too old to work in the fields or moved out of the village. After the major walls had been restored, they decided to plant irises there instead of rice. When these bloomed for the first time, the club members celebrated together, partying and appreciating the flowers. This was the first of the now familiar annual gatherings around the terraced rice fields. Since then club membership has grown rapidly, reaching around 80 members in 2009, and it now holds three annual festivals, as noted.

These events, however, were not exclusively inspired by the club members. Instrumental to them was another outsider, the then director of the local office of the Ministry of Agriculture, Forestry and Fisheries (MAFF), who was also lecturing at Kochi University at the time. Drawing on his previous experience in overseas projects, he felt that the abandoned rice fields, along with the houses standing upon steep slopes, could be a valuable community resource and began to encourage local people to capitalize on this. Through a series of workshops organized by the university students aimed at "discovering the local treasures", proposals for the events were formulated. But although the ideas might not have been the club's originally, their organization should be credited almost solely to members, except for the first time when the MAFF director was around to give encouragement and assistance. The club members added their own tastes and upgraded the infrastructure by building storage and other amenities. The space around the once-abandoned rice fields is now a place where local people can feel a sense of festivity, and provides them with collective excitement and enjoyment.

As the festivals became something for local residents to look forward to, two important advances were made. First, owners of other rice fields started giving up their lands for the free use of the Dan-dan club; thus private properties have been "communized" for the good of the community. Second, the network of people regenerating the village has grown. Not only does the Dan-dan club have more members now, but the formation of the community council with the Hoshigakubo-kai, Kochi University and Niyodogawa-cho has brought it to the next level. An application was prepared with active encouragement from the town council; the community council originally received a state subsidy of ¥1 million, and then another million for two years from the town council. This would require them to be more forward-looking and conscious of Choja as a whole rather than just enjoying the events around the rice fields. These two issues are explored further in the following subsections.

The symbolic value of terraced rice fields and the communization of private lands

The terraced rice fields are without doubt the focal point of regeneration. One of the remarkable things about the development of regeneration activities there is what may be called the "communization of private lands". Several people own a total of 20 or so sections of rice field. Only three still cultivate six or seven sections as rice paddies; the other owners have given permission to the Dan-dan club to use their lands as the club members wish. This process began rather humbly with the use of a small paddy at the bottom of the cluster to plant irises. After a couple of years, though, with Kochi University stepping in with the festival proposal, it became necessary to use larger fields that are more accessible from the approach road. The owner of the main ones that now stage the event had been out of the village and was not likely to come back. He recalls:

> It was just through a phone call. They [the club] asked me if they could use my rice fields. I didn't really know what they were up to, but I said yes because I wouldn't want to go back and forth to keep on farming anymore anyway. Then, I was invited to the club's AGM at the end of that year. That was when I first saw what they were doing on my fields, and I was quite happy with that. (Taro, landowner)

Other owners followed him. Although most live in Choja, they think they have become too old for work in the fields. They uniformly appreciated the work of the Dan-dan club, and said they would have liked to continue cropping rice, and felt bad and even embarrassed that the fields were left weedy. They all missed the beautiful scenery of golden rice plants, but were content that their lands were kept tidy and they could enjoy the flower blooms and festival events.

A significant case is the owner of the local construction company, who had acquired several paddies relatively recently. He started up the company in his 20s and almost singlehandedly grew it into the most prominent local contractor, with 85 employees in 2009. Although it is not entirely clear for what purpose he originally wanted to acquire fields, he now willingly contributes to the Dan-dan club. He has allowed the club to use his paddies to erect storage sheds and set up the main stage for the events, and mobilizes his employees and machines to help it put up the wire to hang *tanabata* decorations. Club members say it has been a pleasant surprise to see him show such commitment to the local community. He himself once admitted that, having come from a settlement adjacent to Choja, he never tried to mingle with the local people when he was younger.

It is interesting, however, that the terraced rice fields were never thought of as community resources before they were abandoned. Much qualitative evidence suggests they were regarded as private property when they were being cultivated, merely the largest cluster of rice fields located in the centre of Choja. One owner thought them something of a status symbol, since they were notably large and comparatively fertile. Some might speculate that the fields have been symbolic of the local power relations. While it used to be common practice for farmers to help each other when they needed manpower during the planting and harvesting seasons, those who owned the larger fields used to hire temporary workers, mostly women, who would receive either money or a portion of rice in return for their work.

Outsiders' "eyes" were certainly instrumental in discovering the value of the terraced fields as the "stage" for the festivals. It is true that the landscape of Choja in general and that of the rice fields in particular appeal to visitors. A newly appointed schoolteacher had been impressed with the scenery since moving to Choja earlier that year; she was coincidentally doing "discovering Choja's treasure" workshops in her class when the author visited Choja to run a similar workshop. Two workshop participants from Kochi University, accompanying a friend born and raised in Choja, were also very excited about the views.

It is worth noting that there are still many terraced rice fields being cultivated in Choja. For instance, there is a particularly large, well-maintained cluster in one of the peripheral subsettlements. This is kept in a perfect condition as rice fields, and people agree they are as beautiful as the abandoned ones used to be. However, in terms of symbolic power to bring people together, the latter seem to have an advantage. This could be because to appreciate the fields in the peripheral settlement, you have to go further up the mountain to have a good view, whereas those in the centre of Choja are located along the approach road to the main settlement cluster and are very easy to view from many different angles. What decides the symbolic value of a particular place is an issue to be explored elsewhere.

Development of a regeneration network and its challenges

In spite of the rapid and steady increase in club membership during the first few years and the launch of the community council, the community regeneration effort has not been without its problems. First, there seem to be significant gaps in the network of regeneration (Suzuki and Matous, 2010; Suzuki, 2011a, 2011b). Figure 8.1 shows the network of verbal communication about a workshop. As participants were recruited using the personal contacts of core Dan-dan club members, this could be seen to reflect their ability to reach other community members. It indicates that two gaps must be bridged: that of generation and that between Choja's subsettlements (Suzuki and Matous, 2010).

The age distribution is not shown in Figure 8.1, but in fact seven of the 10 small components (on the left) detached from the main one (on the right) are cases "where young members of the community, such as primary school pupils, high school and university students, and a woman in the early twenties, only referred to their classmates or family members, and for some reasons a link to any of the adults connected in the main component is missing" (ibid.). The Dan-dan club, composed mainly of people in their 60s and over, has worked quite closely with the local primary school, giving children opportunities to experience agricultural work using club fields; thus the presence of pupils in the workshop was not surprising, but there was an obvious lack of people in their 20s to 50s – the working population.

However, of perhaps more direct relevance to the concern of this chapter is the geographical gap. The large cluster on the right consists mostly of those living in settlements close to the terraced rice fields, whereas those from more peripheral settlements tend to appear separate on the left. Indeed, much qualitative evidence suggests that those who live in more peripheral settlements tend to distance themselves from the activities of the Dan-dan club, the simplest explanation for this being that they have little business there in their daily lives.

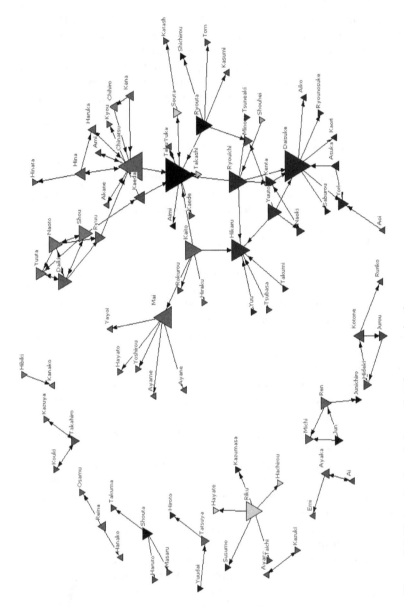

Figure 8.1 Network of workshop-related communication
Source: Suzuki and Matous (2010).

An extended study is being conducted to explore what might be the more precise factors determining these gaps. While the quantitative data analysis has just got under way, early indications through the qualitative data have concerned the local dynamics revolving around the Dan-dan club. First, the attitude of the Hoshigakubo-kai has been rather ambivalent. It is quite evident that its launch was inspired by the "success" of the Dan-dan club. The town council's educational committee at first attempted to contract out the maintenance of Hoshigakubo to the Dan-dan club, but the club declined the offer, apparently due to a lack of capacity. Then Tomio, a town councillor from Choja, gathered his friends and established the Hoshigakubo-kai to take charge of it.

Although there is some membership overlap between the two groups, the core members are mainly from different subsettlements, with most Hoshigakubo-kai members residing higher up and thus nearer to their site. The two cooperate to some degree, in that they put up shops for each other's festivals; but they also keep some distance from each other. Asked if he would like to collaborate more with the Dan-dan club, for instance in organizing a tour to Hoshigakubo in conjunction with the club's Tanabata festival, Tomio was very clear that competition rather than collaboration was the way forward:

> We can't possibly take their customers away. It is good that we have separate responsibilities. If they do that, then we do this. You know? Competition makes us better. (Tomio, core member of the Hoshigakubo-kai)

While "rivalry" might be the word to describe the relationship between the two groups, a larger challenge would probably lie in getting the locals who are not part of either group involved. Some of them just look indifferent, and others may be described as bystanders or free riders.

The most notable among the indifferent mass are the tenants of the mining company's dormitories, who constitute the large proportion of Choja's working population. While the core members of the Dan-dan club have been keen on recruiting younger people to succeed them, only a few of the 80 or so dormitory tenants are members of the club. This may be natural, as most come from outside Choja and thus are not well integrated with the natives. However, if the regeneration effort is to be sustained, it will be necessary to involve this group. Now, though, they may be more concerned with family life than with volunteering in the community.

Other groups among the natives are conscious of what the Dan-dan club has been doing but do not participate in it for different reasons. For example, Naoyuki, a postman in his late 50s who is well respected in the community, considers it would be better for him not to help out, at least for now:

> I am not going to help them for now. It is good for them to do that by them-selves. It keeps them fit and motivated for a while.

Other people clearly state that volunteering is not for them, as it is a "luxury" they cannot afford while coping with daily life. The most com-mon answer to the question "Why don't you participate in the Dan-dan club?" is "I'm too busy taking care of my own fields/forests." They have their own ways of enjoying their spare time, however, which will be ex-plored in a future study. Also noticeable are those who clearly like the events held at the rice fields and look proud that Choja is able to host such festivals. The Candle Night, in particular, seems to be very popular among the locals. This might not necessarily mean they would be willing to take the time to help out with event preparation, not to mention the rather routine maintenance work of the terraced fields. Indeed, the regular participants in such work seem to be limited to six to eight core members.

The rice fields as "rediscovered" community resources

The development process of the Dan-dan club, or that of community re-generation in Choja on the whole, illustrates how abandoned agricultural resources may become symbolic and function as the focal point of regen-eration to mobilize people in and out of the area in maintaining and pro-moting a sense of community. This process has been characterized not only by cooperation and integration but also conflicts of different kinds, sometimes inflicted by outsiders' interventions and sometimes provoked within local communities. Nevertheless, the community has made signifi-cant progress in terms of revitalization over the last few years. This sec-tion discusses what implications this example may have in terms of resource governance and community development.

The restored terraced rice fields are no doubt the symbol of Choja's regeneration. Few could dispute the positivity that the Dan-dan club and its now famous festivals have brought to Choja. The restoration of the stone terraces, in particular, provides an interesting example of private properties becoming communized to serve the community. The rice pad-dies were abandoned simply as a result of personal decisions when they had become too costly for their owners to maintain. However, that is when people realized the positive externality they had enjoyed. The owners were willing to open up their lands for communal use and are thankful to the club for keeping the paddies as something valuable to the community.

That said, the Dan-dan club finds it challenging to gain more support from the locals. A number of locals now appreciate the value of their festivals and look forward to them, but not as many are willing to give up their spare time for volunteer work. If we call this attitude "free riding", it might be another piece of evidence, though ironic, that the club's work has the characteristics of a public good. It should not be overlooked, however, that the restored rice fields probably serve as "resources" for a limited number of people as yet. The presence of the Hoshigakubo-kai is an illustration of this. It is clear that the location of the places significantly influences the membership of the two organizations. It is also evident that a significant proportion of the locals are fairly indifferent to what the Dan-dan club has been doing.

In what sense, then, are the terraced rice fields "resources" to the community? What do the landowners gain from giving up their lands? What drives the core members of the Dan-dan club to do the rather mundane volunteer maintenance work? What has motivated other members to join the club, when they are not so keen on volunteering? What keeps the non-members away from the club? And can we really call them "community resources"?

First, for the landowners, the land has little personal utility. The cost of maintaining the rice fields is simply unbearable, and it is much cheaper to purchase the rice they need. However, they are well aware that leaving the paddies unmaintained incurs negative externality to the community – such as the deterioration of scenery and added costs for the maintenance of surrounding paddies – and feel embarrassed about it. Seeing their lands kept not just neat and tidy but even beautified must be pleasing; they can live the community life without being embarrassed, but proud. Thus their gain is a psychological one coming from being part of the community.

Second, it is worth noting that most core members of the Dan-dan club are permanent settlers who moved in from adjoining villages to work and "u-turners" born in Choja who moved out for work and came back after quite a long time. They are not complete outsiders, but they might feel, overtly or subconsciously, more or less marginal in the community. Indeed, the "putting something back into the community" mentality is evident in some of them. Some even claim they are consciously acting as a "disturbing factor", in hopes that people will become more outward looking. The ironic fact that the "core" members are in fact on the "periphery" of the community might be one of the driving forces in their

dedication to the club activities. Thus, what they seek through the restoration of the rice fields and the organization of the festivals may be a
sense of belonging to the community.

Third, more observation is needed to understand the motivations of
the other, less frequent, participants in the club. There seem to be at least
two different types. One is the "next generation" aged 50–60, who are
close to the core members but still have full-time jobs and so have limited spare time for volunteering compared to the core members. The
other is an older group, mostly female, who come out for lighter tasks
such as weeding but are too old to do more physically demanding tasks,
like mowing and putting up the stage, wires and tents for the festivals.
Despite these limitations, however, they are supportive of what the core
members do, and, notably, they may not be as marginal in the community
as the core members. Thus their support might be construed as a sign that
they now regard the core members as part of the community.

Finally, non-members can be broadly classified into three groups. One
is the indifferent group, who do not consider themselves part of the local
community; the typical example being employees of the mining company,
who are probably only temporary residents. This group may have no business at all with the terraced rice fields. Another category is the bystanders
and free riders, the natives who have not joined the club but are not particularly hostile to it. This group enjoys the benefit of the rice fields' restoration to some extent, most likely as customers of the festivals. The
final category is the more hard-core natives, who are not happy about the
club and probably still consider its core members as "outsiders".

This latter category seems to coincide with geographical remoteness
from the rice fields. They tend to live in one of the relatively peripheral
subsettlements and identify themselves with their own settlement rather
than the whole of Choja. Thus the rice fields have likely not been "resources" to them, nor have they been anything that represents their sub-
community. However, now that the Dan-dan club and the restored rice
fields are increasingly recognized as the "symbol" of Choja in outsiders'
eyes (including in the media), some might have felt their identities threatened. The Hoshigakubo-kai may have rediscovered its own community
resource as a counter to the Dan-dan club's rice fields. By doing so, however, they have come to work together with the Dan-dan club, so they
could have their presence felt in the community as well. In that sense,
they might also be dependent on the restored rice fields to a significant
extent.

Hence the "rediscovery" of the rice fields as "community resources"
could be understood as the consequence of distinct acts by different
groups of people seeking their own gain. The rice fields are "resources"
for different people in different senses. They may not provide the com-

munity with material benefits, yet they play a central role in the dynamics of community development. They work as the catalyst of interaction within the community, which otherwise would be quieter and less connected (Suzuki and Matous, 2010).

Resource governance and community development

This case provides us with a basis for critiquing the current dominant discourse of resource governance and rural regeneration in Japan, and that of community development in general. The main argument for rural regeneration is that the community needs to restore its capacity to manage its "invaluable" natural resources. Community development is considered the means to natural resource management. Choja's case may indicate the opposite – that the management of the resources is the means to community development.

First, the restoration of the rice fields has aimed to preserve neither biodiversity nor the tradition of rice cropping – the "important natural resources" in Miyazaki's (2000) sense. The stone terraces were restored, but rice paddies were turned into flowerbeds. The club has deliberately chosen to do so, balancing the limited amount of time they could allocate to volunteering and the rather humble returns of enjoying the festivals three times a year, along with a small income from the vegetables they have recently started producing. They admit that it would be "ideal" if they could go back to rice cropping, but they must also know very well that this is only nostalgia and beyond their capability. They may not have met the general criteria of rice field restoration, but they have found a sustainable balance which satisfies their own interests.

Second, notwithstanding the club members' dedication to the community, "development" in the sense of economic and/or demographic growth could probably not be expected of Choja. The macroscopic trends of ageing and depopulation are too powerful for one community to reverse singlehandedly. Some might argue that it is still possible to create employment and grow the local economy through community enterprises, referring to many cases of "good practice" which can be found nationwide (METI, 2011). Choja does not seem to follow any of the conventional models, though. Its approach so far differs from popular ones, like the invention of a community brand and the promotion of either agricultural or event tourism. Its festivals do attract visitors from Choja and beyond, but there is only one hotel, with a capacity of about 20 people per night. It is not that they have given up hope of creating business; in fact, they often talk of the necessity of generating income, and a "farmers' restaurant" has been envisioned from the beginning. That said, the major changes this regeneration movement has brought have remained internal, with the typical ingredients of community development: community members seem more connected with each other, confident in carrying out the events by themselves and linked with external support such as the town council, prefectural government officials and several universities. In short, the effect of capacity building is evident, yet the "end product" of economic prosperity still seems a long way away – if it ever comes.

Indeed, the conventional models of regional regeneration may rely too much on "community branding" and the expected increase in the "non-resident population". It seems inevitable that this will lead to competition among regions and create "winners" and "losers". When the national population is projected to shrink, it is more likely you end up on the side of the "losers". Choja may not be a "winner", but has been invigorated nonetheless. Community development there is not directed towards the preservation of either "important" natural resources or the "tradition" of rural farming villages, nor is it likely to lead to economic and demographic development. It may still be important in itself, however, allowing the community to remain a community. Hence it may not be the resources themselves but the interactions within the community provoked by the process of managing those resources that are necessary for sustaining the community.

The material environment may not change easily. However, this case study may illustrate how a community can adjust itself to cope with this reality by making innovative use of the given environment. Zimmerman (1951), using the phrase "resources are not; they become", suggests that a resource does not pre-exist the human discovery of the use of something for some purpose (De Gregori, 1987). Thus resources are inherently transient, and certain materials can be resources in different senses for different people at different times. On the other hand, Park's (1936) ecological definition of "community" suggests that communities are also transient. In Park's sense, a community is essentially a symbiotic system in which people live interdependently on the ecological resources available within a territory. In much the same way as plants and animals do, human beings compete for resources to achieve a balanced state in which a certain group appears dominant, but this state is eventually disturbed in one way or another, and competition intensifies again to reach another balanced state.

The point is that a community itself is destined to change as it alters its own environment. In other words, who becomes dominant within the system depends on adaption to the change in available resources. The local dynamics in Choja, including the formation of the Dan-dan club, the Hoshigakubo-kai and the community council, may be understood in light of this. In Choja, like many other rural villages in Japan, fewer resources are available for people to rely on. Jobs have been lost and public services – such as public transport, road maintenance, schools and hospitals – are being "rationalized" and closed down. However, a community striving to live in its given environment can do so by making the most of the remaining scarce resources or even exploiting resources seemingly of little use. Choja's regeneration movement may be one such example. There is no way back to its "traditional" community practices, nor could it afford to "preserve its natural resources", but it can still struggle to be a community, with members sometimes competing against and sometimes depending upon one another. The complex process of discovery and rediscovery of resources could be understood as an essential part of a community's struggle for survival. A more profound understanding of such complexity would provide insights into effective ways of intervening in struggling communities.

Notes

1. The term might literally translate as a "settlement pushed to the limit", though the answer to "the limit of what?" is not entirely clear. Translated more freely, a "settlement on the verge of extinction" might represent its nuance more precisely. Some might prefer the term "marginal community", which could embrace a broad range of minority groups and thus is avoided here.
2. The names of informants in this chapter are pseudonyms.

REFERENCES

Cabinet Office (2012) "Heisei 24nen-ban Kourei Shakai Hakusho" ("White Paper on Aged Society, Year 2012 Edition"), available at http://www8.cao.go.jp/kourei/whitepaper/w-2012/zenbun/24pdf_index.html (in Japanese).
Chinese Academy of Social Sciences, Indian National Science Academy, Indonesian Academy of Sciences, National Research Council of the US National Academies and Science Council of Japan (2010) *Preparing for the Challenges of Population Aging in Asia: Strengthening the Scientific Basis of Policy Development*, Washington, DC: National Academy Press, available at www.nap.edu/catalog/12977.html.
Chusankan Chiiki Forum (2010) "Chusankan Chiiki Forum No Mezasumono" ("Aims of Chusankan Chiiki Forum"), available at www.chusankan-f.net/ (in Japanese).
De Gregori, T. R. (1987) "Resources Are Not; They Become: An Institutional Theory", *Journal of Economic Issues* 21(3), pp. 1241–1263.

East-West Center (2002) *The Future of Population in Asia*, Honolulu, HI: East-West Center.

Latouche, S. (1993) *In the Wake of the Affluent Society: An Exploration of Post-Development*, London: Zed Books.

——— (2004) "Why Less Should Be So Much More: Degrowth Economics", *Le Monde Diplomatique*, English edn, November, available at http://mondediplo.com/2004/11/14latouche.

METI (2011) *Social Business Casebook: Chiiki Ni "Tsunagari" To "Hirogari" Wo Umidasu Hinto (Social Business Casebook: Hints to Create "Connections" and "Breadth" in Areas)*, Tokyo: Ministry of Economy, Trade and Industry (in Japanese).

Miyazaki, T. (ed.) (2000) *Kankyo Hozen To Kouryu No Chiiki Zukuri: Chusankan Chiiki No Shizen Shigen Kanri System (Environmental Preservation and Community Development through Population Exchange: The Natural Resource Management System in Mountainous and Semi-Mountainous Areas)*, Kyoto: Showado (in Japanese).

Nakajima, M. (1999) *Nippon No Tanada: Hozen He No Torikumi (Terraced Rice Fields in Japan: Effort towards Preservation)*, Tokyo: Kokonshoin (in Japanese).

Nishimoto, H., K. Nagai and N. Suzuki (2010) "A Study on the Living Space of the Residents in a Remote Mountainous Village: A Case of Choja Village in Niyodogawacho, Kochi, Japan", *Journal of Society for Social Management Systems* SMS10-141, available at http://management.kochi-tech.ac.jp/ssms_papers/sms10_141Kohei%20Nagai100118_0559_Web.pdf.

Niyodo-sonshi Henshu Iinkai (2005) *Niyodo-sonshi Tsuiho (History of Niyodo Village, New Edition)*, Niyodo-mura: Niyodo-mura Educational Committee (in Japanese).

Ohno, A. (2005) *Genkai Shuraku to Chiiki Saisei (Genkai-shuraku and Regional Regeneration)*, Kochi: Kochi Shinbunsha (in Japanese).

——— (2008) *Sanson Kankyo Shakaigaku Josetsu (An Introduction to Environmental Sociology of Mountainous Villages)*, Tokyo: Noubunkyo (in Japanese).

Park, R. E. (1936) "Human Ecology", *American Journal of Sociology* 42(1), pp. 1–15.

Pieterse, J. N. (1998) "My Paradigm or Yours? Alternative Development, Post-Development, Reflexive Development", *Development and Change* 29, pp. 343–373.

——— (2000) "After Post-Development", *Third World Quarterly* 21(2), pp. 175–191.

Suzuki, N. (2011a) "A Study of the Development Process of a Voluntary Organization Aimed for Rural Regeneration: Combining Qualitative and Quantitative Approaches", paper presented at Eighth Workshop on Social Capital and Development Trends in the Japanese and Swedish Countryside, Nara, 20–22 May.

——— (2011b) "Measuring the Process of Rural Regeneration: A Social Network Approach to Understanding Community Dynamics", in K. Kobayashi, H. Westlund and H. Jeong (eds) *Social Capital and Development Trends in Rural Areas*, Vol. 7, Kyoto: Kyoto University, pp. 57–67.

Suzuki, N. and P. Matous (2010) "The Relevance of Symbolic Physical Environment to the Formation of Social Networks for Rural Regeneration", *Journal of Society for Social Management Systems* SSMS10-158, available at http://management.kochi-tech.ac.jp/ssms2010/ssms_paper2010/sms10_158%20Naofumi%20Suzuki100117_2201_web.pdf.

US Central Intelligence Agency (2009) "The World Factbook", Japan, available at https://www.cia.gov/library/publications/the-world-factbook/geos/ja.html.

Zimmerman, E. (1951) *World Resources and Industries*, New York: Harper & Bros.

9

Fishermen's plantations as a way of resource governance in Japan

Tomohiro Oh

Introduction

Typical studies on natural resources from a social science perspective tend to choose one type of resource – forests, for example – and ask what factors contribute to the sustainable use or wasteful exploitation of that resource. This approach, however, downplays the very definition of resources as a "bundle of potential use" (Sato, 2007). In other words, the resourcefulness of a material lies not in its material characteristics but in its potential to be utilized, and this particular potential must be discovered by society. Resources should therefore be defined as one outcome of the interaction between humans and nature (Hunker, 1964). This definition helps us to differentiate the otherwise indistinguishable concepts of "raw materials" and "resources" – while the former refers to materials that have set objectives (such as oil, which is used for energy), resources only have potential that has yet to be harnessed in any specific form.

The original concept of resources as having predefined uses has far-reaching implications in both rhetoric and practice. Focusing instead on the unrealized potential (or multiple possibilities) of resources forces us to consider the trade-offs between options for using a particular resource and the way resources are transformed into goods. This distinction is important because, supposing that environmental problems can be attributed primarily to the way humans consume goods, we must not only address our consumer culture but also the way in which resources are made into goods.

Governance of natural resources: Uncovering the social purpose of materials in nature, Sato (ed.), United Nations University Press, 2013, ISBN 978-92-808-1228-2

Ensuring an analytical scope that accurately captures the advantages and disadvantages of various possible resource uses is particularly important in the modern age of environmental conservation and economic development, where concerns about inequality with respect to resource use and access have become unavoidable. But how can we identify these key trade-offs when they are often so hard to observe directly? The examples illustrated here aim to provide a starting point in answering this question.

Before proceeding, however, it is crucial to keep one thing in mind – in contrast to typical international discussions, I discuss Japan not as an "advanced" case where various dilemmas have been successfully addressed by the government through the optimal use of technology, but rather as a nation seeing an emerging trend that is based on a new awareness of the connections between resources and the environment. This movement is, in a way, a reaction to the excessive division of labour encouraged by the market economy, and the resulting fragmentation of government structure that has failed to address local ecological problems holistically.

This study pays particular attention to interactions between coastal and forest resources through the medium of local society. These interactions form the basis of the local resource system. Broadleaf trees offer one clue to understanding this system. In addition to supplying timber or pulp, forests perform a number of functions and provide various utilities for humans. From multiple possibilities, these functions are derived from interactions among resources, including culture, technology and capital.

To understand the relationship among forests, sea and local society, one must scrutinize the mechanism by which, in the presence of several potential options, humans extract particular chosen functions or a combination of functions from natural resources. Also, before effective rules regarding resource use can be implemented, the local system already in place must be thoroughly understood. For these reasons, local movements for resource conservation warrant attention; such movements represent the final outcome of the history of interactions among humans, society and nature.

Why do fishermen plant trees?

The cost of economic growth in Japan

While Japan is often considered synonymous with high population density and scarce natural resources, this is not the case for the entire country. It is true that Japan's economic growth was boosted primarily by the industrial sector, which manufactured exports using raw materials imported from abroad. However, Japan also has the world's sixth-widest exclusive economic zone (4.5 million km^2), which is about 12 times larger than the country's land area (0.38 million km^2). Forested areas cover 67 per cent of this land area and have been maintained at around 25 million ha since the end of the Second World War.[1] Although the supply of raw materials necessary for industry, such as oil and minerals, is low, a broader definition of what comprises natural resources reveals that Japan is relatively resource rich. But on the other hand, it can be said that people have suffered from the negative side of resources, i.e. the risks of natural disaster, such as tsunamis in coastal regions or landslides in the mountainous areas in an age of frequent earthquakes.

After the Second World War, Japan experienced impressive economic growth, particularly during the period between 1955 and 1972. This rapid growth caused significant problems in both natural and social environments nationwide. Serious economic gaps became apparent, especially between rural and urban areas, spurring a labour migration from the countryside into the cities (Okado, 2006). The mass exodus of people from rural areas caused environmental degradation in urban spaces and a shortage of labour in primary industries, and in some cases the disappearance of rural villages.

Large areas of previously undisturbed nature, such as coasts and tidal lands, were exploited for industrial purposes, such as reclamation for developing coastal industrial areas. As a result, tidal lands decreased by about 40 per cent (from 82,000 to 49,000 ha) over the 54 years between 1945 and 1998. The proportion of natural coasts, in contrast to the largely man-made beaches on the main islands, is now only 45 per cent (Policy Research Association on Biodiversity, 2002: 106). Such reckless consumption of coastal resources eventually led to a decrease in fishery resources.

Turning attention to the forest, *Satoyama*, broadleaf trees that were once major vegetation and provided firewood and materials for daily use, have been losing economic value with the drastic change in lifestyles and the conversion of energy source from charcoal or firewood. A large part of the secondary forest was felled for pulp material and became conifer plantations in the 1950s and 1960s. In fact, about 40 per cent of Japan's forests are artificial, created primarily by a nationwide project to plant high-value (at that time) conifers that displaced many of the lower-value broadleaf trees. However, artificial forests cannot be maintained without proper care. Biodiversity is also considered to be poor.

Planners in central government expected technical innovation and scale efficiency to resolve regional imbalances and expand production capacity rather than conserve the resource base. However, in forestry this strategy had limited effectiveness in a country made up of primarily mountainous areas. Furthermore, Japan's ageing society and the decrease in the working population have caused its forestry to lose a certain degree of market competitiveness; e.g. the self-sufficiency ratio of timber in Japan is only about 27 per cent. This situation seems paradoxical given that the proportion of forest cover in Japan, around 67 per cent, is among the highest of any nation in the world.

In short, Japan's industrial development came at the cost of damaging its ecological foundation. Excessive land use by industry, including the agriculture, dairy and forestry sectors, ended up transferring the environmental burden to downstream coastal villages, especially fishing communities.

The spread of fishermen's plantations in the 1990s

Ignoring for a moment the plentiful examples of failure in each form of resource management, there is one success that warrants attention: the gradual expansion of tree planting by fishermen in various parts of Japan. Several cooperative fishery associations started their own individual tree plantations in the late 1980s. Later, in the 1990s, fishermen's tree plantations began to emerge as a social movement. The movement gradually came to life as Japanese society began to pay more and more attention to environmental problems. With government assistance, the practice has now spread throughout the country.

Of course, this movement does not represent the first time coastal fishermen have taken action against environmental problems. Resource conservation in Japan first began to gain momentum in the 1960s and 1970s. Environmental pollution that was a mere nuisance in certain parts of Japan in the early 1950s was shown to have devastating health effects – for example, the notorious Minamata disease – by the 1960s. During this period more than 300 organizations and sufferers developed campaigns against pollution and environmental destruction (Ishi, 1996: 27). Fishermen, who live on coastal resources, were direct sufferers from pollution and reclamation.

Because the primary goal of these campaigns was to protect the health or livelihood of humans rather than to protect the environment, the scope of their activity was often limited to obvious and immediate damage. After governmental regulations began to take effect, particularly following the establishment of the Environment Agency in 1971 and the oil shocks of the 1970s, the pollution problem gradually receded from the centre stage of public attention. Monetary compensation for the cost of pollution or reclamation worked as an incentive for giving up fishing and accelerated the decline in the labour force of the fishing industry.

A striking difference between the recent plantation movement and the "traditional" environmental movement is that, in the former, the fishermen are more aware of the ecological functions of broadleaf trees in watershed areas. Japanese fishermen have long been sensitive to the condition of forests, as almost all materials necessary for fishing (materials for boats and tools, for example) are collected from forests. Mountains also play a key role in enabling ship navigation – "reading the mountain" is one of the most essential skills for fishermen (Hatakeyama, 1994). Local fishermen even knew the forest provided nutrients and valuable shade to fisheries, and trees controlled the outflow of rainwater and soil. Based on the long-held awareness of the connection between forests and fishing, logging was traditionally prohibited in forests along coastal or riverside areas. This tradition was institutionalized with the Forest Law (established in 1897) and the establishment of national forest reserves for fish breeding, both of which remain in place today (Nakata, 2004: 121).

In addition to these official forest reserves for fish breeding established in the past, the plantation movement was triggered by fishermen's newfound appreciation for broadleaf trees and by additional support from the scientific community. Besides providing organic nutrients in the form of fallen leaves, leaf mould supplies a critical substance – iron ions – to coastal ecosystems (Matsunaga, 1993). In the early 1990s marine scientists found that fulvic acid, derived from the deterioration of fallen leaves by microorganisms, delivers iron to coastal zones. Without this additional iron, seaweed and phytoplankton, which require iron to absorb nitrogen, could not grow. The precise mechanism was beyond the fishermen's knowledge, but the fishermen's plantations reflected an accurate insight into the connection between forest and sea resources.

The characteristics of fishermen's plantations can be described in terms of scale and distance. Plantation sites are located near the headwaters or upstream areas of rivers that flow into fishing grounds. Fishermen's incentives to conserve forests originate from a desire to protect their livelihood – the same desire that spurred them to petition for protection against coastal reclamation or pollution. Now, the benefits of their planting activities are being seen far inland and are making significant contributions to the general public, e.g. the improvement of the deteriorated forest environment due to the decline in numbers of mountain villagers accessing the resources.

Because the idea behind the plantation movement was connected to the popular concept of ecosystems, the practices of these fishermen attracted remarkable support and participation from the public and even triggered interest among scientists – not only natural scientists but also social scientists and workers interested in bottom-up community development. Considering the connections between resources, achieving more systematic conservation was found to be essential in overcoming environmental problems, since the root cause of resource degradation is believed to be the fragmented relationships among individual resource uses in a connected system.

Similar movements are found throughout Japan, yet the exact practices differ depending on geographic and social conditions. The conservation movement and incentives leading to conservation-oriented action might offer a wealth of lessons for other areas seeking a path towards sustainable development. Furthermore, understanding the fishermen's practices, and their social and geographical contexts, provides hints about the kind of assistance they might need from outside, and also helps us discover the shortcomings of developmental policies that have failed to address these needs.

I first focus on the case of oyster farmers in Miyagi prefecture. Their successful approach is considered to be the origin of the plantation movement and a flagship practice. I look at what kinds of context urged their pioneering work and how they came up with the idea of fishermen's plantations. Moreover, because Miyagi prefecture, located in northern Japan, was severely damaged in the great east Japan earthquake in March 2011, I discuss the significance of oyster farmers' plantations in the process of recovery from disaster.

Then I turn to the case of Yakushima, an island located in southern Japan, to examine further the social conditions that encouraged fishermen to plant trees and point out the limitations of these activities in addressing resource problems on a regional scale. In an increasingly interconnected world, examination of an island case provides useful analogies and enables us to ask the right questions, revealing in detail how resource systems behave under certain institutional arrangements. A key model for sustainable local development may be extracted from an island context that has limited industrial capability but ample renewable resources.

Restoring the connection between forest and sea: Kesennuma

Plantation against dam construction

Today, fishermen's plantations are frequently mentioned in various media and even school textbooks, and have now achieved nationwide recognition as a symbolic activity of environmental conservation in Japan.[2] The plantation established by the oyster farmers of Karakuwa town in Miyagi prefecture is considered to be one of the most famous. It can also be said that this pioneering activity in the late 1980s triggered the nationwide movement. One oyster farmer suspected that the successful farming of oysters was connected to the forest environment upstream through the river flowing into his oyster farm, Moune Bay, a part of Kesennuma Bay. With his colleague, he began planting broadleaf trees upstream of the Okawa River in 1989. However, the reason the oyster farmers came up with the idea of planting trees in an area far away from the river mouth needs to be scrutinized in more detail, given that the effects of the plantation are not clear immediately and might not be so for decades.

One interesting fact behind their activity is the existence of the Niitsuki Dam project 8 km upstream from the mouth of the Okawa. In 1974 Miyagi prefecture designed the multipurpose dam upon the request of Kesennuma city located next to Karakuwa town. The plan remained under contemplation until the late 1980s. The basic agreement on construction operation between the city and the prefecture was concluded in 1988, after construction expenses were earmarked in the draft fiscal budget in 1987.

It was no coincidence that the oyster farmers' plantation started just before the groundbreaking of the Niitsuki Dam. Oyster farmers are sensitive to the condition of the river water and the growth of their oysters. As a result of economic growth and improvements in living standards, the coastal environment had deteriorated, with pollution from sewage, agricultural wastewater and oil spreading from fish-processing facilities. The oyster farmers experienced an outbreak of red tide plankton in the 1970s; the oyster meat became red-coloured and lost its market value. It was not difficult for a group living in the coastal areas to imagine the negative impact of the dam construction. Once it began, the coastal area could suffer an outflow of muddy water for a decade due to the construction work to reline the road and railway, in addition to the regional development plan with its large-scale forest cutting and land reclamation.

At the same time, it is not difficult to understand why almost everyone living in the district hesitated to argue about the necessity of the dam. Such a large-scale public work was implemented as an economic stimulus to the rural areas, and even though the effect might be short-lived, a large majority of the population would benefit, more and less, from this public enterprise. Although Kesennuma is one of the major ports and a fishery centre in the northern part of Japan, it seemed less concerned about conservation of the coastal area – the large-scale offshore fishery is dominant compared to small-scale fishing in estuarine or coastal areas. As mentioned, the fishermen's earlier action against the degradation of coastal environments had been an exasperating struggle in such an intricate resource system with powerful stakeholders.

How did the oyster farmers, a minority with less political power to work on resource governance, overcome a situation that could induce serious damage to their resource base? In such a seemingly no-win situation, the plantation was the answer to broaden their support and attract potential stakeholders, i.e. the general public, without discussing the contested dam project. One farmer, who later became the leader of the plantation activity, came up with the idea of planting trees in the mountainous area 20 km from their oyster farms, in the upper reaches above the planned construction site (Obitani, 2000). His statement shows that their action was a sophisticated strategy which did not involve speaking out clearly against the dam construction.

> Not to speak with a political tone. We decided to plant trees as the way to capture the mind of people living in the whole watershed area. (Obitani, 2000: 153)

Several tactics were crucial in bringing their activity to public attention (ibid.). First was putting out a catchphrase, "The forest is longing for the sea, the sea is longing for the forest", which is the essence of a Japanese 31-syllable verse produced by a local poet living in the mountainous area upstream of the Okawa River. With the help of this poet, they successfully attracted public attention by using the mutual affection between a loving couple as a metaphor for the relation between the forest and the sea.

Second was the evocation of the local and historical relationship between mountain villages and fishing villages. The oyster farmers involved Murone village, which is located at the southern end of Iwate prefecture, 30 minutes inland from Karakuwa town. They created the first plantation along the lines of the traditional Murone festival, a famous event that has continued for more than 1,000 years. In the festival, different kinds of ceremonial roles are handed down from one generation to another. For example, at the beginning of the festival the fishermen of Karakuwa have the task of collecting tidewater from Kesennuma Bay and offering it to the Murone shrine located at Mt Murone, in the headwaters of the Okawa River. Following the traditional style of this festival, oyster farmers offered tidewater and oysters to the Murone shrine in advance of the plantation being created nearby. Their plantation thus evoked the historical and spiritual bond existing in the local society.

The planting site was called the forest of oysters, and the group the club of longing for oyster forest. The plantation in the mountainous area far from the sea, under the waving flags which are usually used to pray or indicate a large haul of fish, caught the attention of the media and the people. The annual afforestation festival became popular and attracted increasing numbers of participants year by year, and also improved awareness of environmental problems.

Before long, a marine scientist whom the leader consulted about the scientific significance of planting broadleaf trees confirmed the farmers' suspicions (Hatakeyama, 2003: 17). It became clear that the leaf mould of the forest area was playing a critical role in delivering iron to the coastal area via the river. The scientist's opinion, although controversial at the time, gave the farmers the justification and incentives they needed for planting trees in the mountain forest 20 km from their oyster farms.

Besides the direct influence of enhancing the natural environment of the river basin, empowering the fishermen in the resource system was a significant consequence of their activity. The oyster farmers were in the vanguard in conserving the environment as a whole with their dramatic action, which was different from previous conservation focusing on single resources. Their activities were rewarded by the freezing of the dam construction project in 1997.

From growing forest to building society

Fishermen's plantations, first begun as a clever measure against the dam construction, gradually had a ripple effect around the nation at different levels. As described, wood products are no longer indispensable in daily life and have been replaced by other convenient industrial products. The local relationship between the coastal and mountain areas through the use of forest resources, e.g. to get materials for vessels or fishing tackle, had also become poor in the process of modernization, especially from the 1950s. Besides being good practice in environmental conservation, the plantations served as an alternative way to revitalize the rural society through exchanges between mountain and coastal peoples, and also as hands-on ecological education.

Their effect is not limited to improving the coastal environment, which leads to the enrichment of fishery resources, but motivates revitalization efforts in mountainous villages. The people of Murone village, inspired by the oyster farmers' plantation, decided to restore their waterwheel as a symbol of an environmentally conscious development. This promotes organic farming, instead of depending heavily on agricultural chemicals that might be an environmental burden, especially in downstream areas. The oyster farmers welcomed this coast-conscious plan and supported it by selling marine products at cut-rate prices at every opportunity. This old power supply, the waterwheel, tree plantations to conserve the source of water and pro-environmental agriculture indicate a shift from the revitalization of local society through public works to the recovery of the local ecological system and restoration of the connection between upstream and downstream areas.

The impressive and dynamic efforts of the oyster farmers became good educational tools for children to learn about the vague and elusive relationship between resources and the environment. The plantations served as a way for children to learn about the unity of nature and how river pollution damages the fisheries. This enhanced the mutual concern and communication between families living in coastal and mountain areas. The leaders spoke of the critical role of the people in determining methods of resource utilization: "To grow a tree takes fifty years, but it takes just twenty years to raise the children" (Hatakeyama, 2004: 90).

In the 1990s fishermen's plantations became a nationwide movement with the participation of fisheries' cooperatives around the country. This expansion of activities led to enhanced institution building for environment conservation. The National Cooperation of Fisheries decided on plantations as practical tasks to be carried out by its branch organizations. The National Summit on Fishermen's Forests was held in 1998, and the National Forum for Fishermen's Forests in 1999. When the Forest Law was revised in 2001, the newly planted fishermen's forests were annexed into the conservation forest. The government enhanced the action by setting out a five-year project to promote fishermen's forests from 2001, followed by two-year project on "Plantation for fish ground conservation" from 2007. These government schemes promoted the spread of fishermen's plantations nationwide in the 2000s. Activity that had first begun as an environmental conservation measure gradually turned into the creation of an environment and a society that are more sensitive to how they relate to resources, then enhanced the institutional movement.

Now, in the context of the earthquake disaster, the local society will recover from the tragedy through the various links with mountain villages, scientific groups and their supporters around the country which they have formed through the activities. The plantation festival of 2011 was held with such help. At the same time the concept generated from the plantation, the connection between forest and sea, is considered one of the basic ideas on which a future society will be built. When the fishermen's leader was invited to a Ministry of Agriculture, Forestry and Fisheries committee for policy assessment, he insisted the reconstruction plan should utilize problematic conifer plantations around the nation.[3] Because millions of houses have been destroyed and damaged by the tsunami, it is anticipated there will be a great demand for materials for rebuilding the homes of disaster victims. From his holistic view and experience, using the long-abandoned conifers will lead to improvement of the forest, which will eventually enhance marine productivity.

The lesson that can be learned from the oyster farmers' practice is that exploitation of one resource often has repercussions on other resources. Seeking a balance in resource use, then, is more important than the optimal exploitation of a single resource. The scope of use should be carefully evaluated with regard to the possible influences that excessive use might have on the local resource system. The local system consists of relationships between fisheries and forests and links between the different uses of these resources. Fishermen's tree plantations are a reflection of this unity of natural resources, embodying a holistic view of nature that is often downplayed by developmental government strategies. However, the practice does not mean just resource conservation. Relationships built through the plantations could enhance the resilience of society against the negative aspects of nature, i.e. disasters, bringing new ideas that the so-called vertically divided administration finds it hard to come up with.

Plantations in an island of World Natural Heritage: Yakushima

Disturbance of local resource systems and firewood shortage

Yakushima island is geographically isolated and people have traditionally lived on renewable resources. It is located on the stream of the Black Current, which provides excellent fishing grounds. Abundant moisture brought by this warm current fosters the island's rich and varied flora (Yumoto, 1995). Yakushima is therefore regarded as a resource-rich island, despite its location at the periphery of the industrialized centre of mainland Japan. This setting might be analogous to developing countries in the southern hemisphere, where control of rich renewable natural resources is dominated by industrialized centres in the northern hemisphere.

The island is well known for its 1,000-year-old cedar trees, called Yakusugi, which are now strictly protected along with the rich natural environment surrounding them. But despite its international reputation as a World Natural Heritage site, Yakushima could not escape the ecological problems experienced by the rest of the world. This section focuses on the utilization of forest resources and changes in this use during periods of rapid social transformation in Japan. It aims to identify the reasons behind the failure of past developmental policies imposed on Yakushima by showing how they are linked to natural resources and local society.

Dried fish from Yakushima have been a valued commodity for decades and were ranked in the first grade of Japan's dried bonito in 1822 (Miyashita, 2000: 315). Despite its possible geographical disadvantages from being located on the periphery of the archipelago, the island's richness in natural resources, such as forests and fish, has been the major factor contributing to the flourishing fishing industry on Yakushima (Figures 9.1 and 9.2).

Of course, it is not practical to insist on traditional values and local practices alone as the solution to sustainability in every region, and the

Figure 9.1 Dried fish factories located beside Isso River

Figure 9.2 Sun-drying fish, 2006

fishing industry is too small to support the island's entire population today. However, even more important on a small island are the multi-layered coexisting institutions that serve as a buffer when an external economic shock hits. I focus on the local resource exploitation on Yakushima by examining the connections between a firewood shortage and fishermen's tree plantations. Smoke from burning broadleaf trees provides an aroma component that helps to protect dried fish from oxidation. Broadleaf trees have thus been essential to traditional dried fish production on Yakushima. Through discussion of actions concerning broadleaf trees, plus government and market involvement, this study aims to evaluate how social interaction via resource exploitation influences the local resource system.

Yakushima witnessed dramatic changes in forest utilization during the period of modernization in the late nineteenth century. In 1868 the newly formed Meiji central government established nationwide political control and began to carry out national land-use surveys and land tax reforms. Previously, in the Edo era, daily use of wood, such as for firewood and building materials for homes and fishing boats, was not strictly regulated by the local government. However, large portions of the forested areas on Yakushima were designated as the exclusive property of the state in 1882 (Editorial Committee of Kamiyaku Town History, 1984). That state-owned forests account for almost 78 per cent of the wooded areas on Yakushima is an indispensable factor in understanding the history of forest exploitation on the island.

Figure 9.3 shows the broadleaf timber yields from the national forests on Yakushima from 1950 to 2002. After the war, logging and conifer planting operations were started in response to the sudden expansion of national demands for timber. The government enacted several laws to enhance the productivity of the national forest; yields on Yakushima began to increase in the 1950s and expanded sharply in the 1960s.

Meanwhile, broadleaf forests became less important as primary energy resources and were gradually replaced with electricity, gas and oil. In the late 1950s, however, these trees began to attract the attention of the pulp industry. Technological innovation enabled the use of broadleaf trees as raw material for pulp. The Yakushima Forest Development Company, co-founded with several pulp companies outside the island in 1963, undertook pulp chip production.

The demand for pulp material encouraged intense logging in secondary forests composed of broadleaf trees (ibid.: 507). Social and economic situations encouraged local people to plant cedar for future sources of building material rather than leaving the land as secondary forest with almost no market value. The broadleaf timber yield reached its peak during the late 1960s. In the forested areas near Isso village, where most of the dried fish manufacturers were located, broadleaf trees began to decrease, being replaced by cedars, and areas with easy access to Isso residents were almost transformed into cedar forests.

After 1970 the amount of broadleaf timber production began to decrease gradually, triggered by environmental movements to protect 1,000-year-old cedars from excess logging. The problem escalated to the national level, and the Forest Agency was put under pressure to revise its operation policies to be more pro-environment. This re-examination resulted in lower production and a shift from full-scale logging to selective cutting. The step-like decrease in hardwood logging in Figure 9.3 after 1970 was partly because of the opposition campaign.

During this period, fishermen on Yakushima also experienced dramatic changes in their mackerel catch (ibid.: 524). Figure 9.3 shows the catch statistics for the years between 1950 and 2003. Periodical ups and downs in mackerel catch were common throughout this period, suggesting that fluctuations in catch could be attributed not only to the efforts of the fishermen but also to the ecological characteristics of the mackerel habitat.

Around 1980, dried fish manufacturers began complaining of a firewood shortage around Isso (Isso Brokers Union, 1981). By this time the national forestry had already reduced the logging yield in response to pressure from conservation movements to stop logging in natural broadleaf forests. The drastic decline in yield sparked a chronic shortage in broadleaf wood and increased its price on the market, resulting in a tough year for fishermen. Figure 9.3 clearly shows the exploitation of broadleaf trees, which was unfortunately carried out regardless of the needs for wood for dried fish production.

During the decline in the mackerel catch in the 1960s, extensive logging took place in the national forest, with wood yields abundant enough to satisfy the needs of both the pulp companies and the dried fish manu-

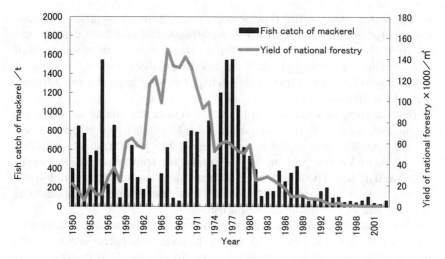

Figure 9.3 Transition of broadleaf tree production from national forest and changes in mackerel catch in Kamiyaku town
Sources: Forest yield 1950–1980 – Kumamoto Forestry Office (1982, 1981–2002); fish catch 1950–1957 – Tsutsumi (1959); fish catch 1958–2003 – Kagoshima Statistical Research Office (1958–2003).

facturers. Incentives to manage broadleaf tree forests were thus lower during times of abundance – even for dried fish manufacturers, because their needs for firewood were affected by fluctuations in fishery resources. The firewood shortage in the dried fish industry shows that marine resources are a critical component of the resource system. Indeed, this causal linkage among natural resources through local society development demonstrates what the concept of "resources" is all about; forest policy cannot be discussed without also considering fishery resource conservation.

Forests protected and fisheries exploited

In the 1990s, when Japanese society began to pay increased attention to global environmental issues, several symbolic events took place on Yakushima with respect to broadleaf forests. First, Yakushima was designated as a World Natural Heritage site in 1993. This prestigious designation was due not only to the existence of the attractive Yakusugi but also because of the island's nearly undisturbed broadleaf forests.

A second and lesser-known event was the planting of forests by fishermen, starting in 1996, demonstrating that the fishermen's tree plantation movement had diffused to the southernmost edge of Japan. In Yakushima tree planting was carried out by fishery cooperatives on the northern half of the island. Due to differences in the availability of natural resources, the socio-economic conditions in the northern and southern districts are different. In the northern part of the island, fishermen catch spotted mackerel in the fishing grounds off the island. Isso, one of the villages belonging to Kamiyaku town in the north, has long been the main fishing port of the island.

Tree planting by fishermen was carried out during the three years between 1996 and 1998. In this period, 11,600 young trees were planted, covering 5.6 hectares of the national forest. The plantation site is called the forest of Yaku-saba (the popular name for spotted mackerel caught near Yakushima). These spotted mackerel are famous for their high quality and market value, making them an important fish species for the local industry and raw material for dried fish.

Clearly, the decrease in fishery resources motivated the fishermen's union to plant trees. Figure 9.3 shows the mackerel catch in Kamiyaku. In recent years a clear decreasing trend in the catch is apparent – it decreased sharply after reaching a peak around 1977. The fluctuation in mackerel catch subject to a constant fishing effort is considered to depend on two factors: the mackerel population size and their migration rate to the fishing grounds. Even after taking into consideration the decreased fishing effort due to depopulation and the ageing of fishermen, a decrease in the catch is still apparent. Furthermore, flying fish, which came to the island to breed, gradually began to disappear after the 1960s, which was a source of concern among Yakushima's fishermen.

During this period the broadleaf forests were subjected to the operation of full-scale logging (Kumamoto Forestry Office, 1982; Hirata, 2005). The damage to the natural environment caused by the forestry industry is effectively demonstrated by the author's interview with a local elder: "When it rained, the clear cutting caused the streams to be filled with mud, and the mouth of the river was coloured red."

Deforestation in Yakushima, however, is not the sole cause of the fishermen's problems. Overfishing, for example, is a critical underlying factor contributing to the depletion of mackerel. Historical studies suggest that the continuous pressures of overexploitation and severe competition with mainland fishing in coastal areas have constrained the island's fishery over many years.

In the post-Second World War period the fishing industry recovered against a background of national food scarcity. The total size of the fish catch in Kamiyaku town reached its maximum, almost 2,400 tonnes, in 1955 (Editorial Committee of Kamiyaku Town History, 1984: 524). During this period many villagers worked in the fishery and the number of fishing vessels also increased steadily. However, soon after the mid-1950s, due perhaps to increased competition with mainland fishing vessels, the catch dropped sharply and the fishery stock began to deteriorate. The effect of overfishing around fishing grounds can be confirmed from an inconstant annual catch. Differences in the fishing methods used by the islanders and the mainland fishing vessels were also a critical factor – the islanders used pole-and-line fishing, while outsiders used seine fishing. Seine fishing is more effective and efficient. The motorization of vessels and improvements in equipment used by outsiders created additional disadvantages for local fishermen, who had previously enjoyed the benefits of the island being surrounded by rich fishing grounds.

During the period of economic growth in Japan the catch level remained unstable, due primarily to a decrease in the number of fishermen on the island. The number of people working off the island began to increase around 1955 and the number of fishermen on Yakushima – which had been as high as 600 in 1955 – had diminished to just over 100 by 1975. Thus the fishery industry in Kamiyaku was clearly in decline during the period of economic growth.

One factor that made the expansion of the fishermen's conservation movement possible was the establishment of 200-mile economic zones. This arrangement took effect from 1977 in Japan; it imposed severe restrictions on Japanese deep-sea fishing, and resulted in re-evaluation of coastal resources. The decline in coastal fishing areas was of increasing importance at this time. The plantation movement in Yakushima was thus, in a way, a public expression of dismay over their economic difficulties. In fact, a rally against overfishing conducted by overseas boats was staged in the same year tree plantations began to appear on Yakushima.

Both forest and coastal resources of Yakushima have been exposed to a wave of industrialization as part of an effort to boost national economic growth. Such moves, in general, deprived the island of resources and caused serious uncertainty about supplies of raw materials for the long-standing dried fish industry, which had fully utilized the local ecological system.

Raw materials for dried fish production are no longer provided by fishermen in Yakushima. After the late 1990s, manufacturers relied on "import" materials from the mainland (News Crew of Minami-Nippon Shimbun, 1990: 181). The catches of the island's fishermen are mostly distributed as *sashimi*, which is more profitable, and the Fisheries Cooperative Association of Yakushima is even limiting the fish catch to avoid an excess of supply and a fall in the market price of mackerel. In a climate of strong societal division, the unity in resource use that once existed within the dried fish industry seems to have severely diminished.

Forest conservation by the fishermen on Yakushima is a consequence of unequal resource systems, evidenced by the obvious gap in resource access between the forests – which are well-protected sources of tourism revenue – and the desperate fishermen who are forced to plant trees in the mountains in attempts to secure their livelihoods. The case of Yakushima offers an important lesson with regard to natural resource governance in other regions: having a variety of uses for natural resources, rather than maximizing a single resource use, can lead to sustainable development. Certainly, the World Heritage site on Yakushima is a major potential income source, but not all island residents are directly engaged in the tourism industry. It is therefore unsuitable to frame the question of resource use in terms of either logging or tourism, considering that an increasing number of visitors could actually threaten the forest (Baba and Morimoto, 2007).

What about the dried fish industry as another option for economic development? As noted, dried fish production, however small in scale, has been carried out on Yakushima for at least 400 years, and yet has never been appreciated as a medium through which to achieve sustainable development. My findings indicate that resource conservation has not been carried out successfully enough to allow the dried fish industry to grow steadily, suggesting that the decay of the industry in modern times is not an inevitable result of rapid modernization.

Unity of resources and policy implications for developing countries

A holistic view of natural resources, as demonstrated by fishermen's tree-planting activities, is critical in achieving balanced local development, especially for renewable resources. Despite its intuitive appeal, however, local innovation alone is far from resolving the resource problem. As demonstrated in Yakushima, forest and coastal resources are no longer under the autonomous management of the local people. Large portions of forest, now designated as a World Heritage site, are out of the hands of island residents. In addition, fishery resources have become scarce, not only because of a natural decrease in fish stocks but also due to competition with outsiders. Yakushima's forest and fishery resources have become entangled in a property system on a larger regional and national scale. To make resource conservation in places like Yakushima an attractive agenda for national policy, cooperation among local practices across the nation is essential. The expansion in fishermen's tree plantations has done just that by drawing national attention to the issue, improving the position of fishing among industrial activities and encouraging local and central governments to provide assistance to various local initiatives in the process.

Despite institutional limitations, much remains to be achieved by local initiatives for successful conservation, but this requires local communities to unite and focus on a common problem. The unity of society is a necessary precondition for local resource conservation. The problem of natural resources cannot be treated within the economic sector or by particular resource sectors alone. Societies, where people use several resources simultaneously to support their livelihoods, become vulnerable unless resource conservation and related institutions can be designed under a unified plan. This point is particularly relevant in situations where social division of labour has progressed to a large extent.

The cases described here have several implications for developing countries. First, hasty concentration on the development of the most profitable resource may undermine resource sustainability. There remains much to be learned – not necessarily from traditional resource use but from locals' awareness of recent changes in resource conditions. Second, once the causal link between multiple resources is established in the minds of stakeholders, overexploitation of one resource may encourage investment in another, just as the declining fish industry became a stimulus for tree planting. For this to happen, however, institutional arrangements are necessary. Third, empowerment of the people may have powerful effects on resource conservation. We have seen how scientific confirmation of the tacit knowledge of local fishermen boosted their activities in broadleaf tree planting. The process of this empowerment revealed the power of those who were able to assume the roles of catalysts connecting otherwise distinct forces (e.g. scientists, public officials, government agencies), and the potential of these individuals to contribute to the recovery of the resource system.

A now-famous oyster farmer from the town of Karakuwa once described himself as an "estuarine human being", by which he meant a person whose livelihood is exclusively dependent neither on the forest nor on the sea but on the intermediate domain between the two (Hatakeyama, 2003: 300). Those who use several resources simultaneously – including seaweed farmers and dried fish manufacturers – are in many ways the most vulnerable to social and environmental turbulence affecting the resources on which they depend. The case of the tree-planting fishermen in Japan illustrates the importance of empowering these individuals by giving them the autonomy to secure their own livelihoods; in fact, in today's fragmented world, the responsible governance of resources requires the active participation of local individuals in positions at the heart of threatened ecosystems.

Notes

1. For statistical information regarding agriculture, forestry and fisheries see www.maff. go.jp/j/tokei/sihyo/index.html.
2. See www.maff.go.jp/j/pr/aff/0906/spe1_05.html.
3. For the minutes of the committee, see www.maff.go.jp/j/assess/pdf/record_23_2.pdf

REFERENCES

Baba, T. and Y. Morimoto (2007) "The Visitor's Recreational Manners and Evaluations to Actions against Overuse of Forest Region on Yakushima Island, Japan", *Journal of Japanese Institute of Landscape Architecture* 70(5), pp. 547–550 (in Japanese).

Editorial Committee of Kamiyaku Town History (ed.) (1984) *The History of Kamiyaku Town*, Kagoshima: Kamiyaku Town Educational Board (in Japanese).

Hatakeyama, S. (1994) *The Forest Is Longing for the Sea, the Sea Is Longing for the Forest*, Tokyo: Hokuto Publishing (in Japanese).

—— (2003) *The Japanese Estuarine Journey*, Tokyo: Bungeishunju (in Japanese).

—— (2004) "The Forest Is Longing for the Sea: A Home Fragrant with Estuary", *Studies of Regional Policy* 6(3), pp. 81–91 (in Japanese).

Hirata, K. (2005) "Multiple Use and Management of Forest: Case Example in Yakushima", *Journal of Forest Economics* 51(1), pp. 15–26 (in Japanese).

Hunker, H. (1964) *Zimmermann's Introduction to World Resources*, Tokyo: Sanryosyobo (in Japanese).

Ishi, H. (1996) "The Changes of Awareness of Global Environment in Recent Years", *Environmental Information Science* 25(1), pp. 24–31 (in Japanese).

Isso Brokers Union (1981) "Petition to Sustainable Supply of Firewood", archived at Yakushima Forest Environment Conservation Center, Yakushima, Kagoshima (in Japanese).

Kagoshima Statistical Research Office (1958–2003) *Annual Report for Statistics on Agriculture, Forestry and Fisheries of Kagoshima Prefecture*, Associations of Agriculture and Forestry Statistics of Kagoshima (in Japanese).

Kumamoto Forestry Office (1981–2002) *Statistics of Kumamoto Forestry Enterprise*, Kumamoto Forestry Office (in Japanese).

—— (1982) *Forest Management of National Forestry of Yakushima*, Kumamoto: Kumamoto Forestry Office (in Japanese).

Matsunaga, K. (1993) *Once Forest Disappears, Marine Life Goes Too*, Tokyo: Kodansha (in Japanese).

Miyashita, A. (2000) *Dried Bonito*, Tokyo: Hosei University Press (in Japanese).

Nakata, H. (2004) "Fish Breeding Forest", in Japanese Association for Coastal Zone Studies (ed.) *Encyclopedia of Coastal Zone Environment*, Tokyo: Kyoritsu Shuppan, pp. 121–122 (in Japanese).

News Crew of Minami-Nippon Shimbun (1990) *The Home of Yakusugi*, Tokyo: Iwanami Shoten Publishers (in Japanese).

Obitani, H. (2000) "The Development and Character Change of Planting Movement by Fishermen – From Watershed Area Conservation to Environment and Resource Creation", *Journal of Environmental Sociology* 6, pp. 148–162 (in Japanese).

Okado, M. (2006) "Development and Agricultural Areas in Post-War Japan", in T. Mizuuchi, Y. Suzuki, M. Okado, S. Morita and M. Okamoto (eds) *Change in Development and Local Culture*, Tokyo: Seikyusha, pp. 93–119 (in Japanese).

Policy Research Association on Biodiversity (ed.) (2002) *100 Key Words of Biodiversity*, Tokyo: Chuohoki Publishing (in Japanese).

Sato, J. (2007) "Formation of the Resource Concept in Japan: Post-War Efforts in Knowledge Integration", *Sustainability Science* 2(2), pp. 151–158.

Tsutsumi, H. (ed.) (1959) *Report of the Survey on Agriculture, Forestry and Fisheries*, Kagoshima: Kamiyaku Town (in Japanese).

Yumoto, T. (1995) *Yakushima*, Tokyo: Kodansha (in Japanese).

Index

A

AAC. *See* Anglo American Corporation (AAC)

adaptive co-management, 146

African development, 4

anatomy of state and society, 6–8

Anglo American Corporation (AAC), 166

AQSIQ. *See* General Administration of Quality Supervision, Inspection and Quarantine [China] (AQSIQ)

Asian Development Bank, 108, 126–27

B

Brazil, 44, 46, 48–52, 54–56, 62–67, 70n1

British South Africa Company (BSAC), 166, 168–69

BSAC. *See* British South Africa Company (BSAC)

C

Cambodia

  agro-industry, 99

  Asian Development Bank Sustainable Forest Management Project, 108

  "Cambodia Forest Policy Assessment," 102–3

  Cambodia's land law classifies forests, rivers, temples as "state public property," 110

Chup, state-owned rubber company, 110–13

constitution (1993) granted tenure over all forest areas, 101

Department of Forestry, 106–7

Dipterocarp (tree species), 99, 104–6, 108, 115n11

"directive order" by Hun Sen suspending the cutting of resin trees, 107

farmers encouraged to plant rubber on a family scale on their own small chamkar land, 112

fishery lot owner has "property" right to fish during the flooded season; and the landowner cultivates his or her land in the dry season, 2

forest areas enclosed in plantation businesses, 101, 109–13

forest concessions promoted public interest in "sustainable management" of a state-owned asset, 110

forest exploitation, 99, 102

forest governance, 114

forest laws inscribed rights to resin tappers by restricting the cutting of resin trees, 106

forest management, sustainable, 100–101, 104, 108–9, 113

forest policy reform, 98